Climate Capitalism
Global Warming and the Transformation of the Global Economy

Can capitalism effectively respond to climate change? Do we need a different type of capitalism that is able to deliver growth but on a low-carbon basis? If so, how do we get there?

These are the ambitious questions addressed in this book. These are not just technical questions about whether the technologies or policies exist to confront these challenges. They are about questions of strategy, politics and power. How do we begin to assemble the alliances and coalitions that are necessary to transform the global economy? How do we get those with power to support efforts to fundamentally change the way we develop?

Climate Capitalism shows that new, interesting and surprising things are happening in the world of climate politics. Confronting climate change is now understood as a problem of 'decarbonising' the global economy: ending our dependence on carbon-based fossil fuels. This book explores whether such a transformation is underway, how it might be accelerated, and the complex politics of this process. Given the dominance of global capitalism and free-market ideologies, decarbonisation is dependent on creating carbon markets and engaging powerful actors in the world of business and finance. *Climate Capitalism* assesses the huge political dilemmas this poses, and the need to challenge the entrenched power of many corporations, the culture of energy use, and the inequalities in energy consumption across the globe.

Climate Capitalism is essential reading for anyone wanting to better understand the challenge we face. It will also inform a range of student courses in environmental studies, development studies, international relations and business programmes.

PETER NEWELL is Professor of International Development at the University of East Anglia. He has worked on climate change as a researcher, consultant, teacher and activist for over 16 years. He has undertaken work for international organisations such as the United Nations Development Programme and the Global Environment Facility, provided policy advice to a number of different governments and worked for non-government organisations such as Climate Network Europe and Friends of the Earth. He is an Economic and Social Research Council Climate Change Leadership Fellow and is the author of *Climate for Change* (Cambridge University Press, 2000), the first book on the role of non-state actors in global climate politics.

MATTHEW PATERSON is Professor of Political Science at the University of Ottawa. He has been researching climate change politics since 1989. He wrote the first book in political science focused solely on climate politics, *Global Warming and Global Politics* (Routledge, 1996), which is still widely used as a key text for understanding climate-change politics. His book *Automobile Politics: Ecology and Cultural Political Economy* (Cambridge University Press, 2007) won the prestigious International Political Economy Book Prize.

Praise for *Climate Capitalism*:

'The question of whether and under what terms capitalism can cope with climate change is the most important and challenging of our age. *Climate Capitalism* addresses this issue in an accessible and timely manner. It is required reading for all.'

Sir David King, former Chief Scientific Adviser to the UK Government and Director of the Smith School of Enterprise and the Environment, University of Oxford

'This is the best book yet written on the complex connections between climate change policy, markets and capitalism more generally. Written in an impartial and balanced way, the work should become a standard text in the field.'

Professor Lord Tony Giddens, London School of Economics and Political Science, author of *The Politics of Climate Change*

'It is now clear that capitalism as usual is not up to tackling the challenge of climate change. Under what conditions might capitalism be transformed to generate growth through low carbon development? *Climate Capitalism* addresses this most pressing of issues in an informed and accessible way. It is essential reading for governments, businesses and concerned citizens alike.'

Rt. Hon Michael Meacher M.P. and former UK Minister of the Environment

'*Climate Capitalism* by Peter Newell and Matthew Paterson provides a comprehensive review of the market in carbon reductions as well as the challenges that tackling climate change poses to capitalism more generally. While accepting that the model of global capitalism being followed so far in most of the world may need to be changed to a new, more sustainable, paradigm in the longer term, we need to start from where we are and harness the positive forces of capitalism towards solving the climate change problem rather than exacerbating it. It is an excellent book that anyone interested in the economics of climate change should read.'

Saleemul Huq, Senior Fellow, Climate Change Group, International Institute for Environment and Development

'Climate change we know is intrinsically linked to the model of economic growth in the world. Neo-liberal economists today accept that climate change is the market's biggest failure. But still the world is looking for small answers to tinker its way out of the problem of growth. It is time we looked for new ways of "business unusual". This is why this book, *Climate Capitalism*, is timely. It helps us understand the crisis, but also provides the opportunity to reinvent growth without pollution. Read it because you must.'

Sunita Narain, Director of the Centre for Science and Environment, New Delhi

'Governments, businesses and people the world over are grappling with how to tackle climate change, preferably without sacrificing living standards and lifestyles. Is "green capitalism" possible or a contradiction in terms? Will emerging forms of governance manage the potential and pitfalls of carbon markets in ways that achieve climate justice? Informed by two decades of climate scholarship, the authors provide an accessible entry to these big policy questions of the day. Backed by careful research, their balanced analysis will help inform not only all those interested in climate regulation, but all those who see climate change as a harbinger of broader debates and choices about forms of global governance and the future shape of the global economy.'

Farhana Yamin, former Research Fellow, Institute of Development Studies, University of Sussex

Climate
Capitalism

Global Warming and the Transformation of the Global Economy

PETER NEWELL
University of East Anglia

MATTHEW PATERSON
University of Ottawa

CAMBRIDGE UNIVERSITY PRESS
Cambridge, New York, Melbourne, Madrid, Cape Town, Singapore,
São Paulo, Delhi, Dubai, Tokyo

Cambridge University Press
The Edinburgh Building, Cambridge CB2 8RU, UK

Published in the United States of America by Cambridge University Press,
New York

www.cambridge.org
Information on this title: www.cambridge.org/9780521194853

First published 2010

Printed in the United Kingdom at the University Press, Cambridge

A catalogue record for this publication is available from the British Library

Library of Congress Cataloguing in Publication data
Newell, Peter (Peter John)
    Climate capitalism : global warming and the transformation of the global
    economy / Peter Newell, Matthew Paterson.
        p.   cm.
    Includes bibliographical references and index.
    ISBN 978-0-521-19485-3 – ISBN 978-0-521-12728-8 (pbk.)
    1. Emissions trading.   2. Climatic changes–Economic aspects.
    3. Pollution–Economic aspects.   4. Capitalism.   5. Globalization.
    I. Paterson, Matthew, 1967– II. Title.
    HC79.P55N49 2010
    363.738'746–dc22   2010012380

ISBN 978-0-521-19485-3 Hardback
ISBN 978-0-521-12728-8 Paperback

We dedicate this book to Ana and Freya, who have even more of a stake than we do in whether we manage to get climate capitalism, and what shape it takes.

Contents

Preface

Can capitalism effectively respond to climate change? Do we need a different type of capitalism that is able to deliver growth but on a low-carbon basis? If so, how do we get there?

These are the ambitious questions we address in this book. These are not just technical questions about whether the technologies exist to get us out of this mess or whether the right policies exist to confront these challenges. They are about questions of strategy, politics and power. How do we begin to assemble the alliances and coalitions that are necessary to transform the global economy? How do we get those with power to support efforts to fundamentally change the way our economies develop?

Climate Capitalism shows that new, interesting and surprising things are happening in the world of climate politics. Advances can be made when environmental activists get together with city financiers, or when carbon traders and development NGOs put their minds together to get money to flow into low-carbon development. This is not politics as usual. Nor can it afford to be. But like it or not, in the short- and near-term, responses to climate change will be shaped by the way that capitalism currently works. So it is crucial to understand how capitalism has shaped responses to climate change to date and to explore the different ways in which it might do so in the future.

Responses to climate change have so far been organised for the most part around the construction of markets in carbon emissions. The official aim behind these carbon markets is to 'put a price on carbon' – to make the costs of emitting carbon explicit to those polluting. But at the same time they open up climate politics to being manipulated by financiers for short-term profit. This has made many people very uneasy. We write this book at a time when the financial crisis and the climate crisis co-exist, and when the idea that financial actors might have a role to play in responses to climate change will seem an anathema to many. But responses to climate change, if they are to be effective, need to mobilise all actors in the business and financial community to bring about a transformation to a low-carbon economy.

Our aim is not to tell you what to think about these markets. It is more to understand the forces driving them, and the nature of the dilemmas we face. We want to allow you, the reader, to decide which proposals for change are worth supporting, which are not, and why. We don't, therefore, provide a blueprint for action. Many have already been produced. Most rapidly become outdated and irrelevant because of the pace of events in the contemporary world of climate politics. Instead, we end the book with a series of scenarios which sketch different ways in which carbon markets might develop. We finalised the book shortly after the UN Climate Change Conference in Copenhagen in December 2009. Such events show the futility of blueprints, but at the same time we believe it is nevertheless consistent with the broad argument we develop here.

We come to this book as academics who have spent nearly two decades researching and writing about climate change politics. We have been both highly critical of the responses of governments and business to the issue to date, and highly sceptical of the idea that capitalism can deliver either a socially just or sustainable future. But we also write as concerned citizens and activists that want to see urgent action within short time-frames. This means that post-capitalist futures, while in many ways very attractive, will not provide the political and social context within which we have to tackle this most pressing of issues. This gives rise to a series of dilemmas about working with or against carbon markets: strengthening the rules by which they operate or campaigning to abandon them; trying to ensure they deliver at least some benefits to the majority of the world's poor or decrying them as carbon colonialism, as an insidious attempt to regain control of developing countries' resources.

So the book is an attempt to get a grip on a story that is rapidly unfolding in new and challenging ways. It represents our effort to share what we have learned and observed about climate change since it hit the international political agenda in the late 1980s. It is an attempt to show that the issues we face are more complex than a simple battle between 'the good guys' and 'the bad guys', and to lay out the nature of the tricky dilemmas that anyone concerned with the issue must grapple with.

Acknowledgements

Though this book has been fairly quick in the making, we have managed to accumulate a number of debts along the way.

Peter Newell would like to thank both Diana Liverman at Oxford University for allowing him the time and space to make progress on the book as a James Martin Fellow at the Environmental Change Institute and Bruce Lankford at the School of International Development at the University of East Anglia for enabling him to take up the fellowship. He would also like to acknowledge the support of the UK Economic and Social Research Council for his Climate Change Leadership Fellowship to work on areas closely related to the themes of the book. From PhD supervisor to collaborator, working with Mat has always been a pleasure and he is grateful to him for driving this project to conclusion when it could have fallen behind so many other competing commitments. Lastly, and most importantly, he would like to thank Lucila for her patience, love and support.

Matthew Paterson's research for this book has been supported by a Social Sciences and Humanities Research Council grant, as well as by the University of Ottawa in supporting his application for teaching release. He thanks both institutions. He also thanks Peter for initially suggesting working together on a book with the theme of 'climate capitalism,' and for being such a fun person to work with. Finally, he thanks Jo for bullying him with reasonableness, a steady stream of ideas and articles from the new social media sources he resists unreasonably, and for the constant companionship of daily life which make writing feel easy.

Both would like to thank the following people. Firstly, Matt Lloyd for his encouragement and commitment to the book and hands-on approach to editing. Matt read the manuscript and gave extensive comments which have helped enormously to tighten the text. Second, Anice Paterson (Matthew's mum – our guinea-pig lay-reader!), who meticulously poured over an earlier draft of the manuscript and highlighted areas of academic jargon and climate-ese which we have sought to make accessible for the non-specialist reader. We are truly grateful for the effort she made. Four readers for Cambridge University Press commented on various chapters and helped us clarify various parts of the argument. We have benefited from research assistance on different chapters by Koffi Yenkey, Robert Macneil, Philippe Descheneau and from Helen Colyer in putting together the glossary. We interviewed a great many people during the research for this book – carbon traders, officials from government and international organisations, corporate executives, environmental activists – and we owe them a debt of thanks for their time, generosity, information and insight. Some of them are named here, many others are, however, anonymous.

Abbreviations

AAU	Assigned Amount Unit
AIJ	Activities Implemented Jointly
BA	British Airways
BP	British Petroleum
CCB	CCBA standards
CCBA	Climate Community and Biodiversity Alliance
CCX	Chicago Climate Exchange
CDCF	Community Development Carbon Fund
CDM	Clean Development Mechanism
CDP	Carbon Disclosure Project
CERES	Coalition for Environmentally Responsible Economies
CERs	Certified Emissions Reductions
CFC	chlorofluorocarbon
CFL	compact fluorescent light
CICERO	Center for International Climate and Environmental Research – Oslo
CO_2	carbon dioxide
CO_2e	CO_2 equivalent
COP	Conference of the Parties to the UNFCCC
CSR	Corporate Social Resposibility
DEFRA	Department for Environment, Food and Rural Affairs
DNA	Designated National Authority
DNV	Det Norske Veritas
DOE	Designated Operational Entity
ERU	Emission Reduction Unit
EU	European Union
EU ETS	Emissions Trading Scheme
EUA	European Union Allowance
FACE	Forests Absorbing Carbon Emissions

FERN	Forests and the European Union Resource Network
FSC	Forestry Stewardship Council
GATT	General Agreement on Tariffs and Trade
G77	Group of developing countries (originally 77 that signed a declaration in 1964)
G8	Group of eight countries – Canada, France, Germany, Italy, Japan, Russia, the United Kingdom and the United States
GCC	Global Climate Coalition
GDP	Gross Domestic Product
GEF	Global Environment Facility
GHG	greenhouse gas
GM	genetically modified
GNP	Gross National Product
GWP	Global Warming Potential
HFC	hydrofluorocarbon
ICCR	Interfaith Centre for Corporate Responsibility
IEA	International Energy Agency
IETA	International Emissions Trading Association
IMF	International Monetary Fund
IPCC	Intergovernmental Panel on Climate Change
ISO	International Organization for Standardization
JI	Joint Implementation
LFG	landfill gas
LULUCF	Land Use, Land-Use Change and Forestry
MDG	Millennium Development Goal
NAFTA	North American Free Trade Area
NGO	Non-governmental Organisation
N_2O	nitrous oxide
ODA	Official Development Assistance
OECD	Organisation for Economic Cooperation and Development
PCF	Prototype Carbon Fund
PDD	Project Design Document
PEMEX	Petroleos Mexicanos
PP	Project Participant
PR	public relations
REDD	Reducing Emissions from Deforestation and Forest Degradation
RGGI	Regional Greenhouse Gas Initiative
SEC	Securities and Exchange Commission (US government)

SME	Small and Medium Enterprises
SGS	Société Générale de Surveillance
SO_2	sulphur dioxide
SRI	Socially Responsible Investment
SUV	Sports Utility Vehicle
UK	United Kingdom
UN	United Nations
UNCTAD	United Nations Conference on Trade and Development
UNDP	United Nations Development Programme
UNEP	United Nations Environment Programme
UNEP FI	United Nations Environment Programme Finance Initiative
UNFCCC	United Nations Framework Convention on Climate Change
UNICE	Union of Industrial Employers' Confederations in Europe
UNICEF	United Nations International Children's Emergency Fund
USA	United States of America
VCS	Voluntary Carbon Standard
VCU	Voluntary Carbon Unit
VCM	Voluntary Carbon Market
VER	Verified Emissions Reductions
WBCSD	World Business Council for Sustainable Development
WMO	World Meteorological Organization
WRI	World Resources Institute
WTO	World Trade Organization
WWF	World Wide Fund for Nature

1

Introducing climate capitalism

Never before has humanity as a whole embarked on a project to radically transform the way its societies work. Sure, there have been revolutionary projects, many national, some aiming at global transformation. Through empire and war, countries have sought to assert their view of the world in order to re-model it along new political lines. And revolutions have certainly happened, both political, and more importantly in the current context, social and technological. We can think of the inventions of agriculture, printing, the steam engine or the computer. All of these have wrought vast changes upon societies. But all of these were the result of initiatives by individuals, particular companies or countries. In responses to climate change, we have the first instance of societies collectively seeking a dramatic transformation of the entire global economy.

For that is the basic claim we want to make in this book. On the one hand, responding to climate change entails radical changes in how the global economy and daily life are organised. The term 'decarbonisation of the economy' is increasingly in common use. It refers to the process of taking the carbon out of the energy we use to run the economy. But its implications for how the economy is organised are rarely drawn out or understood – it is rather seen as simply a technical question. The result of decarbonising the economy is what we call *climate capitalism*: a model which squares capitalism's need for continual economic growth with substantial shifts away from carbon-based industrial development.

On the other hand, we are not just making an idealist plea for this transformation, although we certainly believe it is necessary. We also claim that we are – at least potentially – currently in the early stages of this transformation. That is, the processes that might lead to decarbonisation, albeit still in their infancy, are being put in place. Often these processes are weakly understood, even by those participating in them. But the various elements we now see in climate policy, in particular the most innovative elements of the carbon economy, are those which *might* serve to effect the transformation most now recognise is necessary.

This is, however, where for many it gets scary. The world we are referring to is that of the financial markets (whose credibility is not currently at a historic highpoint) and large transnational corporations, who have been empowered to turn climate change into a question of trading and investment. This is the world of carbon trading and carbon offsets, about which many of us are confused and hold conflicting views, if we do not regard them with total hostility.

You may have thought that climate change was about sea-level rise, heatwaves, hurricanes and droughts, about scientific controversies and uncertainties, and perhaps about global inequalities and moral responsibility. So you can be forgiven for being confused when you see that major city banks are trading carbon just like dollars, oil, grain or sub-prime mortgages, and that this is seen as the cutting edge of responses to climate change.

How did we end up with this way of responding to climate change? And are efforts to buy and sell units of carbon little more than a scam, where business people and financiers get to make money without delivering real cuts on greenhouse gas (GHG) emissions? Or, do these new markets represent the start of the greening of the global economy, a serious attempt to mobilise those with power in the global economy to address perhaps the greatest challenge we have ever collectively faced? More specifically, can they lead to the decarbonisation we need?

CLIMATE CHANGE: FROM THREAT ...

Many people have increasingly come to realise that climate change is the issue of the age. It impinges on every aspect of the things that keep us alive – food and energy – as well as the ways we make money, such as trade, industry and transport. Whereas once climate change was a quirky subject discussed in obscure scientific journals or amongst people who get excited about technology, it is now part of everyday discourse. As these connections are understood, we recognise the need to mainstream action on climate change into policy on agriculture, transport, energy and trade. And we start to understand climate change not as a discrete environmental problem like forests or acid rain, but as something that affects everything we do. It is not just an issue which will change how we live in the future, but how we live today.

Increasing evidence has transformed climate change from a potential, long-term issue of uncertain consequences, to an immediate issue of food production, heatwaves, hurricanes, water shortages and the loss of iconic landscapes such as alpine glaciers or species such as polar bears. Indeed, in the latter case we are in an unprecedented historical situation where we for the first time know that a species is probably in effect already extinct; what is left is the endgame as polar bears die out during the next 30–40 years, as the climatic impacts of emissions already produced reap their damage.

The anxiety associated with these events has been reinforced by the growing drip-feed of news stories which appear to confirm our sense that something has irrevocably changed. Each year there is a new piece of evidence. Even just regarding hurricanes, we have a new first almost every year – 2004 giving us the first hurricane ever in the southern hemisphere, 2005 giving us Katrina, the most destructive in modern history, 2007 the first year with two category 5 storms in the same year.

While no individual event can be attributed to climate change, extreme weather events provide timely reminders of what we can expect in a world of accelerated climate change. It may not be sensitive to say so, but it is probably true that unprecedented floods in the UK in 2007, which wreaked havoc across the country, including several deaths, brought home the severity of the issue to people normally protected from the effects of climate change. Certainly more so than the floods in Mozambique the same year, which, while shocking, were ultimately less visible to those in the rich North. Of course, the floods in Mozambique displaced many more than in the UK (the 2007 floods killed around 30 people, while earlier flooding in 2000 killed around 700). But while the rich can protect themselves better from the effects of climate change, they are less and less immune from its effects.

The pressure to recognise the seriousness of the climate crisis has also been built by a flurry of books and films which have summarised recent research and information on the subject for a broad public (and provoked increasingly hysterical responses from climate deniers such as Margaret Thatcher's former Chancellor of the Exchequer Nigel Lawson). With titles like *Fieldnotes from a Catastrophe*, *The Weathermakers*, *Six Degrees* and *Heat*, such books have deepened the already existing broad consensus for action on climate among public opinion (in rich countries at least), moving it centre-stage in political debates.[1] Al Gore's documentary *An Inconvenient Truth* has been the highest profile of these,[2] reflecting the dominance of screen over print in contemporary culture as well as Gore's particular profile as almost US President, long-time campaigner on environmental issues and co-recipient with the UN's Intergovernmental Panel on Climate Change (IPCC) of the Nobel Peace Prize in 2007.

These books and Gore's film summarise the ever-strengthening scientific consensus, but also put in place a number of key pieces in the puzzle that help us realise the severity of the situation. They more or less all talk about the slow-down of the Gulf stream (of course dramatised in the wildly exaggerated climate disaster movie *The Day After Tomorrow*), changes in El Niño patterns, the acceleration in the collapse of the Greenland ice sheet, melting of permafrost and rapidly diminishing Arctic ice (the cause of the extinction of the polar bears). The latest addition to this list has been the acidification of oceans, an issue which emerged on the scene in 2009. These sorts of changes, occurring more rapidly than anyone thought possible, have given credence to the concern that climate change may indeed make human life on the planet extremely tenuous. The polar bears may be the least of our worries.

To bolster this sense that climate change threatens human civilisation, these books also follow Jared Diamond's lead in re-investigating a series of civilisational collapses that can be associated with changes in climate – the failure of Vikings in Greenland, the collapse of the Akkadians of Sumeria or the Mayan civilisations, the Justinian plague from AD 536 onwards, among others. What is striking here is that all of these historical collapses occurred as a result of (among other things) climate changes significantly less serious than those we are currently in the early stages of. During the century after 1340, global average temperatures declined by only 0.2 °C – this was enough to force the hardy Norse to abandon Greenland. This shift is insignificant compared to the temperature increases already experienced in the twentieth century (around a 0.6 °C rise) and an order of magnitude

---

[1] N. Lawson, *An Appeal to Reason: a Cool Look at Global Warming* (London: Gerald Duckworth & Co., 2008); E. Kolbert, *Fieldnotes from a Catastrophe* (London: Bloomsbury, 2007); T. Flannery, *The Weathermakers* (Toronto: HarperCollins, 2006); M. Lynas, *Six Degrees* (London: HarperCollins, 2007); G. Monbiot, *Heat* (London: Penguin, 2007).

[2] Though at the time of writing the independently produced film *The Age of Stupid*, which takes a far more critical look at climate politics, is a success on the independent cinema circuit.

smaller than those projected for the twenty-first century (between a 1.5 and 4.5 °C rise, according to the IPCC).

The figure of 2 °C higher than pre-industrial temperatures has been widely talked about as a target for the maximum temperature change that human societies might be able to tolerate. The European Union (EU) has even made it a formal aim in its negotiations for the agreement to replace the Kyoto Protocol – the international community's main treaty to date designed to reduce emissions, agreed in 1997 – and they were joined in 2009 by the G8 declaration which said that 'global average temperature above pre-industrial levels ought not to exceed 2 °C'.[3] Despite its various weaknesses, the 'Copenhagen Accord', produced at the UN Climate Change negotiations in December 2009, also affirmed this goal.

Two things here are sobering. First, unless you make the most optimistic assumptions about the sensitivity of climate to CO_2 changes, this threshold is basically *already passed* – to achieve this would require CO_2 concentrations in the atmosphere which are lower than current levels.[4] The organisation 350.org was set up precisely to campaign for policies that aim to reduce overall concentrations to that level, 350 parts per million (ppm). If you make less optimistic assumptions about climate sensitivity and demanding but plausible emissions scenarios, then it's hard to avoid the conclusion that we are likely to be headed for more like 4 °C or even more.

Second, the last time the climate was 2 °C higher than the present was around 129,000 years ago (palaeoclimatologists call this the 'Eemian interglacial period'). At that point, sea levels were 5–6 metres higher than at present, much higher than the 60 cm increase that the IPCC's 2007 report suggested would be the likely maximum.[5] So even

---

[3] 'World powers accept warming limit', BBC News, see http://news.bbc.co.uk/1/hi/world/europe/8142825.stm, accessed 9 July 2009.

[4] An excellent short explanation of the logic here can be found in A. Dessler and E. Parson, *The Science and Politics of Global Climate Change* (Cambridge: Cambridge University Press, 2006), pp. 155–8. Briefly, the logic is this: according to IPCC models, to achieve a maximum temperature rise of 2 °C, you can have a maximum CO_2 atmospheric concentration 510 ppm if you assume low climatic sensitivity to CO_2 concentrations, 370 ppm with a mid-range sensitivity assumption, and only 270 ppm if climate is highly sensitive to CO_2 levels. Given that CO_2 concentrations are currently at around 380 ppm, we are already past that threshold unless climate only has a lower sensitivity. That we don't yet have the temperature changes is because of the delays in how the atmosphere–ocean system responds to the CO_2 increases.

[5] See Mark Lynas' summary of this evidence in M. Lynas, *Six Degrees: Our Future on a Hotter Planet*, (London: 4th Estate, 2007), pp. 71–3.

if we manage to limit temperature increases to 2 °C, we may be in serious trouble. At 4 °C higher, even on the conservative IPCC assessments of a 60 cm sea-level rise (their minimum projected increase for that temperature rise), large areas of cities like London, Boston, New York, Alexandria, Mumbai and Shanghai will be inundated. But in the longer term (the only question is how quickly), with this amount of warming, sea level will rise by between 6 m and 25 m as the Greenland and Antarctica ice sheets melt (the variation depends on how much of Antarctica melts at this temperature). At a 6 m rise, London's flood defence experts suggest that much of London can no longer be defended. But again, the last time the world was 4 °C warmer than today (around 40 million years ago), there was no ice at either pole, and sea levels were more like 50 m higher than today's.[6] This is the science-fiction world of J. G. Ballard's 1962 novel *The Drowned World*, where Greenland is the most habitable part of the planet. The novel is set in London where the spire of St. Paul's Cathedral just manages to peak out above the water level.[7]

... TO RESPONSE

So recent evidence gives us good cause to believe that it is highly probable we are on course for a very bumpy ride, and that our window of opportunity for trying to achieve a soft climatic landing is there, but quickly closing. Writing in mid 2008, Andrew Simms of the New Economics Foundation claimed that we have '100 months to save the planet'.[8]

While this evidence is crucial in building a sense of the necessity of radical action on climate change, it tells us little about how societies are already both adapting to climate change and developing strategies to mitigate it. Apart from in George Monbiot's *Heat* and Anthony Giddens' *The Politics of Climate Change*, the best we get is a series of 'what you can do to help the fight against climate change', as in books like *The Climate Diet: How You Can Cut Carbon, Cut Costs, and Save the Planet* or *How to Live a Low Carbon Life* or former chief scientist for the UK government Sir David King's *The Hot Topic: How to Tackle Global Warming and Still Keep the Lights on*.[9]

[6] M. Lynas, *Six Degrees*..., pp. 178–82.

[7] J. G. Ballard, *The Drowned World* (London: Gollancz, 1962).

[8] A. Simms, '95 months and counting', *The Guardian*, 1 January 2009. http://www.guardian.co.uk/commentisfree/2009/jan/01/climatechange.

[9] J. Harrington, *The Climate Diet: How you can cut carbon, cut costs, and save the planet.* (London: Earthscan, 2008); C. Goodall, *How to Live a Low Carbon Life*,

In Gore's film, the question of what needs to be done is barely an after-thought – relegated to the credits – and left in the realm of the most individualised of actions – buying a hybrid car or turning down the thermostat or the air-conditioner.

The premise for this book is that we need to understand how societies might *collectively* address climate change. Dealing successfully with climate change entails a wholesale transformation so that the economy can be 'decarbonised'. Our central question is: 'What will determine whether, as a society, we can avoid the most dangerous aspects of climate change?' And our central argument is encapsulated in our title *Climate Capitalism*.

We are not endorsing a blind faith in capitalism to adequately address climate change. Those at all familiar with our other work would be surprised if that were the case. We are suggesting, however, that the origins of climate change are in the ways that the economy has been organised; the technologies, sectors, imperatives and patterns of growth that have led to increasing CO_2 emissions. These have all been also central to the growth of the capitalist economy as a whole over the last two centuries.

As a consequence, the attempt to decarbonise the global economy presents a huge and unprecedented challenge. The transformations involved are not easy to pursue, will not be smooth and most likely unpopular. There are plenty who would lose out from such a transformation – coal companies, miners, oil companies and exporting countries, those addicted to their cars, flying round the world or other aspects of high-consumption lifestyles, in particular. They can be expected to resist, and have already done so vociferously.

Behind the cosy language used to describe climate change as a common threat to all humankind, it is clear that some people and countries contribute to it disproportionately, while others bear the brunt of its effects. What makes it a particularly tricky issue to address is that it is the people that will suffer most that currently contribute least to the problem, i.e. the poor in the developing world. Despite often being talked about as a scientific question, climate change is first and foremost a deeply political and moral issue.

The origins of climate change are implicated in the choices we all make every day, throughout the day. From the moment you wake

(London: Earthscan, 2007); G.Walker and Sir D. King, *The Hot Topic: How to Tackle Global Warming and Still Keep the Lights on* (London: Bloomsbury, 2008); A. Giddens, *The Politics of Climate Change* (Cambridge: Polity Press, 2009).

up in the morning and decide what to eat for breakfast (assuming you have that luxury) you are engaging, mostly unconsciously, in sets of choices about whether the food you eat is sourced locally or has been transported half way around the world to get to your breakfast table. How you heat the water for your shower implies a decision to use a particular source of energy which will have an impact (malign or benign) on climate change and how you decide to get to work also determines how much CO_2 you add to the atmosphere.

It is easy to see then why politicians talk about personal carbon allowances, making us individually responsible for our carbon footprints. But if decarbonisation of the economy is really to take off, the challenge has to be addressed at many more scales. The suppliers of our energy have to have incentives to switch to renewable options. We have to have transport systems that do not create incentives for individual and unnecessary car use, which in turn implies changes in planning systems for a carbon-constrained world.

This is not only an issue of ethical consumerism and individual choice. Persuading people to buy CFC-free deodorants may have worked in helping to address ozone depletion. Persuading people to fly less in a world of cheap flights, to leave their cars at home when their nearest shops are out of town is harder because food, energy and transport systems, currently organised, assume a world unconstrained by limits on carbon use. This is why capitalism as it currently operates is not working when it comes to tackling climate change. Fundamentally, capitalism does not have a concept of sufficiency, of how much is *enough*. If it doesn't continue growing, it implodes in crises such as those of the 1930s.

But if one premise for this book is that climate change entails an enormous transformation of how capitalism operates, then our other premise is that despite resistance, in fact an embryonic form of climate capitalism is already emerging. The chapters that follow elaborate how the ways that governments, corporations and non-governmental actors have responded to climate change are best understood as an effort to decarbonise the global economy. Of course this development is patchy – some governments are more active than others, some businesses much more entrepreneurial and far-sighted than others – but the foundations of such an economy are nevertheless in the process of being built. These foundations can be characterised as different types of carbon markets, which put a price on carbon, and thus create incentives to reduce emissions.

These sorts of response to climate change are also highly problematic of course. Many readers will already have prejudices against, or at least worries about, treating the atmosphere like a commodity to be bought and sold, or about buying carbon offsets to enable the rich to continue their high-consuming lifestyles with a clear conscience. We share these worries.

But there is something about climate change that makes it unique amongst environmental problems. The origins of climate change are deeply rooted in the development of the global capitalist economy. The ways the world has responded to climate change have been conditioned by the sort of free-market capitalism which has prevailed since the early 1980s. To respond to climate change successfully entails decarbonising that economy, to re-structure or dismantle huge economic sectors on which the whole of global development has been based. This is in sharp contrast to efforts to deal with ozone depletion, which involved the elimination of a relatively small batch of chemicals with specific uses by a handful of leading companies. Likewise, we can deal with most forms of water pollution by banning certain applications of fertilisers, dealing with human and animal wastes, and controls on what chemical industries can discharge into rivers and lakes. To ban these practices, while often inconvenient for the companies involved, is hardly a challenge to the whole edifice of global capitalism.

In contrast, to propose to ban all further coal and oil use, as some have done, is both unrealistic and deeply problematic. The use of these fuels is currently so widespread that simply to ban them would cause economic growth to collapse. And a lack of growth is something that the capitalist system in which we live simply cannot tolerate – it would collapse as a system.

So the challenge of climate change means, in effect, either abandoning capitalism, or seeking to find a way for it to grow while gradually replacing coal, oil and gas. Assuming the former is unlikely in the short term, the questions to be asked are, what can growth be based on? What are the energy sources to power a decarbonised economy? Which powerful actors might be brought on board to overcome resistance from the oil and coal companies? And for those worried (including us) about the image of unbridled free-market capitalism as managing the climate for us, then we are forced to address the questions: What type of climate capitalism do we want? Can it be made to serve desirable social, as well as environmental, ends? And what might it take to bring it about?

In this context, a response that focuses on creating markets, where money can be made for trading carbon allowances within limits set by governments, is rather appealing. Against the backdrop of the problems of recalcitrant industries and reluctant consumers, it creates the possibility of economic winners from decarbonisation. What's more, those winners – financiers – are rather powerful, and can support you as you build the policies which might produce decarbonisation overall. Trading on its own clearly won't be enough, but it does provide a powerful constituency that benefits from climate-change policy, which is crucial politically.

Turning this into a successful project for decarbonisation requires constructing altogether different models of growth that do not depend on abundant and cheap fossil fuels, one that may actually reward reductions in energy use and its more efficient use. This means decoupling emissions growth from economic growth. The key question is whether capitalists can find ways of doing new business in a way that helps to achieve decarbonisation. They need to be able to do this in a way which brings on board those that will be doing less business in a low-carbon economy, or at least to provide enough growth overall for policymakers to be able to override their resistance.

What we try to do in the chapters that follow is elaborate the central elements in this emerging economy, and the central political dilemmas we face as it comes into being. Will it in fact enable us to decarbonise the global economy? Does it need to be regulated to do so or will climate capitalism arise 'naturally' out of the practices of corporations and markets? Will it come at the expense of the world's poor and marginalised, or could it rather enable redistribution of wealth from rich to poor countries at the same time?

At the end of the book, we draw out various possible scenarios for what sorts of climate capitalism we might end up having to live (or die) with. We invite you, the reader, to decide which one you feel is most likely and which one you would like to see. None are inevitable. All result from the complex interplay of a wide array of actors, institutions and decision-making processes. And the financial crisis of the last couple of years gives us unusual room for manoeuvre in shaping these responses. Getting involved as consumers, activists, entrepreneurs and concerned citizens will allow us all to shape the sort of future we want in a carbon-constrained world.

2

Histories of climate, histories of capitalism

Sometimes, in order to look forward, we have to start by looking backwards. What determines how we can respond to climate change is whether we can transform the economy by decarbonising it. Given this, examining how the global economy has evolved in the past may hold the key to understanding how we might transform it in the future. How does the global economy operate? How has it developed over the last 30–40 years? How do these developments shape the way we respond to climate change?

This chapter traces the intertwined history of modern capitalism and climate change. By this we mean the emergence of climate change both as a fact (the trends in emissions, changes in climate) and as an issue (its scientific and policy development and how people have mobilised around it), along with the key shifts in the global economy going on at the same time. This history shows that by the time responses to climate change became well established, notably in the Kyoto Protocol of 1997, the sorts of strategies being developed had been determined by the dominance of financial actors, free-market ideologies, global inequalities, and rise of network and partnership forms of organisation.

CARBONIFEROUS CAPITALISM AND THE ORIGINS OF CLIMATE CHANGE

Other writers have told modern history through the life of a particular commodity whether it be sugar, coffee or, more immediately relevant for our purposes, coal and oil.[1] By the same token, the rise of

[1] S. Mintz, *Sweetness and Power: The Place of Sugar in Modern History* (London: Penguin, 1986); A. Wild, *Black Gold: A Dark History of Coffee* (London: Harper Perennial, 2005); B. Freese, *Coal: A Human History* (London: Arrow Books, 2003).

contemporary forms of capitalism is closely connected to the large-scale exploitation and use of fossil fuels. Oil, coal and, more recently, natural gas have provided the basic input to all of the production upon which our societies have been based.

Lewis Mumford wrote in the 1930s that the contemporary world should be understood as embodying a form of 'carboniferous capitalism'. By this he meant that it was based on the extraction and use of dead plants laid down in the carboniferous period, transformed through long geological processes into coal. In other words, the carbon those plants had extracted from what might be called 'ancient sunlight' was turned into a source of easily obtainable and highly intensive energy.[2]

War, social struggle, modern industry and mass transportation are intimately related to the access, use and distribution of fossil fuels. Think of resource conflicts in the Middle East, including wars in Iraq in the late twentieth and early twenty-first century; the rise of car culture from the 1920s; and, way before that, struggles to improve the social condition of people blighted by the industrial revolution, described so vividly by Friedrich Engels in *The Condition of the Working Class in England*.[3] These are just a few illustrations of how fossil fuels have come to define who we are, where we have come from and how we live.

But let's go back further in time. In 1769 James Watt made decisive improvements on Newcomen's original steam engine design. During the nineteenth century, this technology was used to industrialise large parts of the world, heat homes and offices, and move more and more people round faster by train. Oil has assumed an equally central role in transforming society. Historian Eric Hobsbawm argues:[4]

> New raw materials, often only to be found outside Europe, therefore acquired a significance which was only to become evident in the later period of imperialism. Thus oil already attracted the attention of indigenous Yankees as a convenient fuel for lamps, but rapidly acquired new uses with chemical processing. In 1859 a mere two thousand barrels had been produced, but by 1874 almost 11 million barrels (mostly from Pennsylvania and New York) were already enabling John D. Rockefeller to establish a stranglehold over the new industry by the control of its transport through his Standard Oil Company.

[2] L. Mumford, *Technics and Civilization* (New York: Harcourt, 1934).
[3] F. Engels, *The Condition of the Working Class in England* (London: Penguin, 1987).
[4] E. Hobsbawm, *The Age of Capital* (London: Abacus), p. 59.

By the late nineteenth century, oil was discovered in Pennsylvania and the internal combustion engine was developed, fuelling the development of a car-oriented economy in the twentieth century. At the same time, electricity generation was developed, enabling the use of oil and coal to light and heat homes, and make all sorts of home appliances possible, from fridges to plasma-screen televisions. Shortly after, engines were developed for aviation. Common to all these developments were technologies that expand and intensify the amount of 'ancient sunlight' that we use.

By the early 1960s, it became clear that this use of ancient sunlight had triggered a noticeable change in the gases in the atmosphere. We had known in 1827 that the CO_2 in the atmosphere was one of the determinants of climate. Swedish scientist Svante Arrhenius argued for the first time in 1896 that burning coal and oil could increase the amount of CO_2 in the atmosphere and thus lead to warming. By 1963 we knew that CO_2 in the atmosphere was going up year on year, based on measurements of atmospheric CO_2 started by Charles Keeling in Hawaii in 1958.[5]

ENERGY USE AND ECONOMIC GROWTH

While the scientific understanding of climate change was developing, the expansion of energy use proceeded apace. The series of inventions from the steam engine onwards – the railways, mechanised industrial and agricultural production, the internal combustion engine, fossil fuel electricity production, through to the jet engine – continued to require and enable a constant expansion in the use of coal, oil and gas. Overall consumption of fossil fuels grew tenfold, from to 200 × 10^18 joules[6] between 1900 and 1970, by which time carbon emissions from such fuels were four billion tonnes a year. The growth of such consumption was strongly concentrated in the industrialised countries in the North, who still accounted for 70% of global emissions in 1990 (despite only having around 25% of world population). But the model of growth based on fossil energy was also progressively globalised,

[5] S. R. Weart, *The Discovery of Global Warming* (Cambridge MA: Harvard University Press, 2004), pp. 43–4.

[6] See M. Jaccard, *Sustainable Fossil Fuels* (Cambridge: Cambrdge University Press, 2006), p. 17. An exajoule or EJ is 10^18 joules. For comparison, a 100 watt light bulb uses 100 joules per second, or around 3 ×10^9 joules if it was running continuously for a year. So it would take 333 million such bulbs running constantly to use an EJ.

through imitation by newly independent countries and by the lending practices of international institutions like the World Bank.[7]

There was a broad consensus through to the mid 1970s that energy use and economic growth were intimately related. The growth of energy use and the growth of industrial economies seemed in lock step. Growth stimulates increases in energy use as expanded economic activity requires more throughput of energy for production and consumption. But growth is also dependent on those increases; without increases in energy use, the transport of goods, the heating of houses, the powering of industries, and so on, would all be put into question.

Then in 1973–1974, the conflict in the Middle East between Israel and its neighbours triggered a four-fold increase in oil prices in six months. Many countries, in particular in Europe and newly industrialised Japan, depended heavily on the Middle East for their oil, and consequently put into place a series of policies designed to reduce such dependence. For some, such as the UK and Norway, this stimulated the search for an exploitation of oil resources within their own territories. But most didn't have this option available to them, and thus they pursued aggressive policies designed to promote energy efficiency and conservation. They increased taxes on petroleum consumption, introduced subsidies for home insulation, and changed building codes to increase the efficiency of new homes. Some also worked hard to develop alternative sources of energy; notable was Denmark's early promotion of wind energy, and Brazil's methanol programme.

One consequence of this was that the energy intensity of these economies – the amount of energy used for each unit of output – declined significantly. Some suggested that energy use and economic growth were being decoupled. However, two awkward facts muddy this picture.

First, energy efficiency has a more complicated relationship to overall energy use than it first seems. Translating efficiency gains in particular uses – in car engines, in light bulbs or appliances, for example – into reductions in consumption overall, is a complicated business. And while the energy *intensity* of European and Japanese economies has declined considerably since the early 1970s, the overall energy *use* of those economies has nevertheless continued to increase. This is largely because of the overall growth of their economies. At the level of *individual* energy use, the question is, if I save some money by buying a highly

---

[7] I. Tellam, (ed), *Fuel for Change: World Bank Energy Policy – Rhetoric and Reality* (London: Zed Books, 2000).

efficient fridge, heating system and car, what do I do with the extra money? If I spend it on an outdoor patio heater and cheap flights, then energy use may well still go up, even if the intensity of the economic activity I generate declines. So the lesson of the 'decoupling' of energy use from growth in the 1970s is not a simple one.

Second, and perhaps more telling, is that if one looks at the overall energy intensity of the global economy, it is possible the decoupling doesn't even exist. That is, energy use per unit of gross world product is largely similar to that existing before the oil crisis.[8] This is largely because one of the significant effects of the energy price increases was that it stimulated a de-industrialisation of Europe and Japan, and the shifting of many industrial processes to other countries. European and Japanese economies became increasingly centred on services, which are relatively less energy intensive, while newly industrialising economies such as Korea, Taiwan, Mexico, Brazil, and more recently China and India, expanded industrial production. Many of the end products from this production are still destined for European, Japanese or American markets – but the energy involved in producing a fridge that is consumed in Germany but produced in Taiwan appears in statistics as part of Taiwanese energy consumption not German. One recent study found that in 2005 China emitted 1.7 billion tonnes of greenhouse gases (GHGs) from its export-related sectors, 33% of the national total.[9]

Facts such as these suggest a serious shortcoming of approaches that set emissions targets on a nation-by-nation basis and at the point of production rather than consumption. The overall story, however, is of a close correlation between global energy use and global economic growth. The challenge for climate policy is how to decouple the two.

TOWARDS CONSENSUS ON CLIMATE CHANGE

Charles Keeling had established by the early 1960s that CO_2 levels were in fact rising. But the link between CO_2 and climate change still needed to be established. We knew that, in general, CO_2 is a component in the climate system, but it doesn't necessarily follow

---

[8] See for example A. Meyer, *Contraction and Convergence: The Global Solution to Climate Change*, Schumacher Briefings 5 (Totnes: Green Books, 2000), p. 28.

[9] Carbon Positive, 'West exporting emissions to China,'. See http://www.carbonpositive.net.

(climate being a complicated thing) that the observed change in CO_2 has or would lead to climate change, let alone that if it did, the changes implied would be dramatic or dangerous. But by around 1990, we also started to have strong evidence that in fact the world had warmed, by around 0.6 °C, during the twentieth century. There were many efforts from 1979 onwards to firm up the state of knowledge, organised primarily by the UN's World Meteorological Organization (WMO). This included: palaeoclimatic research building up a picture of past climate changes; the development of models, known as general circulation models, to simulate existing climate and thus the effect of increased GHG concentrations; research on the interaction between the atmosphere and the oceans, known to be crucial to the global carbon cycle; and a focus on possible alternative explanations (such as sunspots or natural climatic variation) for the observed rise in global average temperatures.

Increasingly, a series of measures of past climates (other than direct measurements) showed a decisive upswing in CO_2 levels and global temperatures from shortly after the time of Watt's invention. These measures include older temperature records plus a series of proxies for temperature found, for example, in tree rings or ice cores. The result of combining these measures has produced what has become known as the 'hockey stick'. When all this evidence is put together, we get a picture of relatively stable temperatures for much of the last millennium, and then a sharp upward trend from around 1900 onwards (there is of course a time-lag between emissions and their effects).

Throughout this period there was (and continues to be, as the recent so-called 'climategate' controversy shows) a small but vocal group of companies with a clear stake in ensuring that climate science doesn't support the case for dramatic cuts in fossil fuel use, while scientists such as Fred Singer and Richard Lindzen have made a name for themselves in spreading doubt about the robustness of the scientific consensus on climate change.[10] More on this in the next chapter.

In the later period, the state of knowledge was organised through the Intergovernmental Panel on Climate Change (IPCC), established by the WMO and United Nations Environmental Programme (UNEP) jointly in 1988. The IPCC's assessment reports (there have now been four of them) have marked key stages in the consolidation of both the

---

[10] P. Newell, *Climate for Change: Non-State Actors and the Global Politics of the Greenhouse* (Cambridge: Cambridge University Press, 2000), pp. 81–2, 101.

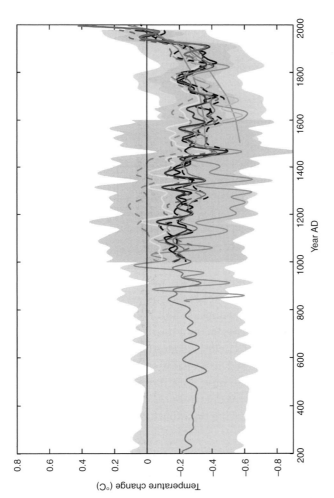

Figure 2.1 The 'hockey stick'. Solid lines are instrument records/reconstructions, broken lines indicate simulations, taken from a variety of sources.

Source: M. Mann C. Amman, R. Bradley *et al.* (2003), 'On past temperatures and anomalous late-20th century warmth,' *Eos Trans. AGU,* **84**(27), doi:10.1029/2003EO270003, available at http://www.realclimate.org/ HockeyStickOverview_html_6623cbd6.png. © AGU 2003.

scientific and political consensus on climate change, and in creating the sense that such climate change constitutes a serious crisis for our societies. Particularly important moments were the statement in the IPCC's Second Assessment Report (1995) that there is now a 'discernable human influence' on global climate. This claim, that observed warming was almost certainly caused by GHG emissions, was made even more assertively in the Third Assessment Report (2001).[11] The IPCC's most recent Fourth Assessment Report came out with the strongest statements yet that 'Warming of the climate system is unequivocal ... Most of the observed increase in global average temperatures since the mid-20th century is *very likely* due to the observed increase in anthropogenic GHG concentrations.'[12]

THE EMERGENCE OF NEOLIBERAL CAPITALISM

While knowledge of climate change firmed up between the 1970s and the 1990s, large changes were also underway in the global economy. In the 1970s, the world economy experienced a series of crises. Since the end of the Second World War the world economy had been governed by what academics and policymakers call the 'Bretton Woods system': the World Bank, International Monetary Fund (IMF), and the General Agreement on Tariffs and Trade (GATT).[13] In 1971, a key part of this, the system through which Western countries fixed their exchange rates to each other, thus providing stability for exporters and investors, collapsed, and the international financial system went into a period of much greater volatility. During the late 1960s and into the 1970s, economic growth went into a slowdown after the sustained expansion of the post-war period. The management of the economy along broadly 'Keynesian' lines (named after the British economist John Maynard Keynes) – using state expenditures and borrowing to smooth out booms and slumps

---

[11] See IPCC, *Climate Change 1995. A Report of the Intergovernmental Panel on Climate Change* (Cambridge: Cambridge University Press, 1995); and IPCC, *Climate Change 2001, Synthesis Report* (Cambridge: Cambridge University Press, 2001).

[12] IPCC, '2007: Summary for Policymakers,' in S. Solomon, D. Qin, M. Manning *et al.* (eds.), *Climate Change 2007: The Physical Science Basis*. Contribution of Working Group I to the Fourth Assessment Report of the Intergovernmental Panel on Climate Change (Cambridge University Press: Cambridge, 2007).

[13] They are known as 'Bretton Woods' institutions after the place in New Hampshire where the guiding rules of the global economy were agreed in 1944. The GATT was turned into the World Trade Organization in 1994.

in the economy, and to promote full employment – went into crisis. Of particular concern was the phenomenon of stagflation – simultaneous increases in inflation and unemployment. And of course, the oil crisis of 1973–1974, already mentioned as an impetus to changes in energy policy, also had a significant impact on the global economy. A similar shock occurred at the end of the decade after the Iranian revolution of 1979.

These events of the 1970s had four key consequences.

You can't buck the market

One is the shift rightward in economic ideology. There was a political struggle to identify the main cause of the various economic problems of the period, but the version that won was best exemplified by Thatcherism and Reaganomics, usually referred to by academics as 'neoliberalism'. This was promoted by a group of economists at the University of Chicago (the 'Chicago boys') who went on to hold influential positions in governments and international institutions where they enthusiastically sought to experiment with the free-market proscriptions advocated by their professors including the father of the 'Chicago school', Milton Friedman.[14]

This approach argued that the crisis in this period occurred because the state had become too involved in the detail of economic management, and the 'natural' effects of markets had thus been distorted. The solutions proposed included an emphasis on free markets, 'rolling back the state', privatisation of publicly owned industries and the retrenchment of the welfare state.

This sort of economic management started with the experiment in Chile in 1973, when General Pinochet overthrew the elected president Salvador Allende in a violent and bloody coup, and brought in the Chicago boys to overhaul the economy and rebuild it along neoliberal lines. But it then took off in the USA and the UK, and afterwards has progressively become the norm across the world. It did so in part because of the dominance of those two countries in global financial markets, but also because of their use of the IMF and the World Bank whose mandate was to promote neoliberal reform agendas in countries from the South (and in the former Soviet bloc after 1989). This

---

[14] See for example, D. Harvey, *A Brief History of NeoLiberalism* (Oxford: Oxford University Press, 2005); or N. Klein, *The Shock Doctrine: the rise of disaster capitalism* (Toronto: Vintage Books, 2007).

ideological preference for markets over state-led economic planning has fundamentally shaped the sorts of climate change policies that have become more or less taken for granted.

Unleashing global finance

The second shift is in the power of different parts of business. In the Bretton Woods period finance was tamed through direct controls on the movement of money around the world, and the major corporations in the global economy were those associated with manufacturing, in particular oil companies and car manufacturers. The regulatory rules were designed to enable manufacturers to flourish – for example the fixed exchange rate system that removed a key source of uncertainty for investors. Neoliberalism aimed to set finance free and stimulated an extraordinary expansion of global financial markets. Margaret Thatcher and Ronald Reagan, followed by other governments in response, deregulated financial markets, removing controls on the movement of money as well as on who can operate in different types of financial markets.

This has had well-known consequences in terms of global volatility – the various currency crises induced by speculation, for example in Brazil, Russia and East Asia – and crises of corporate governance, the classic case being Enron and more recently the sub-prime mortgage crisis. But the other key element that becomes important to understand climate politics is the shift in the power amongst different parts of business. While in the 1970s the key corporations in the global economy were oil companies and car manufacturers, by 2000 or so the key companies were in finance and information technology less.

Rising inequality

The third consequence of neoliberalism is that the world has become a significantly more unequal place. One of the immediate consequences of neoliberal management was a dramatic rise in interest rates. Part of the neoliberal diagnosis of the problem of the 1970s was that governments had not paid enough attention to the problem of inflation, or had attempted to manage it by highly intrusive measures, such as by direct controls on wages and prices.

The neoliberal solution was to 'control the money supply' (hence the name monetarism) on the basis that if you reduced the amount of money in the economy you would reduce the rate that prices could increase. But in a deregulated system, where banks and other institutions are much freer to lend money, the main, if not the only, way to do that is to use interest rates. If you raise the interest rate, you make borrowing more expensive, so people won't be able to spend so much.

But the immediate effect of increased interest rates was what became known as the debt crisis. In a period of two years from 1979 to 1981, 'real' interest rates (actual interest rates minus inflation) in the USA and UK went from 1.4% to 8.6%.[15] In the meantime, countries in the South had borrowed significant amounts of money in the 1970s, in part spurred on by the rise in the prices of raw materials like oil and the availability of 'petro-dollars', and by investment in their economies by Western companies looking for profits during the stagnation of that decade. The repayments on these debts soared simply because of the rise in interest rates and many economies were plunged into crisis.

Mexico made the crisis a global one when it threatened to default on its debt in 1982, prompting emergency action to reschedule its debt and shore up the world's banking system. Many other Southern countries during this period ended up spending the majority of their export earnings on merely servicing the interest on their debt. To add insult to injury, they had to go to the World Bank and the IMF to get emergency loans to stabilise their economies. Those institutions used this new-found power to force neoliberal 'structural adjustment' – read, austerity – measures on them. This frequently made their crises worse, and almost always turned the economic crisis into a social one. For example, forcing the removal of subsidies on basic foodstuffs provoked 'food riots' against the IMF in a number of places.[16]

The debt crisis and its management by the Bretton Woods institutions produced a dramatic reorganisation of power between North and South, and contributed to changes in the situation among countries in the South.[17] Those countries that escaped the IMF's clutches

---

[15] D. Millet and E. Toussaint, 'Figures relating to the debt for 2009', Committee for the Abolition of Third World Debt, available at http://www.cadtm.org/The-Debt-in-figures.

[16] J. Walton and D. Seddon (eds.), *Free Markets and Food Riots: The Politics of Global Adjustment* (Oxford: Blackwell, 1994).

[17] Throughout the book we try to use the terminology of 'North' and 'South' to describe the blocs of countries in the global economy. This of course masks all sorts of complexity produced for example by the rapid growth of China and more recently India, as well as of course excluding some southern hemisphere countries like Australia and New Zealand. But it remains in common usage,

were able to set in train a strong process of growth.[18] This started with
the East Asian tigers, but in the climate change context what is most
significant is the rapid growth of China, from around 1980, and India,
from around 1990. These two countries, the most populous in the
world, have experienced respectively 9.4% and 5.4% average growth
rates in the period 1980–1991 (and have continued at similar rates
since), with China now the world's largest net (though not per capita)
emitter of GHGs. The reorganisation of global hierarchies produced
by this growth has both had the obvious knock-on effects on carbon
emissions, but has also changed the diplomatic landscape on climate
change as elsewhere, in ways we come back to later. The power of the
World Bank has also been important, as it has positioned itself as a
main player in carbon markets and provider of finance for responses
to climate change in Southern countries.[19]

From hierarchies to networks

A fourth shift stimulated by the events of the 1970s is in the way that
organisations operate. If globalisation has changed the nature of international inequalities, it is also frequently described through changing
forms of organisations. Business, governments, NGOs and others have
all undergone shifts in the ways they work, both on their own and
with others, both as cause and consequence of globalisation. These
changes can be characterised as shifts from clear bureaucratic hierarchies, organised through rules and clear procedures, towards much
more fluid forms such as networks and partnerships. Boundaries
between different parts of companies, between different companies,
and between companies, governments and NGOs, are broken down
as actors seek new ways of solving problems. For companies, this is a
response to the perceived competitiveness pressures of globalisation.

especially in diplomatic contexts where the two groups face each other often in
sharp confrontation. Alternative terms like 'developed' (or 'industrialised') and
'developing' are also common ways to express this distinction. In the climate
change negotiations, another layer of jargon is added, with Annex I (in the UN
Framework Convention on Climate Change) and Annex B (in the Kyoto Protocol)
both referring to 'northern' or 'industrialised, countries. We stick to North and
South for continuity and simplicity.

[18] J. Stiglitz, *Globalisation and Its Discontents* (London: Penguin, 2003).
[19] World Bank, *Climate Investment Funds* (Washington DC: World Bank, 2008).
Available at: www.worldbank.org/cifs; World Bank, *Development And Climate
Change: A Strategic Framework For The World Bank Group, Report to the Development
Committee* (Washington DC: World Bank, 2008).

But it also serves as a means to globalise their operations, as they build partnerships with other companies globally in the search for novel sources of economic advantage.

For governments, meanwhile, traditional regulatory and bureaucratic solutions are increasingly seen as ill adapted to the accelerated pace of economic life or to the resolution of problems of ever-greater complexity, of which environmental problems are the perfect example. The notion of 'governance' is in large part an attempt to reorganise government in line with these 'new times'. According to this logic, governments can no longer effectively pursue their goals through simple bureaucratic fiat. They are forced to reorganise themselves internally as well as build partnerships with companies and other social actors to achieve their goals.

We see this in the plethora of public–private partnerships and other similar arrangements. They appear not only at national levels, but also in the UN's Global Compact which sought to make the business community a partner in efforts to advance the goals of UN treaties on labour and human rights and of course environmental protection.

These changes in governmental practice may well be regarded as an extension of neoliberal politics, notably the revived power of business. Certainly, the language of partnerships often serves to obscure the lack of will on the part of governments to regulate powerful corporations. Indeed, self-regulation is often a convenient way for governments to lighten their regulatory load and outsource responsibilities to the private sector.

Whatever their merits, partnership approaches have been influential in the way that actors have responded to climate change as we will see below. And this is not only because they fit with the dominant neoliberal logic. Climate change itself exemplifies the sorts of new complex problem which require novel sorts of organisation focused more on 'problem-solving', 'puzzling through', or 'learning by doing' than the rule-setting that is the focus of more traditional organisations.

NEOLIBERALISM AND CLIMATE POLITICS

The character of neoliberal capitalism has fundamentally shaped how we have responded to climate change. The four key elements we outline above – the ideological fixation with *markets*, the dominance of *finance*, the widening global economic *inequalities*, and the focus on *networks* as means of organising – have all combined to shape the character of responses to climate change.

When people started to talk about climate in political and policy terms in the late 1980s, there was a great proliferation of proposals as to how to respond. Much of this was at the technical level – the prospects for different energy technologies or sources of energy, whether renewable or nuclear and so on. But how might societies best promote these various options?

From early on, the debate reflected the broad shift in the global economy towards the power of finance and neoliberal ideology. In environmental policy debates more generally, there was a growing embrace during the 1980s of the idea of using economic analysis and markets to achieve environmental goals. People talked of the 'New Politics of Pollution'[20] and 'ecological modernisation',[21] which argued that economic growth and environmental protection could be made compatible. This was important in seeking to discredit earlier claims made by the Club of Rome and echoed by environmentalists from the 1970s onwards that there existed environmental limits to economic growth.[22]

Markets, in other words, could be made to work for the environment. Cost–benefit analysis, it was argued, would allow us to weigh up the pros and cons of particular paths to pollution control and allocate values to them accordingly. This way, governments could calculate the optimal rate of pollution. The UK economist David Pearce was a key figure here, promoting the idea that rather than develop policies which specified what technologies business and individuals must use, or to simply ban particular substances or processes (so-called 'command and control' policies) it would be better to use 'market mechanisms' to achieve environmental goals. The book *Blueprint for a Green Economy*, published in 1989, widely known as the Pearce Report, advocated basing policy on the use of market incentives.[23]

Two main mechanisms are particularly important here. On the one hand are environmental taxation measures, where the government

[20] A. Weale, *The New Politics of Pollution* (Manchester: Manchester University Press, 1992).

[21] A. Mol, *Globalization and Environmental Reform: The Ecological Modernization of the Global Economy* (Cambridge MA: MIT Press, 2003).

[22] D. H. Meadows, D. L. Meadows, J. Randers, and W. W. Behrens. *The Limits to Growth* (New York: Universe Books, 1974).

[23] D. A. Pearce, A. Markandya & E. Barbier, *Blueprint for a Green Economy* (London: Earthscan, 1989).

imposes taxes on particular pollutants like carbon dioxide. On the other are emissions trading schemes, where an overall emissions limit is decided, a number of permits adding up to this limit are distributed to actors according to some principle of distribution, and then actors are allowed to trade the permits amongst themselves. With both measures, the main rationale is that they leave the decisions about how to achieve particular environmental goals up to individuals and companies. Governments set either general incentives (in the cases of taxes) or overall limits to pollution levels (in the case of emissions trading) and leave markets to work out who will reduce emissions when and where.[24] In climate change, emerging at precisely this point as a political issue, in the late 1980s, these ideas left a powerful impact. This can be seen most clearly in the way in which emissions trading became the preferred policy approach. We leave the detailed discussion of emissions trading to Chapter 6; here what matters is that it became so popular because it fits with the main elements of neoliberalism discussed above.

EMISSIONS TRADING TAKES OFF

Proposals for emissions trading were made as a means to respond to climate change as early as 1989, in a paper by Michael Grubb[25] and subsequently picked up by others.[26] These are schemes where actors (countries in international systems, or companies in national ones) are allocated permits to emit GHG emissions, and they must either stay within these limits or buy extra permits from other actors who find it easier to reduce their own emissions and thus have surplus permits to sell. The trajectory of emissions trading from the original proposal to its realisation in the Kyoto Protocol encapsulates many of the big economic changes going on at that time. For Grubb and those of many who took the idea up, like Scott Barrett at the London

---

[24] World Bank, *Greening Industry: New Roles for Communities, Markets and Governments* (New York: Oxford University Press, 2000).

[25] M. Grubb, *The Greenhouse Effect: Negotiating Targets* (London: Royal Institute of International Affairs, 1989).

[26] L. Lunde, 'Global warming and a system of tradeable emissions permits: a review of the current debate', *International Challenges*, **11**(3) (1991), 15–28; R. Hahn and R. Stavins, 'Trading in greenhouse permits: A critical examination of design and implementation issues', in H. Lee (ed.), *Shaping National Responses to Climate Change: A Post-Rio Guide* (Washington: Island Press, 1995), pp. 117–219.

Business School, or Frank Joshua at the United Nations Conference on Trade and Development (UNCTAD), it was designed both to be efficient *and* equitable.

Efficiency was fast becoming the most important value in neo-liberal ideology, while equity was the legacy of a dominant framing of global environmental politics since the first UN conference on the environment, the Stockholm Conference on the Human Environment in 1972. Emissions trading systems, in Grubb's or UNCTAD's hands, would enable North–South transfers of wealth and technology and thus respond to the challenge of growth in countries like China and India. The assumption was that a principle of per-capita emissions would be the only legitimate basis for allocating emissions, and thus while countries in the North would be short on permits, those in the South would have a surplus, and thus earn income from selling permits to the North.

Once emissions trading became a formal part of the negotiations, however, it became clear that the equitable part of the equation was to be eliminated. This was largely a result of a diplomatic impasse it provoked. Northern countries baulked at the financial transfers implied, while Southern countries resisted steadfastly the implicit limit on their emissions. The legacy of widening inequalities produced this impasse in climate diplomacy. But it also resulted from the ideological priority attached to efficiency and the way that markets are assumed to produce such efficiency, an idea that was more important to powerful actors than the plea for equity.

In fact this obsession with efficiency and markets also explains the way in which emissions trading was preferred over carbon taxes. Such taxes have also been proposed and implemented in one or two countries such as Sweden and the Netherlands, while the UK's climate change levy was a quasi-carbon tax. But they have failed to get off the ground in most places, for example in the EU where a long carbon tax debate was stalled because of strong industry resistance and a reluctance among some member states to cede tax-raising powers to a regional organisation. Canada provides a classic example of the difficulty in generating support for carbon taxes, where one of the two main parties, the Liberals, ran in the federal election of 2008 with carbon taxes as a high profile part of the campaign, and consequently suffered huge losses at the polls.

In the UN negotiating process, occasional proposals for harmonised introduction of such taxes never got anywhere. Everyday political processes of interest groups defending their interests is important here – big corporations successfully resisted on the grounds of the increased costs, and new taxes are never popular with the public. In a more open global economy, the prospect of relocation also meant that 'carbon leakage' might occur, whereby a tax would simply have the effect of driving the most polluting companies or parts of the production process overseas, resulting in no overall reduction in emissions. This was an argument successfully used by industry groups to prevent taxes from being used in the first place.

So emissions trading emerged as the preferred option because of its ideological fit with neoliberal logic. But it was also more successful because of its fit with the interests of newly dominant financial actors. The USA first formally proposed emissions trading in the UN negotiations in December 1996, and initially there was much resistance from more or less everyone. The US rationale was initially to create flexibility for countries in implementing their commitments. The political resistance to emissions reductions in the USA was considerably stronger than in Europe, and the Clinton administration, while favourable itself to action, was heavily constrained by a Congress which was hostile. Economists in the USA also insisted that the costs of reductions to the US economy were very high, and Clinton was certainly a strong proponent of using market-mechanisms to bring compliance costs down. These factors combined to make the USA propose emissions trading as a means to pursue reductions in a manner that minimised the costs associated with them.

In the Kyoto negotiations up to 1997, countries ended up agreeing to emissions trading mostly because of the USA's single-minded determination to include the flexible mechanisms and the desperate desire of others to keep the USA on board. But the interesting period was the next three years, through to around 2000. In this period, there was a dramatic transformation in the fortunes of emissions trading. The Kyoto process plodded on slowly because of the many unresolved questions about its various innovative elements. But the EU changed its mind about emissions trading shortly after Kyoto, during 1998–1999, becoming a proponent in the Kyoto process but also starting to plan its own system. Individual European countries like the UK and Denmark started also to plan their own emissions trading systems.

Also interested in emissions trading, albeit for different reasons, was a whole range of private market actors that emerged in the late 1990s. Companies such as EcoSecurities (1997), CO2e.com (2000) and Point Carbon (2000) were created. They became key actors in the carbon markets that we discuss at greater length in chapters 5–7. Existing banks, such as Barclays or Dresdner Kleinwort, developed their own carbon trading offices. Annual carbon finance and carbon market conferences were started, and a Carbon Expo – the 'global carbon market fair and conference' – has been held every year since 2004. In 2005 alone emission reduction purchase agreements for more than 100 projects were signed or reached advanced negotiations at Carbon Expo.[27] New associations of actors, like the International Emissions Trading Association (IETA) or the Emissions Marketing Association, and more recently the Carbon Markets and Investors Association, were created or expanded considerably in reaction to the growing momentum of emissions trading systems. But they haven't only reacted to the pressure from politicians; they have become crucial to why politicians didn't abandon emissions trading in the face of various pressures over the next few years – notably the ongoing difficult negotiations in the Kyoto process and the withdrawal of the USA from the process in 2001.

Emissions trading thus became almost unstoppable once the dominant financial actors realised its potential as a new market, with its derivatives, options, swaps, insurance, and so on, and thus as a profitable enterprise. While the key period of take-off of this dynamic was 1996–2000, after that date the process continued to mushroom. We explore the character of these markets in more detail in Chapters 5 and 6. Here, the point to underscore is that emissions trading 'gained traction' because of the intertwining of the need that policy-makers had for flexibility in meeting commitments and the realisation by financial institutions that the emissions market could be the site of significant growth and profits.

Some financial actors also became interested in climate change for another reason. As we show in more detail in Chapter 4, insurance companies started to worry in the early 1990s about large-scale payouts for extreme weather events (principally hurricanes and flooding), which had already increased by that point, and were projected in many models to become even more frequent and intense. Insurers started to act through the 1990s, in conjunction in particular with the United Nations Environment Program (UNEP)'s Finance Initiative which was set up to promote action by financial institutions on climate change and other environmental issues. But their activity exploded in the 2000s, particularly through the Carbon Disclosure Project (CDP).

---

[27] See: http://www.carbonexpo.com/wEnglisch/carbonexpo2/global/ueber_die_mes se/carbon_Expo_2.shtml.

The CDP is a project whereby investors (led by the insurers, but joined by banks and pension funds) attempt to shape the activities of other companies by getting them to disclose their carbon intensity and their strategies to limit emissions. The CDP now has $57 trillion of assets behind it.[28]

Financial companies thus have complicated interests in relation to climate change. They are exposed to all sorts of risks from climate change itself – direct exposure through insurance for homes and businesses, but also indirectly to banks when loans go bad because of weather-related risks. But they have also become the power brokers in contemporary capitalism, capable of moving money around, putting pressure on manufacturers, governments and other social actors. Their power has become a crucial element in the politics of climate change.

NETWORKS FOR CLIMATE CHANGE

As in neoliberalism more generally, organisation around climate change has taken the form of collaborative partnerships, involving networks of all sorts of actors. This can be seen in various projects, from the approach made by Greenpeace's Jeremy Leggett to insurers in the early 1990s, trying to persuade them that climate change was a threat to their interests, to the UNEP Finance Initiative, through to the CDP project.

The Clean Development Mechanism (CDM), one of the central elements of the Kyoto Protocol, has often been described as a huge 'public–private partnership'.[29] Those involved in attempting to put it into practice after its surprise appearance very late in the Kyoto negotiations talk about it precisely as an exercise in 'learning by doing'.[30] If the CDM is described as a public–private partnership, the World Bank's Prototype Carbon Fund (PCF) is described as an 'implementation network',[31] bringing together interested parties from North and South under the rules set out by the CDM.

---

[28] See: http://www.cdproject.net, accessed 19 November 2007.

[29] See for example C. Streck, 'New partnerships in global environmental policy: the clean development mechanism', *Journal of Environment and Development*, **13**(3), (2004), 295–322.

[30] Interview, Christine Zumkeller, former UNFCCC secretariat member, Bonn, October 2007.

[31] C. Streck, 'New partnerships in global environmental policy...'.

Partnerships have also been the preferred way of trying to encourage the uptake of renewable options that will be critical to the achievement of climate capitalism. Initially pushed by the German government, the Renewable Energy and Energy Efficiency Partnership is an international public–private partnership set up in 2002 and funded by governments, businesses and development banks. It is aimed at the development of market conditions that foster sustainable energy and energy efficiency and works to structure policy and regulatory initiatives for clean energy.

Partnership can also be a euphemism for voluntary regulation, however. Proposed as an alternative to Kyoto – critics suggest it was designed to derail Kyoto – the Asia Pacific Partnership on Clean Development and Climate is a public–private partnership that brings together the governments and private sectors of countries that collectively account for more than half the world's economy, population and energy use including Australia, China, India, Japan, the United States and Canada. The partnership does not contain any emission-reduction targets. Rather, it aims to produce forms of cooperation that facilitate investment in clean technologies, goods and services, accelerate the sharing of energy-efficient best practices, and identify policy barriers to the diffusion of clean energy technologies.[32]

At national levels, many organisations have emerged which operate in this partnership fashion. Sometimes arms-length organisations, for example the Carbon Trust in the UK, are used by governments both to implement policy and at the same time act as sites of collaboration amongst companies and between them and NGOs. These bodies aim to foster learning about best practices and provide for the exchange of ideas. Some are based in one country, but operate transnationally. Examples include the UK-based bank HSBC's Climate Partnership. Some of these groups defy traditional categories. The Climate Group, for example, is a body that is technically a non-profit organisation based in London, but which can't be understood as a traditional NGO organised around research and lobbying. Rather, it has transnational corporations and subnational government units as members. They apply to join the Climate Group in order to be regarded as 'leaders' in their CO_2 reductions strategies and use the Climate Group both for public relations (PR) purposes and to be able to network with other similar organisations. The group (both its organisation and its members) acts

[32] APP, Asia Pacific Partnership on Climate and Clean Development, 2008. See http://www.asiapacificpartnership.org/brochure/APP_Booklet_Aug2008.pdf.

to promote CO_2 reductions amongst other companies and subnational actors. The group's close ties to former UK Prime Minister Tony Blair have also provided a high-profile national platform for projecting their ideas into global policy debates on climate change.

These sorts of networks are highly fluid, expanding and changing focus rapidly, aiming to get people to act in ways that neither traditional regulation nor exhortation from governments can. It is certainly the case that the development of some of these networks can be understood as the result of efforts by private companies to avoid such regulation – to show their 'good behaviour' and so prevent a stricter form of action imposed by governments. Chapter 3 shows how climate change has become a leading Corporate Social Responsibility (CSR) issue for companies. But at the same time, as we pointed out in Chapter 1, climate change presents such fundamental challenges to the organisation of capitalist economies that flexible networks, focused on 'learning by doing' as an integral part of strategies for reducing CO_2, are a necessary component of responses. We come back to the interplay between these organisations and larger questions of the 'governance' of climate capitalism in Chapter 7.

CLIMATE CHANGE AND CAPITALISM'S DISCONTENTS

Those seeking new ways of responding to climate change, like the Climate Group, are organised in novel ways. So too are protest groups campaigning both for more aggressive cuts in carbon emissions and against specific types of policies such as emissions trading. Groups like Rising Tide, Climate Justice, Plane Stupid!, together with more loose networks of activists organising protests such as those at the Copenhagen climate summit in 2009 or those disrupting coal power plants or airports in 2008 and 2009 as part of 'Climate Camps', frequently make the connection between the weak response to climate change and the domination of the world by neoliberal capitalism. Some look at the history given above, the close link between energy use and growth, and conclude that to deal with climate change means an end to economic growth, and by extension, to the capitalist way the world is organised.

To act on climate change is, for many activists, to oppose capitalism, or at least its current, finance-led form.[33] Many of these groups

[33] I. Angus, D. Wall and D. Tanuro, *The Global Fight for Climate Justice: Anti-Capitalist Responses to Global Warming and Environmental Destruction* (London: IMG publishers, 2009).

have arisen out of the anti-globalisation protests which were widespread in the late 1990s; most famously those at major economic summits in Seattle, Prague and Genoa have evolved into the regular World Social Forum meetings, where activists share ideas and attempt to build movements around the world against neoliberal capitalism. The Durban Declaration on Carbon Trading produced by the climate justice movement in 2004, for example, makes explicit links between current attempts to turn the Earth's 'carbon-cycling capacity into property to be bought and sold in a global market' and historical 'attempts to commodify land, food, labour, forests, water, genes and ideas'. Groups signing up to the declaration claim, 'Through this process of creating a new commodity – carbon – the Earth's ability and capacity to support a climate conducive to life and human societies is now passing into the same corporate hands that are destroying the climate.'[34]

The aspects of neoliberalism discussed above – the ideological focus on markets, the dominance of finance, and the deepening inequalities, in particular – are precisely what angers many activists. This feeds through into the way that protest groups oppose particular sorts of climate policies. It manifests itself as opposition to emissions trading and carbon offset programmes.

Specific campaigns have been directed in particular at the carbon offset markets, both in the CDM and in the voluntary carbon market. These markets have been widely regarded as a means by which rich consumers in the West merely displace their high-carbon consuming practices by buying offsets for their emissions cheaply in the South. This is referred to as 'carbon colonialism'; a new way of acquiring land and resources in poor countries to sustain profligate consumption of the rich. To this criticism is added that of 'climate fraud'; that many of the projects double-count emissions paid for by other clients or that the scale of the emissions reduction is exaggerated or non-existent.[35] Groups have lodged complaints over the carbon-neutral claims of companies and wealthy individuals, challenging what they consider to be the 'scientifically dubious practice of planting trees to compensate for pollution'. Their arguments are informed

---

[34] Durban Declaration, 'Climate Justice Now! The Durban Declaration on Carbon Trading,' 2004, signed 10 October, Glenmore Centre, Durban, South Africa.

[35] L. Lohmann, *Carbon Trading: A Critical Conversation on Climate Change, Privatisation and Power*. Development Dialogue No. 48, September (Uddevalla Sweden: Mediaprint, 2006).

by a broader position adopted by many environmental NGOs on this issue that such practices 'distract attention away from the fundamental changes urgently necessary if we are to achieve a more sustainable and just future'.[36]

These policies are opposed because they turn climate change into yet another opportunity for financiers to make money through creating new commodities, and because they create new North–South inequalities or exacerbate existing ones. What is interesting is that as well as questioning and contesting the limits of commodification and exposing 'fraudulent' practice in carbon markets, such forms of activism also force advocates of market approaches to legitimise themselves. For example, they have led to restrictions on the sorts of projects that can be included within the CDM and temporary dismissals of organisations approved to validate projects where acts of climate fraud have been uncovered. They have also helped to create ways to govern the carbon offset markets, as in the Voluntary Carbon Standard or the Gold Standard. These set higher standards for those buyers and sellers of emissions reductions wanting to distance themselves from the scandals and controversy that activists have generated around 'climate fraud' and 'carbon colonialism'. We discuss these further in Chapter 9.

So the ways neoliberalism and climate policies are opposed by activists are closely intertwined. But opposition to both also helps to shape how neoliberalism and climate policy are developed. Neoliberalism has been 'softened' during the 2000s, in part because of recurrent economic crises, and the current crisis may well produce more reforms. But it has also changed because of sustained campaigning against many of its worst effects. Business-led voluntary codes of conduct and certification schemes offer an attempt to allay consumer fears and NGO pressure about increasingly mobile companies taking advantage of poor working conditions and lower environmental standards in a globalised economy. Similarly, carbon markets are being shaped precisely by the protests against them. Neoliberalism has been plagued by constant crises over its legitimacy; neoliberal climate change politics can be expected to be subject to similar crises.

---

[36] CTW (Carbon Trade Watch), 'Environmentalists Cry Foul at Rock Stars Polluting Companies Carbon-Neutral Claims' (2004) (press release, 6 May). See http://www. tni.org/ctw, accessed 19 November 2004.

CONCLUSIONS

By the time the Kyoto Protocol had been agreed in 1997, it had become absolutely normal to think that the appropriate way to deal with climate change is not so much to focus on restricting fossil fuel use, but on the creation of markets. Governments, international organisations and private actors were all focused on the *creation* of markets for emissions, of *new or expanding* markets for renewable energy technologies and of new *investment* opportunities.

Shortly afterwards, the term 'carbon market' was coined to describe the totality of these sorts of approaches to climate change. What they have in common is that they all turn carbon into a commodity that can be traded. Neoliberalism had definitively placed its stamp on the character of climate politics: its market-orientation; the opportunities it creates for finance to invest in a variety of new markets; its struggle to deal with the global inequalities it generates; and its organisation through fluid networks rather than traditional hierarchies.

Meanwhile, however, global capitalism has continued as normal. Neither the development of ideas about climate change, nor the novel sorts of policy developed to deal with it, have yet had any significant impact on emissions levels. Global carbon emissions continue to grow, largely in line with global GDP. Many states and businesses still take no account of climate change in their routine planning, and assume that the future will look largely like the past, that is, based fundamentally on growth in fossil fuel consumption. Some states seem to have started on a path of decarbonisation, but even they have only been able to do so stimulated by external accidents. In the UK, for example, often taken as a leader in climate policy, emissions have gone down principally because of the 'dash for gas' in the early 1990s, triggered by electricity privatisation and the Thatcher government's determination to break the power of the unions by taking on the striking coal miners. Another leader, Germany, was helped greatly by reunification of East and West in 1990, and the collapse of East German industry that followed. The current obsession with 'energy security' in the USA is another possible accident that could trigger investment in renewables and energy efficiency (alternatively, it could stimulate investment in offshore oil drilling and tar sands). But while there are some leaders, others resolutely follow the 'carboniferous' approach, digging up 'ancient sunlight' to promote economic growth, and new poles of growth such as in China and India dwarf efforts of some countries and businesses to limit emissions. Meanwhile, the vast majority of the World Bank's lending for energy projects continues to go to fossil fuels, despite the organisation having made a pitch to play a positive role in leading responses to climate change.[37]

This history provokes a number of questions. If business actors are newly empowered under neoliberalism, how have they responded to the challenge of climate change? How do the approaches of different parts of business vary? How has business changed position since the early years of climate politics? These are questions we turn to in the next chapter.

[37] WRI, 'Correcting the World's greatest market failure: Climate change and multilateral development banks' (2008). See http://www.wri.org/publication/correcting-the-worlds-greatest-market-failure; WWF-UK, 'The World Bank and its carbon footprint: why the World Bank is still far from being an environment bank' (2008). See http://www.wwf.org.uk/filelibrary/pdf/world_bank_report.pdf.

3

Climate for business: from threat to opportunity

It may seem hard to believe today, but there was once a time that business denied there was such a thing as climate change. Vast amounts of money and effort went into discrediting the scientific basis on which the case for action was made. Business lobby organisations were set up and funded by those companies that felt threatened by action on climate change. Aggressive lobbying which aimed to derail national and international responses to the issue was commonplace on Capitol Hill in Washington or at UN climate negotiations.

From the mid 1990s onwards, however, a fascinating transformation took place. Though a handful of companies continue vociferously to resist tougher forms of action, many started to sense that regulation of greenhouse gases (GHGs) was on its way, and that they were better off preparing themselves to compete and survive in this new business environment. Some then learned what a smaller number of companies had already worked out – that beyond just being a question of risk management, there were in fact many good business opportunities in a carbon-constrained economy. There was a strong 'business case' for action on climate change. The US Climate Action Partnership, for example, an organisation that is 'committed to a pathway that will slow, stop and reverse the growth of US emissions while expanding the US economy'[1] includes among its members companies like Alcoa, British Petroleum, Ford, General Electric and Shell, all of which were previously among the ranks of the industry lobbies resisting calls for action. Even Exxon Mobil, the last of the big US oil companies to concede ground, now officially accepts the existence of climate change

[1] See http://www.us-cap.org/.

and the need to reduce emissions, although it still also funds organisations like the Heritage Foundation which deny the existence of climate change.[2] Many now accept the need for action, are taking action themselves and increasingly see in climate change the opportunity to make lots of money.

This shift in attitude among key corporate actors is crucial to the possibility of a transformation towards climate capitalism. Without the support of business, widespread transformations of the economy are impossible to imagine. But how do we explain such a seemingly dramatic transition? How much of it is little more than good public relations? Or is business indeed at the forefront of bringing about a shift to climate capitalism? What does the character of the transformation tell us about the likely shape of climate capitalism that might emerge?

A CLIMATE OF DENIAL

Climate change first registered on the radar screen of fossil fuel companies in the late 1980s and early 1990s amid growing demands for an international treaty to address the issue. The UN's Intergovernmental Panel on Climate Change (IPCC) had been set up in 1988, and, at the end of 1990, negotiations were set in train to agree a treaty in time for the Rio conference of 1992. Businesses whose interests were threatened by the prospect of action to reduce the use of fossil fuels realised they were under attack. They moved into gear to hire lobbyists and form coalitions to defend their interests. Two organisations in particular stood out; the Global Climate Coalition (GCC) and the Climate Council. Members included all the main companies involved in oil extraction, car or steel manufacturing, and electricity generation, as well as industry associations like the US National Association of Manufacturers and the National Mining Association. Though now disbanded, it is difficult to overestimate the importance of the GCC during the early to mid 1990s as *the* voice of concerned industry in the international climate negotiations. As Robert Reinstein, former head of the US climate delegation and then-industry lobbyist told us back in 1996: 'When GCC, which represents companies constituting a very significant proportion of the country's GDP start making noises, they obviously get attention.'[3]

---

[2] D. Adam, 'ExxonMobil continuing to fund climate skeptic groups, records show', *The Guardian*, 1 July 2009. See http://www.guardian.co.uk/environment/2009/jul/01/exxon-mobil-climate-change-sceptics-funding.

[3] Quoted in P. Newell, *Climate for Change: Non-State Actors and the Global Politics of the Greenhouse* (Cambridge: Cambridge University Press, 2000).

At national levels, powerful groups sought to fight off policy measures that threatened their interests, such as the proposed EU carbon tax in 1992. These groups included the Confederation of British Industry (UK), the World Coal Institute, the American Petroleum Institute or Western Fuels Association (US), as well as regional groupings such as employers' organisations like the Union of Industrial Employers' Confederations in Europe (UNICE, now called Business Europe) and the European Round Table of Industrialists.

A multi-pronged strategy was developed to get the message across loud and clear: that climate change was not happening; that if it was then it was natural and nothing to do with human activities (certainly not fossil fuel use); and that to act to limit emissions would cripple industrial economies and result in politicians being kicked out of office. This chorus of opinion helped make a 'wait and see' approach sound like common sense. 'Cool heads in a warming world', was one of their slogans. The strategy was to kill off climate change as an issue before it got too serious and gathered too much political momentum. And for a long time it worked.

SHOOT THE MESSENGER

One approach was to challenge the science behind climate change. Scientists such as Fred Singer, Robert Balling and Patrick Michaels were (and are) only too happy to receive funds from fossil fuel lobbies for their work, which raised questions about human contributions to climate change and the very existence of the problem itself.[4] Industry bodies such as the American Enterprise Institute, as recently as 2007, were offering individual scientists sums of $10,000 each to discredit the prevailing IPCC consensus.[5] The fossil fuel lobby was particularly well linked to those governments that contribute most to global warming. In the USA, Bush senior's Chief of Staff John Sununu played a key part in ensuring that President Bush senior only got to hear doubts about the science and studies that emphasised the costs of taking action. Sununu's director of communications in the White House was none other than John Shlaes who went on to head the Global Climate Coalition leading the assault on a treaty on climate change.

[4] P. Newell, *Climate for Change...*, pp. 81–2, 101.
[5] I. Sample, 'Scientists offered cash to dispute climate study', *The Guardian*, 2 February 2007.

Insiders such as Sununu certainly made the job of industry lobbyists a whole lot easier. When in 1989 NASA scientist James Hansen found his warning to Congress about the urgency of action on climate change had been watered down by the US Office of Management and Budget, the scale of political gate-keeping that was going on became clear for all to see.

CREATE CONFUSION

As it became more obvious that those challenging the science were often industry stooges, another strategy started to appeal. Who do the public trust most in environmental debates? Government? Rarely. Business? Never. NGOs? Most of the time. QED.

The next strategy was therefore to create business-funded environmental NGOs or what critics call 'astroturf' (fake-green) organisations. It aimed at persuading an increasingly anxious public that they had nothing to fear, that protecting the environment is all well and good, but that all this talk of climate change was a load of hot air. In one case, the Western Fuels Association, the Edison Electric Institute and the National Coal Association of the USA created the benign sounding 'Information Council for the Environment', which launched a $500,000 advertising campaign 'to reposition global warming as theory, not fact'. The sum for the campaign was more than the amount spent on climate change campaigns by all the largest environmental NGOs combined. Other examples included the Cooler Heads Coalition and the Coalition for Vehicle Choice, a corporate front organisation that ran an infamous campaign with a woman complaining that 'the government wants to take away my SUV'. In the run-up to Kyoto, these groups spent $13 million in an advertising campaign designed to discredit both the Kyoto Protocol in particular, and fears about climate change more generally.

This strategy involved focusing on schools, local media and 'middle America'. Videos, booklets and posters were prepared which helpfully explained that climate change is perfectly natural and that burning coal and oil is a good thing. We've done it for centuries, right? And in any case trees absorb any CO_2, so let's do the right thing and plant more trees. Elsewhere, more sophisticated critics of action on climate change were enrolled. Bjorn Lomberg, the self-proclaimed 'sceptical environmentalist' was smart enough to engage media and policy elites with his idea that the threat posed by climate change was exaggerated and certainly paled into insignificance when compared with other issues of concern to well-meaning liberals such as HIV/AIDs or the need to tackle global poverty.[6]

Such strategies of creating the appearance of public opposition to action on climate change continue to be used by some companies in the USA. Indeed those that have stated their support for emissions cuts have come under pressure to resign their membership of the American Petroleum Institute which in 2009 called on its members to encourage their employees to attend 'citizen energy rallies' in protest against President Obama's Waxman–Markey bill of climate legislation.[7] This strategy has also involved attempting to undermine the credibility of mainstream climate scientists. In 1996, there was a vicious attack against Ben Santer over alleged changes to an agreed IPCC document. In 2009, in the run-up to the Copenhagen negotiations, illegally hacked emails were used to attack climate scientists from the University of East Anglia.

WHO PAYS?

The next battle ground was economics: how much would it cost to tackle this issue? The fossil fuel lobby set to work producing economic studies suggesting that economies would be driven into recession if they adopted measures proposed by leading scientists. A popular figure in the early 1990s was that reducing CO_2 emissions by 20% – the amount proposed by a high-profile conference in Toronto in 1988 and repeated by many groups as a first step – would cost the US economy $3.6 trillion. This figure was used in the 1990 Economic Report of the President, and came from analyses by US economists Alan Manne and Richard Richels. In the spin of the GCC and right-wing think tanks, however, what got lost was that this was the high end of a wide range of possible costs. These ranged from $800 billion to $3.6 trillion – other economists like William Cline, Jae Edmonds, or those at the Organisation of Economic Cooperation and Development (OECD) gave lower figures still. Furthermore, the figure was for the cumulative costs between 1990 and 2100 – in other words spread over 110 years! As many pointed out, once the figure was translated into a more sensible framing, it amounted to something like a three-month delay in the

---

[6] B. Lomberg, 'Climate change can wait. World health can't', *The Observer*, 2 July 2006.

[7] T. Macalister, 'BP and Shell warned to halt campaign against Obama's climate change bill', *The Guardian*, 20 August 2009.

doubling of GDP. But the huge numbers proved very effective in creating the sense of a calamity induced by emissions reduction goals.

Related to this was the argument that if we reduce emissions in the North, businesses would merely move overseas, producing a loss of jobs and competitiveness and no net gains in emissions reductions. In a globalised economy of capital mobility and internationalised structures of production, companies argued, there is no point in one country taking action if others don't do the same. This has become known as the problem of 'carbon leakage'. The argument was used effectively in particular to block proposals for a carbon tax in the EU in the wake of the UN Rio summit in 1992. The prospect of the tax, according to *The Economist*, 'spurred the massed ranks of Europe's industrialists to mount what is probably their most powerful offensive against an EC proposal'.[8] Shocked at the intensity of business mobilisation against the tax, Carlos Ripa de Meana, EU Environment Commissioner at the time, described the lobbying offensive as a 'violent assault'.

THE BREAK-UP OF THE ANCIEN RÉGIME

Then came the fall of the old guard or *ancien régime*. The fossil fuel lobby that had held sway for so long saw its power start to wane. It didn't happen overnight of course. But the rhetoric of the fossil fuel lobby and opponents of action on climate change that limiting GHG emissions would have disastrous economic effects ceased to resonate with many business people during the mid 1990s.

If you were manufacturing in an industry where your energy costs were high but new technologies and production processes promised significant cost savings and efficiency gains, or if you were a corporate consumer noticing the steady price reductions for wind or solar energy, would you be persuaded that reducing emissions would be economically disastrous? In addition, if at the same time you became increasingly convinced that climate change was real and would itself have many negative consequences, would you continue to be single-mindedly focused on the price increases for your energy inputs? If, for example, ,you were an insurer noticing increased payouts to extreme weather events, a farmer vulnerable to crop failures or a banker investing in businesses in low-lying areas, would you only think about the increased costs caused by carbon taxes or regulations, or would you also start to make the connection between carbon emissions and climate impacts?

[8] *The Economist*, 'Europe's industries play dirty', 9 May 1992, pp. 91–2.

During the mid 1990s, many businesses started to make these connections and the line peddled by the old guard increasingly seemed less
persuasive. The question of costs remained central to the calculations
of these companies, but they increasingly came to different conclusions about what the costs of acting on climate change were. At the
same time, a shift in the more general landscape of climate politics was
discernible. Amid a strengthening scientific consensus as well as growing public concern fuelled by a series of 'natural' catastrophes like hurricanes Andrew or Mitch, moves were afoot to negotiate legally binding
commitments in the form of a protocol based on the UN Framework
Convention on Climate Change. For some companies, this started to
change the calculations they made. Many were rethinking how climate change could be integrated into their business strategies and that
the costs of responding might not be too bad. And they also started to
judge (less quickly in the USA than elsewhere) that outright opposition
to emissions reductions would be counter-productive and might undermine the credibility of their broader efforts to present themselves in a
green light. Instead, it would make more sense to adapt to and shape
the policies that governments would implement as a result.

DIFFERENT APPROACHES

Responses among businesses took diverse forms. The 'Sunrise' industries energy conservation, efficiency, and renewables – already had a
lot to gain from action. They had been working with some environmental groups to make the case for tough targets to stimulate markets
for their products (for example groups like E7 and the European Wind
Energy Association). In that sense they had always had different interests from the fossil fuel lobby.

For others, the growing attention to the issue also presented
them with new opportunities. This included the nuclear industry, able
to present itself as having a key role to play in meeting future energy
demand in a carbon-constrained future. But it also provided momentum
for innovations to existing products and technologies. Biotechnology
companies, wounded by bruising encounters with activists opposing
genetic modification which damaged their green credentials, raised
the prospect of drought-resistant genetically modified (GM) crops as
a part of efforts to adapt to climate change or GM trees that increase
the absorption of CO_2 serving as carbon sinks. Biofuels were also promoted heavily by governments such as Brazil where ethanol-based

combustion has been hailed as an 'agro-fix' for the depleting supplies of oil with which the world is now confronted.

For some sectors of industry, however, the primary motivation was to gain a *first mover advantage* by innovating in profoundly new ways. Some car companies for example saw tighter fuel efficiency standards on the horizon and spotted a new market niche to be met. Toyota developed its Prius hybrid car with the slogan 'Mean but green' and tellingly 'The power of a good idea'.[9]

For others still, being active on climate change was about reputation management and Corporate Social Responsibility (CSR). Those that had embraced the rhetoric about being a socially and environmentally responsible company in general had to have something to say about climate change, especially in response to questions and pressure from NGOs, consumers and, increasingly, investors. We will see below that this was the case for Shell and British Petroleum (BP) that had both been the target of NGO campaigns about controversial investments in Nigeria and Colombia, respectively.

Meanwhile, it was the fear of regulation that prompted sectors such as the aviation and car industries to become more proactive. As we will see below, in Europe they began to press for emissions trading over taxation in the case of aviation, or voluntary agreements over regulation in the case of the car industry. For others, in the financial sector for example, a strategy on climate change was simply sensible risk management to reduce liabilities and exposure to risk.

Many companies of course are prompted to act by combinations of these motivations. What is interesting is that faced with a similar political challenge, companies have reacted in diverse ways and are motivated to act for a wide range of reasons that combine to produce change in corporate behaviour. The overall tendency, however, was towards seeing failure to anticipate likely policies as a business *risk*.

CLIMATE CHANGE AS RISK MANAGEMENT

Thinking about climate change as a risk rather than a threat has enabled many companies to develop strategies that take account of much more than simply the immediate costs of emissions abatement. Companies came to see many different types of risks to their business in relation to climate change. They faced risks of *incurring*

---

[9] See http://www.toyota.co.uk/cgi-bin/toyota/bv/frame_start.jsp?id=PS2_Exp&Camp aignID=TOY0795&BrochureRCode=AS5623AR002010&TestdriveRCode=AS5623A R002012&LandingPage=PPC_TOY0795_priusg.

costs from later regulation if they didn't plan for them now; risks to their *reputation* (and thus to potential markets if they were seen as unresponsive to societal demands); risks of *legal liabilities* if they were seen to cause damages to others by refusing to cap their emissions; and risks of *losing out* on new market opportunities. All of these combined to produce new corporate strategies, even among some parts of the fossil fuel industry like the oil giants Shell and BP.

The 'sunrise' industries – those involved in renewable energy, energy efficiency and conservation, in particular – were always more than happy for governments to send strong signals to the market that the future was bright in their sector. But frankly they were always too small to make it to centre stage. What became interesting was the way major companies were now acknowledging and acting upon the issue. In May 1997, BP's chief executive officer (CEO) John Browne decided that there was mileage in being seen to be green, announcing the shift of strategy at a high-profile talk at Stanford University. With his backing, the company re-branded itself 'Beyond Petroleum', an ambitious claim for a company whose 2005 accounts indicate that the company invested just $800 million a year into its 'Alternative Energy' division, representing just 5.7 per cent of its 2005 total capital investment, while 72 per cent of BP's new capital investment was spent looking for yet more oil and gas.[10] Browne's strategy reflects precisely this assessment of climate in terms of a number of different, but intersecting, business risks. Assessments of the risks companies face are always subject to change and re-evaluation of course. The current financial crisis seems to have damaged BP's alternative energy budget, which was down from $1.4 billion (£850 million) to between $500 million and $1 billion in 2009, while in April of the same year the company closed a number of solar-panel manufacturing plants in Spain.[11] At the same time the company is increasing investments in controversial oil sands extraction in Alberta, Canada.

One approach to risk management is *to hedge your bets* – in this case positioning yourself in emerging renewable markets in case they take off dramatically while protecting your core corporate assets in the fossil fuel economy. Lord Oxburgh, former Chairman of Shell, explained it the following way:

[10] Friends of the Earth, 'Shell vs. BP: who is performing worst on climate change?', Press release, 27 July 2006. See http://www.foe.co.uk/resource/press_releases/shell_vs_bp_who_is_perform_27072006.html, accessed 19 December 2009.

[11] T. McAlister, 'BP shuts alternative energy HQ', *The Guardian*, 29 June 2009. See http://www.guardian.co.uk/business/2009/jun/28/bp-alternative-energy, accessed 19 December 2009.

If you look at it from oil companies' point of view, effectively what they're doing at the moment is continuing business as usual, and sticking toes in water in a number of areas which might become important in future. But at present there is a relatively poor business case for making significantly greater investment in these new areas if we can call them that, so when I agree that they may not be investing enough, that is if you like the point of view of a citizen of the world rather than a shareholder in one of the companies.[12]

Recent events suggest that Shell, having dabbled in energy alternatives, has decided their core interests remain in oil. The company announced in March 2009 that it will no longer invest in renewable technologies such as wind, solar and hydro power on the basis that they are 'not economic'. Linda Cook, Shell's executive director of gas and power, said 'We do not expect material investment [in wind and solar] going forward.'[13]

Other companies nevertheless followed the lead in taking voluntary action on climate change to reduce their emissions, capitalising on the economic savings to be made and the public relations credit to be earned from being seen to take a lead on the issue. Chemicals giant DuPont reduced its emissions by 65% below their 1990 levels, while IBM has saved $115 million since 1998 through cutting its carbon emissions.

One of the highest profile examples has been General Electric's *Ecomagination* initiative announced in 2005. This involved GE doubling investment in research for cleaner technologies to $1.5 billion a year by 2010, doubling sales of environmentally friendly products to at least $20 billion by 2010 and reducing GHG emissions by 1% by 2012 from 2004 levels. It has received resounding praise from environmental NGOs and the business sector alike. The company is also being rewarded financially, with revenues from the company's portfolio of energy efficient and environmentally advantageous products and services exceeding $12 billion in 2006, up 20 per cent from 2005.[14]

---

[12] David Strahan, author of *The Last Oil Shock*, interview with Lord Oxburgh. See http://www.davidstrahan.com/blog/?p=40, accessed 19 December 2009.

[13] T. Webb, 'Shell dumps wind, solar and hydro power in favour of biofuels,' *The Guardian*, 17 March 2009. See http://www.guardian.co.uk/business/2009/mar/17/royaldutchshell-energy, accessed 19 December 2009.

[14] GE Eco-imagination report, 'Investing and Delivering on Eco-imagination', 2007. http://ge.ecomagination.com/site/downloads/news/2007ecoreport.pdf, accessed 19 December 2009.

Ecomagination was driven by GE's CEO Jeffrey Immelt, who pushed the issue upon taking his post in 2001. He argued that GE was operating in a rapidly changing environment where it had to deal with diminishing domestic oil and natural gas supplies, consumer demands for efficient products and the need to deal with climate change. To remain competitive, GE required a radical change in technology and products. Also, he maintained that instead of being defensive in relation to this changing reality, GE should go on the offensive and take a leadership role in reducing outputs and developing environmentally friendly products that reduce emissions.[15]

For many conservatives such talk was almost blasphemous and highly risky. When under attack from them about his company's proactive stance on climate change Immelt protested, 'Look, I've never voted Democrat, I work for investors!' He was speaking at the 'ECO: nomics' conference in California where he was joined by CEOs from Wal-Mart, Duke Power and Dow Chemicals in making the argument that federal action to cap GHGs 'will unleash entrepreneurs and big business alike to move America towards a clean-energy economy'.[16]

MAKING THE CASE FOR BUSINESS ACTION

A number of NGOs such as the Climate Group in the UK and the Pew Center in the USA have played an important role in making the business case for action on climate change and publicising the benefits achieved by existing leaders in the field. Some companies such as BP and Shell have gone so far as to establish their own intra-firm trading systems that encourage competitive reductions between different parts of the company. This carries benefits such as saving money through reduced use of energy, first-mover advantages that come from developing new technologies and production processes, and public and employee credibility from being seen as an environmentally responsible company.

Given this array of business initiatives, some go so far as to claim that governments are already being outdone by corporations,

---

[15] 'G.E. CEO Immelt Is Bullish On Profitability of Ecomagination'. See http://www.verdexchange.org/node/82, accessed 19 December 2009.

[16] 'GE, Wal-Mart chiefs renew 'green' vows'? See CNNMoney.com, http://money.cnn.com/2008/03/14/news/newsmakers/gunther_scott_immelt.fortune/index.htm, accessed 3 October 2008.

many of which have come out in favour of a binding regulatory framework to lay out clear and strict emissions commitments for the immediate- and long-term future. An impressive group of 150 of some of the world's best known companies signed the 'Bali Communiqué on Climate Change,' calling for 'a comprehensive, legally binding United Nations agreement to tackle Climate Change' in the run up to the Bali climate negotiations in December 2007. The shift towards support for a legally binding treaty in the communiqué marks the most obvious departure from earlier business positions of hostility towards binding action. Moreover, statements contained in the communiqué about action on climate change are suggestive of the logic of climate capitalism:

> The shift to a low-carbon economy will create significant business opportunities. New markets for low-carbon technologies and products worth billions of dollars will be created if the world acts on the scale required. In summary, we believe that tackling climate change is the pro-growth strategy. Ignoring it will ultimately undermine economic growth.[17]

Signatories to the call include Volkswagen, Shell, Nokia, Kodak, Philips, HSBC, General Electric, Nestle, Adidas, Nike, Rolls Royce, DuPont, Johnson & Johnson and Tetra Pak, among many others. Corporations, fearing an uneven playing field and continuously moving targets, want clarity, as well as decisive and early commitments.

Even amid their own financial problems, many leading players were persuaded that a low-carbon economy would create significant business opportunities. Indeed, by February 2007, none other than Lehman Brothers was warning that: 'The pace of a firm's adaptation to climate change is likely to prove to be another of the forces that will influence whether, over the next several years, any given firm survives and prospers – or withers and quite possibly dies.'[18] The fact that the Lehman Brothers went bust in September 2008 was not because of lack of vision on climate change. But their warning that not acting poses a risk to the future survival of companies captures the importance of viewing climate change as an issue of risk.

[17] The Bali Communiqué on Climate Change, http://www.princeofwales.gov.uk/content/documents/Bali%20Communique.pdf, accessed 19 December 2009.
[18] 'FSA warms to climate change risk'. See http://www.finextra.com/fullstory.asp?id=16447, accessed 25 September 2009.

ANTICIPATING AND PRE-EMPTING REGULATION

One risk companies face is the threat of regulation by governments. They have thus generated strategies to anticipate and pre-empt regulation. British Airways (BA) is a good example of a company from the heart of the fossil fuel industry that has moved to engage with the issue of climate change. Andrew Sentance was Head of Environmental Affairs and Chief Economist at BA and is now a member of the Bank of England Monetary Policy Committee. During his period at BA, it underwent a huge transition.[19] Sentance saw the writing on the wall that regulation of carbon emissions was on the way, in one form or another. The challenge was thus to be well positioned relative to competitors in order to survive in this environment.

Like many others in business, he saw emissions trading as a vehicle to avoid less 'business-friendly solutions' such as taxes on fuel and energy use. British Airways argue on their website that 'studies have shown that green taxes have very little effect when compared with carbon trading. In order to receive the same emissions reduction as trading, taxes would have to be at least 23 times more costly than trading.'[20] Engaging early with emissions trading allowed BA to help shape its rules and operations while minimising the financial costs of regulation. Strategically, an emphasis on trading also allowed big corporate players such as BA to build bridges with those elements of the environmental community that saw such market-based mechanisms as the only way of galvanizing momentum around action.

Talking with Andrew Sentance also gives a sense of the battles *within* corporations about how best to engage with climate change as an issue amid prevailing scepticism about whether a strong business case really exists. For BA, action on climate change was relatively easily aligned with existing business models and ideas about CSR. But BA's stance on the issue was met with hostility from other airlines that were worried that conceding the need for action opened up the possibility of other forms of less business-friendly regulation. It was the thin end of the wedge and for Lufthansa, for example, the best ploy was to fight against *any* policy to cut emissions. And there is a potential cost implication for leaders such as BA if others in the airline industry refuse to act.

[19] Interview with Andrew Sentance, Bank of England, 6 June 2008.
[20] 'Carbon footprint-carbon trading.' See http://www.britishairways.com/travel/csr-carbon-trading, accessed 6 April 2008.

Many airlines were still in the 'threat' mode of response –
viewing any regulation of carbon emissions as necessarily a threat to
their interests which they should oppose. British Airways was an out-
lier in that sector. With mounting pressure on the sector to bring down
its emissions, however, BA announced in 2009 that it would reduce
CO_2 emissions from energy use by 30% by 2020 compared with 1990
levels, despite passenger numbers growing by 130% during that time.
The case of aviation highlights another important dynamic in business responses to climate change – regional differences – especially
between Europe and the USA. In an address to the British Airports
Authority, Andrew Sentance coyly observed that 'Global warming is
rightly being identified as one of the key environmental issues which
the airline industry must address in the twenty-first century. There is
no dispute between the industry and policy-makers on this side of the
Atlantic on that issue.'[21] His counterparts in the USA took a different
view.

TRANSATLANTIC DIFFERENCES

This transatlantic difference in strategy is evident in other sectors, and
broadly reflects different assumptions about regulation on each side of
the Atlantic. In the USA, corporations tend to assume that regulation
is to be opposed and relations with governments are often more antag-
onistic, while Europe has a longer history of government–industry
collaboration and mutual accommodation. By the mid to late 1990s,
perhaps nowhere were the divergences in corporate strategies more
visible than in the oil sector. What oil and energy companies could get
away with in the USA, they simply could not get away with in Europe.
There was even a time when Shell in Europe accepted that there was
sufficient scientific consensus to act on climate change, while Shell US
was still fighting battles over whether the science was robust enough
to justify action.[22]

The differences between the more proactive positions of
European companies towards climate change when compared with
their US counterparts could at least in part be accounted for by the
more ambitious policy responses of European governments. But the

---

[21] A. Sentance, 'Addressing climate change – the way ahead for aviation.'
Presentation to BAA Aviation and Climate Change Seminar, 13 October 2003.

[22] D. Levy and P. Newell, 'Oceans apart? Comparing business responses to the environment in Europe and North America', *Environment*, **42**(9) (2000), 8–20.

public positions of companies clearly also reflect their different corporate strategies. For example, the difference between BP and Exxon has been described in terms of 'Beauty and the Beast'.[23] While BP was pursuing a strategy of becoming one of the largest players in the renewables sector (a strategy it has since abandoned), Exxon was still questioning the science underpinning climate change and funding politicians and scientists opposed to action.

Such intransigence led to the company becoming a target for a vocal activist campaign. The 'Expose Exxon' (USA-based) and 'Stop Esso' (UK) campaigns aimed at drawing public attention to the oil giant's opposition to action on climate change. These coalitions claimed a membership of 500,000 in the case of the USA and 10,000 in the UK. They protested outside the company AGM, sought media publicity as an outlet for their claims (even receiving coverage on the global media channel CNN), organised petitions and set up boycotts at Esso/Exxon garages leafleting the public about the company's opposition to action on climate change. Though the campaign ended after three years, the Co-operative Bank calculated that in the UK people who boycotted petrol retailers over a six week period cost the business $742 million in 2003.[24] More recently the company has also come under pressure from the Rockefeller family, a large shareholder in the company, about its stance on climate change.[25] In response, Exxon points to substantial investments in research into renewables at Stanford University – the Global Climate and Energy Project – as evidence of its commitment to action on climate change. On 20 November 2002 Exxon Mobil announced it would give $100 million to a 'groundbreaking Stanford University project dedicated to researching new options for commercially viable, technological systems for energy supply and use which have the capability to substantially reduce greenhouse emissions'.[26]

---

[23] I. H. Rowlands, 'Beauty and the Beast?': BP's and Exxon's Positions on Global Climate Change', *Environment and Planning C: Government and Policy*, **18** (2008), 39–54.

[24] P. Newell, 'Civil society, corporate accountability and the politics of climate change', *Global Environmental Politics*, **8**(3) (2008), 124–55.

[25] A. Clark, 'Exxon facing shareholder revolt over approach to climate change', *The Guardian*, 19 May 2008. See http://www.guardian.co.uk/business/2008/may/19/exxonmobil.oil.

[26] 'ExxonMobil plans $100 Million investment in Stanford University's Global Climate and Energy Project', Business Wire 20 November 2002. See http://www.encyclopedia.com/doc/1G1-94437173.html, accessed 19th December 2009.

In terms of political representation, Shell broke with the likes
of Exxon and the Global Climate Coalition in the late 1990s. Not only
were senior figures within companies such as Shell expressing concern
about the aggressive tactics adopted by groups such as GCC, they even
joined business coalitions promoting renewable energy such as the
Wind Energy Association with the aim of capturing the 5–10% share of
the market for wind energy by 2010. By the year 2000, no major industry federation in Europe was formally opposed to the Kyoto Protocol.
Shell and BP both parted company with the GCC. It was a marriage
of convenience that served a purpose at a particular stage in the climate change debate. But things had moved on and new opportunities
were on the horizon. Shell and BP were then joined by other leading
companies – Ford, DuPont, and the like – who similarly started to see
climate change as a risk to be managed, rather than a threat to their
interests.

The differences between the responses of BP and Shell and those
of Exxon were due to the different regulatory systems that the companies are subject to, the distinct structures of lobbying that are available
to them and divergent corporate strategies. Exxon is a company with a
particular mid-west view of the world, whereas BP's strategy reflects its
origins as a European-based company with a more global orientation.
This perhaps reflects the key role of the company in British foreign policy adventures going back at least to the overthrow of Mossadeq in Iran
in 1953. Individuals at the head of companies also have their own sense
of which way the wind is blowing, so while Lee Raymond of Exxon was
willing to take the flack for an oppositional stance, his successor Rex
Tillerson has pursued a more conciliatory line.

We shouldn't necessarily only look to oil majors as a gauge of
whether industry is capable of moving towards a low-carbon future.
However, it is worth recalling that Shell, BP and Exxon-Mobil are collectively responsible for 8% of man-made emissions of GHGs.[27] Six out
of ten of the world's richest companies are oil companies. It is shifts
among business leaders in these companies that give people like Geoff
Lye of the consultants SustainAbility such hope. Invoking a popular
phrase in climate debates, he argues that we have reached a 'tipping
point' in terms of corporate engagement. Climate change is being
mainstreamed into the business strategies of leading companies as
part of a broader shift from what he calls a 'compliance model' to an

---

[27] G. Lye, SustainAbility, Linacre lecture, 'MNCs and the changing landscape of climate accountability', Oxford University, 24 January 2008.

'accountable business' model, where the court of public opinion is as decisive as the court of law once was in driving business responses.[28]

EVERYONE'S A WINNER: CORPORATE SOCIAL RESPONSIBILITY
AND CLIMATE CHANGE

It is in the court of public opinion that approaching climate change as a CSR issue makes most sense. A large part of the strategy of some corporations results from their being targeted by activists, who dubbed Exxon 'climate criminals' for example, and the need to avoid such bad publicity by engaging proactively with the issue.

The shift of climate change to centre stage as an issue for corporations has to be understood as part of the rise of CSR. Companies increasingly accept that they have both environmental and social responsibilities to their employees, to the communities that host them and to society more broadly. Indeed a veritable CSR industry has grown up over the last decade as a response to a legitimacy crisis about the ability of corporations to deliver benefits to all.

The business case for CSR was put most strongly by the World Business Council for Sustainable Development, which claimed at the time of the Rio summit in 1992 to have 'changed course'.[29] This case suggests that companies could gain a great deal by addressing environmental issues. There were resource savings to be made, better employees to be attracted, new customers to be wooed. It was no longer enough to do the minimum needed to meet government regulatory requirements. Environmental management, eco-efficiency and life-cycle analysis were the new buzzwords.

For some big corporations, climate change has proved to be an opportunity to challenge their reputations as laggards on environmental issues. Wal-Mart, for example, a company that has come under considerable fire for its social and environmental performance, has made climate change a flagship issue, putting pressure on suppliers to reduce their carbon footprint. The company has been fined repeatedly in recent years by various agencies for environmental negligence. For example, in 2005, Wal-Mart paid $1.15 million in fines to the state of Connecticut for the improper storage of pesticides and other toxins that polluted streams near its stores there.[30] The CEO Lee Scott

---

[28] G. Lye, 'MNCs and the changing landscape of climate accountability'.
[29] S. Schmidheiny, *Changing Course: A Global Business Perspective on Development and the Environment* (Cambridge, MA: MIT Press, 1992).
[30] See http://www.WakeUpWalMart.com.

saw in climate change the opportunity to do some re-branding with a vision that includes powering its facilities and fleet of vehicles with renewable energy, cutting back on waste and selling green products. Wal-Mart reportedly crafted their greening plan with the help of former Vice President Al Gore. Commitments include reducing GHG emissions by 2 per cent at existing locations and investing $500 million in environmental improvements each year moving forward.[31]

The CSR approach to managing risk involves engaging your critics and, ideally, forming partnerships with them. This is what many companies have done on climate change. Through HSBC's Climate Partnership, the bank works with the Climate Group, WWF and EarthWatch on projects to raise the awareness of employers about climate change. Nick Robins of HSBC describes this as 'old school philanthropy'. Other companies, such as J. P. Morgan, prefer a more direct approach. You just buy yourself a climate portfolio by purchasing one of the largest producers of carbon offset credits – Oxford-based Climate Care.

While in many examples of CSR the risk is to a company's reputation with its customers (think of the controversies that enveloped Nike or Starbucks), in climate change, one of the principal pressures comes from investors. Those with pensions or life insurance, the base for most of the world's investment capital, can potentially exert a far greater influence than consumers can. Prompted by the crisis in corporate governance exemplified by the Enron and Worldcom financial scandals, the response came in the form of an emphasis on reporting and accountability. Projects to get companies to measure and report on their GHG emissions were developed and flourished in the wake of these scandals. Underpinning these projects is the idea that what matters is what can be counted. A sceptical public wants to know that companies are in fact delivering on their commitments proclaimed in glossy brochures and expensive television advertisements. Systems of reporting and benchmarking are crucial to help persuade them.

The Greenhouse Gas Protocol, jointly created by the World Resources Institute and the World Business Council for Sustainable Development in 1998, is one such project. It is a corporate reporting and accounting standard, and now claims to be 'the most widely used international accounting tool for government and business leaders to

---

[31] 'Wal-Mart's legacy and environmental commitment'. See http://www.buzzle.com/articles/walmart-environmental-legacy-commitment.html, accessed 19 December 2009.

understand, quantify, and manage GHG emissions'.[32] Another is the
Carbon Disclosure Project, which tries to get companies to actually
report their emissions (see more on this in the next chapter). While
for business this was merely another reporting responsibility, for the
financial community, as we will see in the next chapter, it becomes an
important risk-management tool.

Moves by the financial community to shed light on the corporate sector's emissions profile are paralleled by climate activists'
attempts to reposition investments in fossil fuels as liabilities rather
than assets. A report by Platform and Greenpeace warns of increasing financial risk for BP and Shell as a result of their investments in
the Alberta oil tar sands in Canada. The sector now accounts for 30%
of Shell's proven reserves. The report shows that 'tar sands represent
not only an enormous threat to the climate, but also to the security of
pension fund shareholders of the oil companies'. This is because of a
number of factors which the report mentions as threatening the long-
term profitability of the sector including: the prospect of low-carbon
fuel standards, the rising cost of delivering gas to the tar sands, the
unreliability of carbon capture and storage (projects to capture carbon
dioxide from power station flue gases and put it back in the ground),
the extensive clean-up operation and the potential future litigation
from local communities. 'The idea that oil sands will enhance energy
security is delusional', said Andrew Dlugolecki, Director of Andlug
Consulting in the UK, and former director of general insurance at
insurance giant CGNU. 'Investors should do all they can to challenge
this misguided use of shareholders' money, which will make global
warming worse, and instead call for a new approach that is based on
the reality of climate change.'[33]

BUSINESS RISKS FROM CLIMATE CHANGE ITSELF

Of course it is also possible that climate change itself might force companies to change. Climate change is impinging upon business strategy
through the physical impacts that climate change has upon *how* and
where they conduct their business. Companies will thus need to adapt

[32] 'The Greenhouse Gas Protocol Initiative'. See http://www.ghgprotocol.org/, accessed 13 April 2009.
[33] Platform, 'Oil giants "underestimating investor risk" on tar sands'. See http://www.carbonweb.org/showitem.asp?article=352&parent=39, accessed 19 December 2009.

and deal with various risks to their business. Should they withdraw from coasts or from increasingly flood-prone rivers? How should they build given increased risks from hurricanes?

There is growing evidence that companies in sectors vulnerable to climate change, sectors such as tourism and agriculture, for example, are factoring climate change scenarios into their calculations about location and corporate strategy. Barclays Capital for example screens investments according to whether the costs they might face in adapting to climate change will affect Barclays' bottom line. The largest bank in emerging markets, HSBC, is alert to the effect climate change could have on economies where it invests, in particular on port cities such as Mumbai and Shanghai, where it has many billions of dollars worth of assets. There is also some evidence of companies funding adaptation projects as part of their CSR strategy.[34] How far the private sector will go in helping to foot the bill for the $85 billion some think is needed to finance adaptation by 2015 is unclear,[35] but key development actors such as the UK government's Department for International Development are trying to get the private sector on board through their Task Force on Adaptation.

LIMITS TO GREENING BUSINESS

Amid the hype about the opportunities that climate change presents for business, it is worth recalling that climate change presents a different type of challenge for many companies. The rather tired formula of 'win–win' opportunities, which underpins the 'business case for sustainable development', hits its limits with climate change. There are some zero-sum situations. There are trade-offs and there will be losers.

Climate change raises awkward questions about the sustainability of the fossil fuel companies that have underpinned the growth and development of the global economy over the last two centuries. It challenges us to decouple growth from increasing energy use. Whereas tackling ozone depletion was about doing *different business*, tackling climate change is *potentially* about doing *less business*.[36] This doesn't make it

---

[34] Conversation with Chintan Shah, Vice-President and Head of Strategic Business Development, Suzlon Energy India, 4 July 2008, Potsdam Germany.

[35] N. Robins, HSBC, 'Financing the Transition to a Low Carbon Economy', Linacre lecture, 14 January 2008, Oxford University.

[36] I. H. Rowlands, *The Politics of Global Atmospheric Change* (Manchester: Manchester University Press, 1995).

easy to convince your shareholders of the need to get tough on climate change. Indeed most of the future scenarios for energy security that a company like Shell uses do not anticipate an actual drop in emissions, only a levelling off. A world of constraint is not yet one many leaders recognise, it seems, despite the rhetoric. Energy security rather than climate change continues to be the key driver for many. And while this may cause some to seek reductions in oil use, for others it may simply drive projects to expand oil drilling into new areas like the Arctic.

Moreover, though a number of leading multi-nationals are under pressure to deliver on their green rhetoric and do want to reduce their liabilities, it is true that for most companies, most of the time, in most parts of the world, climate change is a non-issue. This is especially the case for small and medium-sized enterprises (SMEs) that constitute over 90% of the volume of economic activity that takes place. These are not generally preoccupied with climate change except when buyers such as Wal-Mart make demands of them. Rarely do SMEs have the resources to comply with demanding standards or to launch elaborate PR initiatives. Whereas BP spent $200 million on convincing the world that it is 'Beyond Petroleum', almost as much as it actually invested in renewable energy in the same period,[37] smaller companies, even where they are making important contributions, do not have a loud enough voice to shout about it.

Climate change also presents some companies with difficult trade-offs where reducing their carbon emissions, for example, may conflict with other elements of their own corporate strategy for good PR. Nowhere is this clearer than in the debate about food miles. The UK-based supermarket Tesco, for example, promised to label all its products according to their carbon footprint. But they then have to face the issue of how to square this commitment with others to support poorer farmers involved in fair-trade schemes, who are reliant on exports to supermarkets. These are the areas that lie beyond the comfortable zone of easy 'win–win' solutions. If handled the wrong way, they could easily be win–lose.

If action on climate change has to be justified in terms of a business case for action and relies upon CSR-type pressures to drive corporate responses, we are left with the issue of what happens in those parts of the world where such pressures do not exist. It would be a

---

[37] See P. Driessen, 'BP – Back to Petroleum', *Review – Institute of Public Affairs*, **55**(1) (2003), 13–14.

brave NGO indeed that spoke out in China about the climate performance of the country's China National Oil Company, Gazprom in Russia,
or the Saudi government within that country. Indeed, a new trend
in the business community in Europe and North America is to argue
that in the absence of commitment to CSR initiatives from these competitors, their own commitment to CSR is untenable and unprofitable.
Just as companies have made such arguments about the need for universal climate policy instruments to eliminate competitive advantages
for those not subject to regulation, the same argument may be made
about voluntary action on climate change.

LOOKING FORWARD

What is the overall picture? The first thing to note is that it is very hard
to paint such a thing, which in itself presents a problem: what is the
net worth of all the voluntary commitments from business? No one
really knows. Different benchmarks over different time-frames covering different gases complicate a comprehensive assessment. Those
who have tried conclude as much.[38]

The picture then, is, perhaps inevitably a mixed one. We find
evidence of significant shifts in rhetoric and evidence of genuine commitments to reduce emissions and invest in technologies and projects
that reduce GHG emissions. Some corporations also seem to be taking
climate change seriously as something which impacts upon their core
corporate strategies, rather than an issue their PR departments can
deal with. At the same time, it is not uncommon to see bold initiatives
on climate change alongside actions which have the reverse effect.
While BP went to considerable lengths to re-brand itself as 'Beyond
Petroleum', it has been at the forefront of those companies making
the most of the extraction of oil from the Alberta oil sands. These
represent the largest source of oil outside of Saudi Arabia, whose
extraction implies a highly polluting process – to say nothing of the
emissions from burning the oil once it is out of the ground. Likewise
airlines increase their fuel efficiency while simultaneously increasing
the number of flights they make.

Rising oil prices and policy momentum around further action
on climate change keep the issue relatively high on the agenda of

---

[38] P. Mann and D. Liverman, 'An empirical study of climate change mitigation
commitments and achievements by non-state actors', conference on the Human
Dimensions of Global Environmental Change, Amsterdam, 24 May 2007.

executives. Interestingly, as many companies point out, the price of carbon per se is not a key determinant of their overall corporate strategy. This is something conceded even by companies that place great faith in market prices triggering low-carbon transitions. The broader health of the economy will also be a determinant of *how far* and *how fast* corporations feel able to move on climate change.

Drivers of change often include regulation, technology and market prices, but also entrepreneurial individuals and supportive corporate cultures. Would BP have moved on climate change in the absence of John Browne's leadership? Possibly in the end, but probably not when they did. Is it likely that Willie Walsh's tenure as Chairman of British Airways will signal a retreat from some of the bolder promises contained in the company's climate change programme? Possibly, but he can't be seen to be retracting too much. How important is the fact that Nicholas Stern, author of the influential Stern Review on the economics of climate change,[39] is an advisor to the Chairman of HSBC, in explaining why this bank has taken a relatively proactive position on climate change? Individuals, even within vast corporate enterprises, can generate significant and widespread change.

Looking at the history of CSR and corporate philanthropy, it is easy to see that fear of regulation has not been the only driver of change. In nineteenth-century England, the appalling conditions documented by Friedrich Engels in *The Condition of the Working Class in England*[40] prompted demands for a Factories Act, but other companies such as Cadbury built their reputation on corporate philanthropy and a concern for the welfare of their employees.

The extent to which regulation is a key driver differs by sector. While oil and aviation are relatively regulated, other sectors are less so. This, combined with ownership and financing structure, has an impact on a company's ability to think strategically and in the long term. For many companies, 2020 or 2030 is the longest time-frame they can imagine. There is an important implication here for policy. Targets set for 2050 or thereafter need to be supplemented by targets closer to home if they are to enter the calculus of corporations today.

The main conclusion of course is that companies are hugely unevenly affected by climate change, and so transitions towards a lower carbon future will inevitably involve a cross-section of sectors

[39] N. Stern, *The Economics of Climate Change* (Cambridge: Cambridge University Press, 2007).

[40] F. Engels, *The Condition of the English Working Class* (London: Penguin, 1987).

from industrial and financial capital. We will return to the issue of
what such coalitions might look like while outlining different future
scenarios for climate capitalism in Chapter 10. But it is clear that the
sorts of responses we have seen to date make perfect sense as either
good CSR or risk-management strategies. In most cases they are not
intended to serve as the basis for a transition to a post-carbon future.
Some companies are trying to align climate change with their core corporate strategies, but such enterprises are the exception rather than
the rule.

   The challenge remains how to move from the politics of token-
ism and displacement to the construction of a low-carbon economy.
This entails more and more companies seeing economic opportunities in such an economy. It thus means the design of regulations and
broader governance structures which enable them to realise these
opportunities. This is one way of seeing the whole apparatus of the
'carbon economy' which we discuss in the next few chapters – a regulatory structure which creates opportunities for companies both to
make money in the carbon markets themselves, and also, by transforming their incentives, to seek out the opportunities in low-carbon
development. It may be these opportunities, more than many other
factors, that will persuade businesses that their future lies in a low-
carbon economy, and that risks they accept now will be rewarded in
the future.

4

Mobilising the power of investors

The scene is the launch of the 2007 report produced by the Carbon Disclosure Project (CDP), in Amsterdam, December 2007. It is a measure of how much attention is now on climate change that this event is going on, and fills a lecture hall with 200 people, at the same time as the UN climate negotiations in Bali. The launch is in the plush headquarters of Dutch bank ABN–AMRO, known outside the Netherlands principally as long-time sponsors of Ajax Amsterdam football club, but one of Europe's largest banks. The audience is mostly fund managers from a range of Dutch financial institutions, as well as a handful of journalists, academics and NGO lobbyists.

The highlight of the event is the talk by Peter Bakker, chief executive officer (CEO) of parcel delivery company TNT. His company is on the *Financial Times* list of the largest 500 companies, the target of the CDP's annual reports. He is engaging and jovial. Someone tells us he's a friend of Bono, clearly the sort of CEO that hangs around at the World Economic Forum in Davos with the in-crowd.

Bakker tells his story of responding to the first CDP questionnaire, and starting to realise that his core business is, from a climate point of view, a very significant part of the problem. He recounts a learning process, finding out about different impacts of different modes of transport, storage systems, and so on. In particular, he focuses on the fact that there is no alternative known to kerosene for aviation fuel. He lets us know that in addition to his fleet of small planes travelling daily across Europe, he's bought two 747s recently, running nine trips a week each between China and Europe carrying the latest iPods and the like. 'Now I love the iPod', he says, but then insists that we have to find a different way to produce and distribute these things, in particular reducing the distances between production and consumption.

You start to think he's talking himself out of a job. But you can see also that he's starting to plan a business model for a sustainable economy. And that he knows there'll still be a central place for logistics companies like his, and that he can make as much money distributing things on bikes (as his company does inside Amsterdam) as on planes, and by train across the medium-sized distances in a newly-localised economy.

So then he moves on to talking about what he's been doing inside TNT. He charts the projected growth of the company's business, its sources of emissions, and what can be done about these. He talks about significant reductions in storage sites through reorganising heating and cooling systems, redesigning buildings, and so on. He discusses the progressive switching of his fleet of trucks to higher-efficiency models, about switching short-distance journeys from air to truck, and procuring electricity from renewable sources. He talks about his company's 'Planet Me' project, working with employees not only to manage the company's emissions better, but also to work with them on improving their domestic emissions, and about changing incentives, for example, to limit access to low-efficiency company cars. He talks about his pain (and that of his son) in having to sell his three-month old Porsche and trade it in for a Prius, in order to lead this transformation from the top.

But he knows that the reliance on aviation is the Achilles heel of his business. Whatever he does about other sources of emissions, there is little to be done about aviation. He recounts conversations with Boeing about possible future purchases. Given that an average 747 lasts around 40 years and takes 5–7 years to build, he knows he'll still be running it in 2050. 'So I says to Mr Boeing, what will the carbon price be in 2050. Will I be able to afford to run this plane then? Will there even be the oil available then?'

STRATEGIES OF FINANCE

Bakker's recognition of the dilemma a company like his faces in relation to climate change has many facets – including the generation he comes from (he's in his mid 40s) and the importance of Corporate Social Responsibility (CSR) to the marketing strategies of increasing numbers of corporations discussed in the previous chapter. But an important component is the way that investors forced him to think about his carbon intensity, that they started to see it as a business risk. So how did financiers arrive at this approach to climate change?

We can broadly discern four sets of strategies adopted by the financial community in response to climate change. One approach, adopted by some in the insurance industry, is to withdraw, protecting assets by taking away certain forms of coverage from some regions and clients.

A second is risk management. Here the actors deal with climate change by limiting, sharing, pooling or hedging the risks of climate impacts. This is how it works: in the 1850s, farmers in the emerging American mid West, and financiers on the Chicago Board of Trade, came together to create financial instruments which acted as insurance for the farmers against bad harvests. For the farmers, this made their incomes less dependent on the vagaries of climate, and enabled them to plan investments and live more securely. For the financiers, it enabled them to find other financial products to sell profitably, which had the handy advantage of not being correlated with the ups and downs of the stock market, thus spreading their own investment risks.[1]

So climate has long been the impetus for people to innovate financially to protect themselves against its changes. In the 1990s, such innovations flourished and proliferated in the face of changes in weather patterns and risks. We saw in Chapter 2 that insurers were among the first businesses to start to worry about the threats climate change posed to their industry, and we return to this history in more detail below. But while some insurers started to develop efforts to invest in renewable energy and lobby governments to develop climate strategies, the dominant approach in the mid 1990s was for the insurers to manage their exposure to the financial risks posed by increases in hurricanes, flooding and other climate-related risks.

This process is known as the securitisation of insurance risks. Traditionally, insurers have insured themselves (a process known as reinsurance) against the sorts of risks that are low in frequency but high in costs when they do occur. Earthquakes, terrorism, flooding, hurricanes, are the sorts of events involved, many of which are weather- or climate-related. But with the rise in payouts for such events from around 1990 onwards, and increasingly confident claims that such a rise is connected to increases in extreme weather events (rather than, say, the simple fact that more rich people now live in risky places like Florida, which is certainly a factor), insurers started to worry that

---

[1] W. Cronon, *Nature's Metropolis: Chicago and the Great West* (New York: WW Norton, 1990), ch. 3.

reinsurance would not be adequate for the task. In the mid 1990s they started, therefore, to turn to the much bigger capital markets to help manage this type of risk.

The outcome was a market in 'catastrophe bonds' and 'catastrophe futures' which by 2006 was worth $5 billion.[2] The logic of these deals is this: the insurer issues a bond which says that if there is no hurricane in a specified area over a certain time period, then the investor who buys the bond will return an attractive rate of interest. If, however, there is such a hurricane, the investor loses their money which is then used to pay out on insured losses from the hurricane. For the insurer it gives access to much more money than that available from the world's main reinsurers – Swiss Re, Munich Re or the syndicates in Lloyds of London. For the investor, it gives not only an attractive rate of return, but also (and importantly) an investment whose performance is not correlated to the stock markets. Hurricanes do not increase or decline in frequency and intensity with the rise and fall of stock prices, while stock prices are not (at least not yet) affected by extreme weather events.

Insurance companies are founded on the idea of risk management – calculating the probabilities of particular types of events, and working out means of spreading, hedging against, minimising or otherwise managing the dangers those events pose. They are perhaps predisposed to be conservative in their reactions to large-scale phenomena like climate change; their first thought is to cover their backs. But others take the risk-management approach to climate change in a much more entrepreneurial direction.

These entrepreneurial actors have developed a series of what are now called weather derivatives products. The classic example is that in many places companies like restaurants and bars can now buy financial products that pay out in the event of rain or snow on a Friday night. This is not an insurance product – they do not have to demonstrate that they lost money because of the rain. It simply pays out in the case of rain. Other examples include a contract where gas distribution companies pay floating interest rates on loans where the fluctuations are seasonal or reflect fluctuations in temperatures, or farmers who can use such instruments to replace traditional crop insurance.

[2] D. Cummins and J. Cummins, 'Cat Bonds and other risk-linked securities: state of the market and recent developments', *Risk Management and Insurance Review*, **11**(1) (2008), 23–47.

The growth of interest in and attention to climate has in effect stimulated other strategies for financiers. There is now a range of products which reflect the entrepreneurial opportunism of some financial institutions in inventing new ways to make money, which nevertheless enable some people to cover themselves against the risks that weather and climate throw at us.[3]

From the point of view of climate capitalism, the risk-management markets are perhaps less interesting than those trying to mobilise investment in decarbonisation. They could, however, play a useful role in making the transition to climate capitalism *possible*, as it enables companies to adapt to climate change in the meantime. But it also could make more widespread an understanding that climate change is a problem to a much wider range of actors – making pub and bar owners aware of their dependence on climate for example. More obviously important, however, is the shaping of investment decisions towards renewable energy, energy efficiency and so on. This is the result of the other two strategies of investors.

The third sort of approach is to see investment in action on climate change as a question of CSR, which, as we saw in Chapter 3, businesses in general have done. Leading financial actors such as HSBC have taken a proactive stance in declaring themselves 'carbon neutral'. Aware of public concern about some approaches to offsetting, however, HSBC claims that its priority is to reduce emissions and only buy offsets for those emissions that cannot be reduced by other means.[4] They also only invest in non-forestry offsets – seeking to avoid the sorts of controversies we discuss in Chapter 7. The CSR element also becomes clear for banks like HSBC in relation to the alliances and partnerships it forms with green groups. For example around 70% of the money in the Climate Group comes from HSBC, and the company also partners with the Earth Watch Institute, World Wild Fund for Nature (WWF) and others.

But as we saw in the previous chapter, CSR has distinct limits as a basis for motivating corporations; interest fluctuates according to the whims of directors or fickle publics, and for that reason is often driven by presentation rather than substance, or responses are concentrated in the public relations (PR) departments of corporations

---

[3] On these, see M. Pryke, 'Geomoney: An option on frost, going long on clouds', *Geoforum*, **38** (2007), 576–88; J. Pollard, J. Oldfield, S. Randalls and J. E. Thornes, 'Firm finances, weather derivatives, and geography', *Geoforum*, **39** (2008), 616–24.

[4] Interview with Nick Robins, HSBC, 19 June 2008.

rather than used as an opportunity to re-think corporate strategy more substantively.

A fourth set of strategies follows from this limit of CSR. It revolves less around improving the information base upon which investors make their decisions. This entails making the operations of companies transparent and accountable to external audiences, specifically investors. Investors, mostly large institutional investors like insurance companies, pension funds and mutual funds, have now started to exert pressure on other companies to disclose their emissions and act to limit or reduce them. For the most part, however, the investors are not motivated by the desire to be a 'good corporate citizen', but rather by the old-fashioned bottom line. While it would be too much to claim this is yet having significant effects on emissions, it nevertheless has significant potential to shape future investment in industries which cause climate change or might successfully mitigate it.

THE CARBON DISCLOSURE PROJECT

This phenomenon is an aspect of climate politics of growing importance. The most important expression of this dynamic is the CDP whose 2007 launch we described above, and which creates the sort of pressure on CEOs like Peter Bakker. The CDP, founded in 2001, is effectively a consortium of investors who write annually to corporations listed on stock exchanges, with a questionnaire asking them to report on their CO_2 emissions, the business and other risks they perceive from climate change or measures to mitigate it, and their strategies for limiting their emissions. They publish the reports as well as the data provided by companies, and do summary analysis on trends (global, by region, by sector).

The key aphorism guiding participation in the CDP is that 'what gets measured can be managed'. Greg Fleming, former president of Global Markets and Investment Banking at Merrill Lynch puts it this way: 'Before CDP, policymakers could only guess at what companies were actually doing regarding climate change. Today we have much broader and more consistent data than ever before which is enabling researchers, policymakers, investors and other interested parties to make more informed decisions and this is due in large part to CDP.'[5]

---

[5] See http://www.cdproject.net/archive-quotes.asp, accessed 3 October 2008.

The business benefits of the CDP are described in the following way:

> The Carbon Disclosure Project (CDP) provides a secretariat for the world's largest institutional investor collaboration on the business implications of climate change. CDP represents an efficient process whereby many institutional investors collectively sign a single global request for disclosure of information on Greenhouse Gas Emissions. More than 1,000 large corporations report on their emissions through this web site. On 1st February 2007 this request was sent to over 2400 companies.[6]

By 2008, the CDP was backed by $57 trillion worth of assets from over 3000 financial institutions.[7] The uptake has been impressive, even if it doesn't necessarily mean that climate change yet features as a normal part of corporate decision-making.[8] The majority of the institutional investors continue to be based either in Europe or North America. The CDP has expanded rapidly though. The numbers of companies who are signatories, or members, has expanded, so that the 2007 report was backed by 315 investors with assets over three times the GDP of the USA in 2006. The reporting rates by companies who are sent the questionnaire have steadily increased, with 77% responding to the 2007 and 2008 questionnaires. The CDP questionnaire and reports are also public and can be accessed via the Internet. Responses from companies are available without restriction.

That the CDP operates on a voluntary basis, means, however, that companies are able to choose which of their operations they include in their emissions disclosure. Indeed most companies signed up to the CDP place a disclaimer that the information they enclose does not include their activities in some Southern countries. Moreover, there is no institutional control mechanism in place to monitor and verify company responses, though the levels of public access do mean other actors are

---

[6] P. Newell, 'Civil society, corporate accountability and the politics of climate change', *Global Environmental Politics*, **8**(3), (2008), 124–55 (p. 142).

[7] See the Carbon Disclosure Project website at: http://www.cdproject.net/, accessed 15 August 2008.

[8] On the limits of what effects the CDP has so far had on company or investor practice, see A. Kolk, D. Levy and J. Pinkse, 'Corporate Responses in an Emerging Climate Regime: The Institutionalization and Commensuration of Carbon Disclosure', *European Accounting Review*, **17**(4) (2008), 719–45.

in a position, at least in theory, to challenge or investigate for themselves claims made by companies submitting data.[9]

The CDP has also become a base for other climate projects focusing on corporations. The Climate Group for example, uses CDP data as the basis for its *Carbon Down, Profits Up* reports,[10] which attempt to show corporations the opportunities for making money while reducing emissions. As Steve Howard, CEO of the Climate Group puts it: 'Many of the companies we work with tell us the Carbon Disclosure Project questionnaire was a real trigger in their decision to start working strategically to address climate change.'[11]

Clearly, if increasing numbers of companies report to the CDP, and start to act on the basis of knowing that the investors behind the CDP will increasingly be reluctant to invest in companies which are either highly carbon intensive, or are doing nothing about their emissions, then significant transitions in what sort of energy companies procure, how they design and operate their buildings, what transport systems they favour both for their business and employees, could occur.

But few analysts of climate politics would have thought that this sort of activity might become important, even central, to pursuing carbon emission reductions. Most were focusing on the intergovernmental negotiations, or on the obvious 'corporate villains' such as Exxon. Even those observers, like both of us, who were following the interest of insurance companies in climate change from the mid 1990s onwards, were taken by surprise by the rapidity with which the CDP (and a few related projects) took off in the early 2000s. So where did this come from?

INVESTORS WAKE UP TO CLIMATE

As we saw in Chapter 2, one of the key developments in the global economy since the early 1980s has been the growth in the importance and power of financial actors. This has posed many problems in the climate change context as elsewhere. It has made regulation or taxation policies difficult, as governments have worried about negative reactions from capital markets which might lead to capital flight.

---

[9] H. Bulkeley and P. Newell, *Governing Climate Change* (London: Routledge, 2010).

[10] Climate Group, *Carbon Down, Profits Up*, 3rd edn. (London: Climate Group, 2007). Available at: http://www.theclimategroup.org/assets/resources/cdpu_newedition.pdf, accessed 9 November 2008.

[11] See http://www.cdproject.net/archive-quotes.asp, accessed 3 October 2008.

But it has also created opportunities. Some financial actors became interested in climate change for their own reasons. In the early 1990s, some insurers, in particular reinsurers[12] like various Lloyds syndicates as well as the world's two biggest reinsurers, Swiss Re and Munich Re, noticed something novel and worrying.

In the 30 years before 1988, there had only been one of what they called a billion-dollar cat (a catastrophe with a billion dollars of insured losses). From 1988 onwards, the numbers of such events exploded. Some of this was attributable to shifting populations, in particular more affluent Americans moving to Florida and elsewhere in the hurricane-prone south-eastern USA. But they also were of the view that the number and intensity of flooding and windstorm events was also changing significantly. This concern was made particularly palpable in 1992 with Hurricane Andrew, which caused $17 billion of losses, the biggest loss in history from a single catastrophe (Katrina has of course since dwarfed it).[13]

Jeremy Leggett, with Greenpeace International at the time, was one of the first to realise this potential, and decided to focus his energies on insurance companies. His idea was to persuade them to think of climate as a serious risk, but one which they could use their financial muscle to mitigate. Insurance at that point was a $1.3 trillion industry, roughly the same size financially as the oil industry, but capable in principle of influencing many others through their investments.

Leggett was acutely aware of the range of strategic options available to insurers that we discussed above. In his view, they had three choices: they could try to ignore the rise in payouts, hoping it was a temporary blip; they could try to respond defensively, withdrawing coverage from high-risk areas and increasing premiums; or they could be proactive and use their investment power to shape carbon emissions and mitigate the sources of the increased risk.[14] The United Nations Environment Programme (UNEP) acted in 1994 on this concern, creating its insurance industry initiative (which later merged with its banking initiative to become its UNEP Finance Initiative, or

---

[12] These are the companies who take on specific risks from the direct insurance companies. They provide extra cover against the low-probability, high-payout risks like hurricanes, floods and the like.

[13] A. Dlugolecki, 'An insurer's perspective', in J. Leggett (ed.), *Climate Change and the Financial Sector* (Gerling Akademie Verlag, Munich, 1996), pp. 64–81.

[14] J. Leggett, *Carbon Wars: Global Warming and the End of the Oil Era* (London: Penguin, 1999).

UNEP FI), along with a number of the insurance companies who had become active on the subject.

But mobilising this power proved remarkably difficult. In the 1990s, the active members of UNEP FI were limited to a small group of individuals from particular companies. Many were from ethical investment companies so committed through their particular relationship to their customers (such as Tessa Tennant at NPI Global Care), or from reinsurance (Swiss and Munich Re, in particular) because of their particularly extreme exposure to climate risks.

For much of the 1990s, it looked like insurers would go, for the most part, for the second of Leggett's options. They did attempt to withdraw coverage from certain areas; they also increased premiums in many places against weather-related risks. They exerted efforts developing new financial instruments such as 'weather derivatives' and 'catastrophe bonds'. It looked like Leggett's and UNEP's hopes would be dashed.

THE TURNING POINT

In the early 2000s, however, the situation changed rather rapidly. One element in the UNEP FI strategy was to develop a tool for 'benchmarking' the CO_2 emissions of companies, which we discuss in more detail below. This became the basis of two projects in the early 2000s which took off: the Global Reporting Initiative and the CDP. The latter in particular expanded rapidly. What happened in the early 2000s to change this situation?

Part of the answer is in the crisis in corporate governance sparked by the scandals that enveloped Enron and WorldCom. These highlighted the need for greater oversight of what corporations were doing with investors' money. This prompted the rise of shareholder activism, and concerns about liability that drove companies, answerable to shareholders, to justify whether their actions (and more importantly inactions) were putting investors at risk.[15] Much of the pressure NGOs started to put on companies went through the finance houses that managed the pension funds and life insurance funds which own most of the shares in the global economy. The question went from being 'can you afford to act?' to 'can you afford not to act?'

---

[15] Greenpeace, Platform and Oil Change International, *BP and Shell: Rising Risks in Tar Sand Investments* (London: Greenpeace, 2008).

By the year 2005 there was a record number of shareholder resolutions on global warming. State and city pension funds, labour foundations, religious and other institutional shareholders filed 30 global warming resolutions requesting financial risk and disclosure plans to reduce greenhouse gas (GHG) emissions. This is three times the number for 2000–2001. Companies affected included leading players from the automobile sector such as Ford and General Motors, Chevron Texaco, Unocal and Exxon Mobil from the oil sector, Dow Chemicals and market leaders in financial services such as J. P. Morgan. Groups such as the Coalition for Environmentally Responsible Economies (CERES) and the Interfaith Centre for Corporate Responsibility (ICCR), a coalition of 275 faith-based institutional investors, have been using their financial muscle to hold companies to account for their performance on climate change. They demand both information disclosure and management practices that reflect the values of their shareholders. Approximately one half of the resolutions filed have been withdrawn by the shareholders after the targeted companies agreed to take actions against global warming that the filers judged to be adequate.[16]

Actions have taken a number of forms. In the USA in 2004, faith-based investor networks filed resolutions against American Electric Power (AEP), Cinergy, Southern Company, TXU Energy and Reliant Energy to disclose their emissions. The companies agreed to prepare and issue reports measuring their emissions and to outline their plans to address the financial implications of their contributions to global warming. Reliant Energy meanwhile agreed to include disclosure of an environmental issue assessment in its filings to the Securities and Exchanges Commission (SEC, the regulator of financial industries in the USA), to amend its Board Audit Committee Charter, annual reviews, and to post environmental information on their website. Overall, the resolutions led to distinctive agreements, but with some common links: acknowledging climate change impacts in securities filings and on corporate websites, assigning board-level responsibility for overseeing climate change mitigation strategy, and benchmarking and GHG emissions reduction goals.

Amid the apparent success of these initiatives in bringing about change, it is important to reiterate the limitations of shareholder activism. There is no obligation upon a corporation to implement resolutions that have been passed. In 2005, CERES and ICCR

---

[16] P. Newell, 'Civil society, corporate accountability and the politics of climate change', *Global Environmental Politics*, **8**(3) (2008), 124–55.

organised a resolution at Exxon's AGM asking for disclosure of plans to comply with GHG reduction targets in Kyoto jurisdictions. The resolution gained the support of 28.4% of Exxon shareholders. But the company's Shareholder Executive Committee authorised Exxon to censor the result, omitting the petition from its report to the SEC. A further commonly acknowledged limitation of shareholder activism is its restriction to countries in the Anglo-Saxon world where finance is particularly dominant. Though there is some evidence of growing interest in Socially Responsible Investment (SRI) in Japan, for example, the global nature of this strategy is limited. Differences in corporate structure and culture mean that the spaces for changing corporate conduct from within are uneven depending on the company in question and the region in which they operate. In the USA shares are more widely held than in Canada where the shares in publicly traded corporations are concentrated in a few hands.

The attraction of targeting the climate investments of key investors is the ripple and spillover effect of this to other investors and the scale of change that can be achieved by shifting the position of just one powerful financial actor. In response to shareholder pressure, for example, J. P. Morgan will now assess the financial risks of GHG emissions in loan evaluations. It will use carbon disclosure and mitigation in its client review process to assess associated risks linked with high carbon dioxide emissions. Others may follow suit with growing attention from activist groups such as BankTrack seeking to embarrass banks into action by exposing their role in fuelling (literally) climate change by providing the credit and capital that underwrites large energy-intensive projects.[17]

So finance is a key part of the risk-management picture. But as climate policy developed, finance also led the way in identifying new business opportunities in climate change.

BENCHMARKING CARBON EMISSIONS

Behind this growth in investor interest in climate change is a tool developed initially amongst UNEP FI members, that of benchmarking carbon emissions. The central strategy of investors has become an attempt to get other companies to make their CO_2 emissions transparent and visible. If you can get companies to report on their CO_2 emissions, according to a standardised format, then investors will be able

---

[17] See http://www.banktrack.org/.

to use this information in their investment strategies. The idea is that companies which are more CO_2 intensive are riskier than less intensive companies, even without taking climate change into account. When the various risks to their business posed by climate change are taken into account – in particular the risk of regulation which will reduce consumption of coal, oil and gas – then investors should be wary of putting money into those companies. Many investors are so large that they have little choice if they want a diversified portfolio – which they need in order to spread investment risk. So if they do have to take these risks of regulation into account, then they have strong incentives to become active in the management of those corporations to make them less CO_2 intensive, through reducing consumption, investing in renewables, and so on.

This process started in 1998 when Tessa Tennant of NPI Global Care, acting for the UNEP FI, proposed a CO_2 benchmarking scheme.[18] Under this, the CO_2 intensity of companies would be made public and investors would be able to use this in their investment decisions. The UNEP FI group developed its methodologies for calculating CO_2 emissions over the next few years.

But these arguments only really became plausible to many investors in the aftermath of the governance scandals of large corporations in the early 2000s (see Chapter 3) and the development of shareholder activism that we document above. As Enron and others went under, activist managers at the UNEP, the Pew Center, CERES and elsewhere were able to add to this melting pot of arguments the advantages of climate change as a means of portraying themselves as good corporate citizens, and thus evade both public criticism and potential litigation. In the aftermath of this crisis, the CO_2 benchmarking proposal, which had lain dormant for several years, blossomed into a series of initiatives – most notably the CDP.

In the same vein, a number of investors in the USA started to put pressure on the SEC to require companies to disclose their carbon emissions. The principle of disclosure in financial regulation is that investors ought to have available to them the information necessary to make well-informed investment decisions. Companies like Merrill Lynch, who also play a leading role in the CDP, argued that companies

[18] C. Thomas and T. Tennant, *Creating a Standard for a Corporate CO_2 Indicator.* Working Document 980526 (Geneva: UNEP Economics, Trade and Environment Unit, 1998).

ought to be required to disclose their carbon emissions, because such emissions would be materially important to investors.

This could be because governments were developing regulations to limit carbon emissions, and thus carbon-intensive companies would become less profitable. Or it could be because they would be exposed to lawsuits for failing to act to limit emissions. A number of such lawsuits have already been prepared against individual corporations who fail to act on their own emissions. The Climate Justice Programme, a coalition of green NGOs and lawyers, for example, sued AEP, Southern Co, Xcel Energy, Cinergy and the federal Tennessee Valley Authority, accounting for about 10% of US emissions between them, for failing to act to limit them.[19]

INVESTMENT, CARBON MARKETS AND PROFITS

Investors were, however, not just motivated by the need to cover their backs against lawsuits. As the emissions trading bandwagon rolled onwards, especially after Kyoto, and the voluntary carbon markets emerged, investors came to identify climate as simply a means to make profitable investments. They poured money into venture capital initiatives to support offset schemes and the official emissions trading markets and they created investment companies to channel money into these.

The history of a company like CantorCO2e is instructive here. It started as Cantor Fitzgerald, a US investment bank, which identified opportunities in the emerging carbon market. The zeal and expertise of a small group of people, some with a background in finance, but others with backgrounds in think-tanks working on climate change and emissions trading, drove the search for attractive investments. Many other carbon finance houses, like EcoSecurities, Climate Care or Climate Change Capital, are similarly the result of a marriage between enthusiastic climate change entrepreneurs and

[19] P. Brown, 'US power giants face landmark climate lawsuit', *The Guardian*, 22 July 2004. See http://www.guardian.co.uk/environment/2004/jul/22/usnews.climate-change, accessed 19 December 2009. On pressure on the SEC, see S. Mufson, 'SEC Pressed to Require Climate-Risk Disclosures', *Washington Post*, 28 September 2007. See http://www.washingtonpost.com/wp-dyn/content/article/2007/09/17/AR2007091701833.html, accessed 19 December 2009; T. Gardner, 'Big investors Urge U.S. to Slash CO_2 Emissions', *Reuters*, 20 March 2007. See http://www.reuters.com/article/environmentNews/idUSN1928444220070320, accessed 19 December 2009.

large financial institutions such as J. P. Morgan looking for new ways to make money.

This development was most rapid in the UK. In part, they were aided by a realisation of the UK government that it was well placed to benefit from emissions trading schemes in particular given the dominance of London in global financial markets.[20] But investors in the biggest market in the world, the USA, feared being left out. Business pressure for the development of an emissions trading scheme in the USA came at least in part from fears of losing market share to Europe after the USA withdrew from Kyoto.

Financiers thus started to lead the way in identifying new business opportunities in climate change. Emissions trading systems and the carbon offset markets were key here. As negotiators in the run-up to Kyoto (and then shortly afterwards in the EU – more recently elsewhere) started seriously to look at these mechanisms, financiers started to wake up to the opportunities presented by such markets. With one or two exceptions, they had not been involved in pressuring countries for emissions trading, or even helping with their design; countries had done this (at US insistence) principally to give themselves flexibility in meeting their emissions commitments and to keep costs down. But once Kyoto was in place, banks like Barclays, Deutsche Bank or Cantor Fitzgerald set up 'carbon trading' arms. Many new start-up small financial institutions were also set up in this period. A few, like EcoSecurities, were established before Kyoto, but most, like Climate Change Capital, came shortly afterwards, to build a product range in the new emissions trading and carbon offset markets. Many of these start-ups were later gobbled up by other large financial institutions like J. P. Morgan.

While initially created by government policy, these markets are in large measure the product of these financial actors. They saw the basic design of an emissions trading system, or an offset mechanism like the CDM, and transformed it into an elaborate market, with the standard features of many other financial markets – with differentiated products to meet diverse client demands, derivative markets (futures, options and the like), information-diffusing mechanisms, and even more recently its own credit-rating instrument (IDEAcarbon).[21] Companies

---

[20] Between the mid 1990s and the mid 2000s, London had taken over from New York as the world's largest financial centre.

[21] IDEAcarbon describes itself as 'an independent and professional provider of ratings, research and strategic advice on carbon finance. Our services are designed

designed particular strategies for trading off the investment risk against the rate of return. They also created spin-off markets, notably the voluntary carbon markets. They have built from these modest policy instruments a market worth $128 billion in 2008.[22]

It is of course possible that all this financial activity is a distraction from the hard politics of reducing emissions. But beyond the important political dynamic which we come back to later in the book, the fact is that emissions trading schemes have built a powerful constituency among financiers who have a vested interest in carbon emissions reductions. It is important not to underestimate the shift towards an 'opportunity' mentality. The previous assumptions about the economics of energy depended on settled, if not lazy, assumptions that energy markets worked optimally, that coal and nuclear were the cheapest, that renewables were expensive and unreliable, and that there were no real opportunities for efficiency improvements. Companies were largely in a complacent mode regarding these things, and thus attempts to reduce emissions looked like a threat.

The shift to thinking in terms of opportunities reverses this logic. A set of ideas has always been present in energy debates which favours investments in efficiency, conservation, renewables, decentralised or 'distributed' production and so on (what Amory Lovins called in the 1970s 'soft energy paths').[23] But they have been marginalised in energy policy circles (except in Denmark), known disparagingly as the 'Cinderella options'. The shift to opportunity as a way of thinking, led by financiers, is helping to produce a reversal of this situation. The ugly sisters become more ugly as a result, and the neatness of the fit between Cinderella's foot (soft energy paths) and the glass slipper (decarbonisation) is increasingly obvious to many. For example, global investments in renewable energy went from $27 billion in 2004 to $100 billion by 2007, with much of the money coming from recently established carbon investment funds.[24] Growth rates for many types of renewable energy have been correspondingly high: annual growth

to provide leading financial institutions, corporations, governments, traders and developers with unbiased intelligence and analysis of the factors that affect the pricing of carbon assets'. http://www.ideacarbon.com/, accessed 21 July 2009.

[22] K. Capoor and P. Ambrosi, *State and Trends of the Carbon Market 2009* (Washington DC: World Bank, 2009), p. 1.

[23] Amory B. Lovins, *Soft Energy Paths: Toward a Durable Peace* (Penguin Books, 1977).

[24] UNEP Press release, 'Climate change worries, high oil prices and government help top factors fueling hot renewable energy investment climate', 20 June 2007 (Paris: United Nations Environment Programme, 2007).

rates of 60 per cent for solar photovoltaics, 42 per cent for biofuels, and 25 per cent for the more mature wind energy, between 2002 and 2006.[25]

CONCLUSIONS

It is by no means certain that investors will keep up the pressure on other companies and on states to disclose CO_2 emissions, or that such pressure will succeed. It is also far from clear that the growth in investment in renewables in particular will be sustained such as to fundamentally reshape the world's energy system. But it is clear that, given the neoliberal context we live in, mobilising the money of private investors, most of whom are large institutional investors like insurance companies and pension funds, will be crucial to achieving this transformation to a low-carbon economy.

For carbon markets to have a substantial effect on emissions, rather than just enable the rich to offset theirs, incentives must be created to shift the behaviour of large-scale financial actors that wield such power in a neoliberal world. A number of these actors, as we saw in Chapter 2, have particular reasons to worry about climate change. Insurers worry about their ability to calculate insurance risks in a changing climate. Bankers worry about their business and housing lending becoming increasingly risky because of increased flooding and extreme weather events. They can deal with this to an extent through the creation of risk-management markets as we saw earlier on, but to rely on this alone is, well, risky.

But translating the concern of the insurance industry into action to shift investments away from carbon-intensive activities is not a simple affair. Clearly, the pursuit of climate capitalism entails shifting investment massively towards renewable energy, energy efficiency and conservation, and new forms of infrastructure, ranging from the high technology solutions like intelligent management of electricity demand[26] to the simple expansion of bicycle paths. At the moment, these institutions, like their public counterparts in the World Bank,

[25] REN21, *Renewables 2007: Global Status Report* (Paris: REN21 Secretariat, 2008), p. 10.

[26] Such as the systems proposed which would trigger high-energy consuming items like fridges to turn automatically off for two minutes during advertising breaks in peak television time, thus reducing the total load needed for the system and increasing the potential share of the supply that renewable energy can make. See G. Monbiot, *Heat* (London: Penguin, 2007), p. 116.

still predominantly invest their money in companies which are both heavy producers and consumers of fossil fuel energy. This is the case even for those who are particularly worried about climate change. What will trigger these shifts in investment? In part, this depends on the construction of a carbon economy which produces a predictable price for carbon emissions, thus giving signals to investors that carbon intensity is, indeed, a business risk.

5

Searching for flexibility, creating a market

If you were sitting in Oslo, Norway, in 1991, as was Ted Hanisch, as the UN climate negotiations started, then two things would have been obvious to you. On the one hand, Norway has a strong tradition of environmental leadership. In the form of previous (and future) prime minister Gro Harlem Brundtland, it provided the chair of the World Commission on Environment and Development that popularised the term 'sustainable development'. The country also has considerable achievements in reductions in various pollutants and a positive reputation for stringent environmental regulation. On the other hand, Norway is an oil producer and exporter, already heavily dependent on oil exports for growth and export earnings, and poised for a significant expansion of its oil operations. Public pressure and diplomatic reputation required Norway to play a positive role in the response to climate change. But emissions were projected to grow significantly because of the role of oil in the economy.

Hanisch was director-general at the Center for International Climate and Environmental Research (CICERO), a newly formed think-tank in Oslo. His response to this dilemma was to propose, in a paper produced in 1991, that countries ought to be able to meet their obligations to reduce their emissions jointly. This could take various forms – investment by one country in projects in another to offset their own emissions, joint projects to limit the emissions of both and so on. But the key was to provide flexibility to allow for the special situations that particular countries found themselves in.

This idea became included in the UN Framework Convention on Climate Change agreed in 1992. US negotiators in particular jumped on the idea, arguing that countries should have maximum *flexibility* – to meet obligations jointly, or to trade off different greenhouse gases (GHGs) amongst each other, or to trade off emissions against increases in sinks which absorb carbon dioxide (mostly forests). And throughout the negotiations leading up to Kyoto, US negotiators took the lead in arguing for both flexibility and cost-effectiveness to be key principles underpinning that treaty.

JOINT IMPLEMENTATION: PUTTING FLEXIBILITY INTO PRACTICE

Hanisch's idea, as developed in particular by US negotiators, is the basis for the Joint Implementation (JI) and Clean Development Mechanism (CDM) elements in the Kyoto Protocol. With JI, countries aim to meet the demand for flexibility in fulfilling their commitments and for cheap emissions reductions through joint projects. Since it is often cheaper to pay for emissions reductions in another country, larger polluters could pay for their emissions to be saved elsewhere, since, in overall ecological terms, it makes no difference where CO_2 (or other gases for that matter) is saved. Many NGOs reacted negatively during the Kyoto negotiations, arguing that this was just a strategy to avoid having to make emissions reductions at home. This criticism would echo in later negotiations.

Negotiators, however, were unsure about two aspects of joint implementation. First, and most simply, how would the system work? This was a sort of arrangement for implementing international agreements of which they had no experience. And second, which countries should be involved? Concerning this, negotiators from the South – that is, the developing countries – argued forcefully that there could be no question of 'joint implementation' involving them, since JI implied that both parties had obligations to reduce their emissions, whereas they had no such obligations.

To respond to these two worries, negotiators agreed at the first Conference of the Parties (COP) to the UN Framework Convention in Berlin in 1995, to run a pilot phase. This started during the Kyoto negotiations and ran through to 2002. It was referred to as 'Activities Implemented Jointly' (AIJ) which neatly got around the South's concerns – the activities would be implemented jointly, but not the targets. The AIJ would allow bilateral projects to be set up between Northern investors and implementing agencies either in the South or in 'economies-in-transition' (ex-Soviet bloc countries) in areas such as renewable energy, energy efficiency, fuel-switching and forestry. And it allowed those negotiating in the run-up to Kyoto and thereafter to have some experience of the issues involved.

Many questions arise in such a system. How should emissions reductions be measured? How should they be attributed to the investing country? Who has the right to approve them? How do you prevent double counting – two countries getting credited for financing the same project? The pilot phase for AIJ activities was set up to 'learn by doing' as a way to trial solutions to some of these challenges. This was a useful political device for exploring the idea further without committing to it as a core element of a future climate regime.

PRESSURE FOR FLEXIBILITY

At Kyoto, pressure (mostly from the USA) for such flexibility mechanisms grew. Even though not enough time had passed to declare the AIJ pilot phase a 'success' (or a failure), negotiators developed the model into a full-blown system. However, following the logic insisted upon by the South, any proper system of joint implementation could only occur between countries in the North, which had emissions reductions obligations. So in Kyoto we have the two instruments – JI, which applies between Northern countries (referred to as Annex B countries in Kyoto jargon) and the CDM which enables investments in Southern countries to be credited to Northern ones.

Both work on a broadly similar basis, however. Any country in the North, or one of its companies, with an obligation to reduce emissions under the Kyoto Protocol, invests in projects in another country. The investing country can then claim the emissions reduced against its own reduction target.

The JI part of Kyoto has very clearly been the poor sister of the CDM. In the pilot phase of AIJ, most of the investment went to economies-in-transition. But in the Kyoto period, investments in CDM projects, and thus in Southern countries, have grown much faster than those in JI projects. In part this is because of institutional questions – there were more technical questions in JI, which slowed down its development.

But mostly the relative success of the CDM was because rich countries, most prominently the USA, wanted to know that the emissions growth in the South would not undo reductions efforts in the North, at the same time giving a commercial advantage to competitor industries that were not subject to emissions cuts. The CDM proposed to enrol the Southern countries in joint efforts to address GHG emissions without requiring them to accept reduction obligations. There was also the stark fact that emissions reductions in the South were simply much cheaper than in the North, so pursuing reductions there was much more cost-effective overall.

THE CLEAN DEVELOPMENT MECHANISM: BRINGING IN THE SOUTH

While Americans were worrying about losing out to rapidly growing countries like China, many in the South started to see opportunities in climate change to attract new investments. Some worried that the hard-line negotiating strategy the South had adopted would prevent them from attracting such investment. Though Southern countries were not obliged to reduce their GHG emissions under the Kyoto Protocol, the interest of investors in capturing the enormous potential that existed within these countries for cheap emissions reductions was growing. Such gains would be delivered not just from offsetting emissions in the North, but through paying for energy and emission-saving projects in the global South. Clean development became the phrase to describe these projects.

Institutions such as the World Bank's Global Environment Facility (GEF), set up in 1991, had played a role in overseeing transfers of aid and technology to the South to help those countries meet the overall goals of the UNFCCC. But there was demand for a new institution that could cope with the expected high levels of demand for investments in projects in the global South that climate entrepreneurs had identified. Given its association with the World Bank, the GEF was never the preferred choice for most in the South, and in any case it had responsibility for tackling many other environmental issues than climate change, such as biodiversity and ozone depletion. The scale of the climate change issue required a new body. The CDM proposal filled this gap.

The CDM started off as a proposal for an international compliance fund whereby revenues raised from fines imposed on Northern countries failing to meet their obligations could be re-directed towards projects and funds for adaptation in the South. It was proposed by Luiz Gylvan Meira Filho, a long-time member of the Brazilian negotiating team. The Brazilians made their proposal just a month before the Kyoto conference. After a little tweaking, the CDM soon became a revamped version of AIJ, reframed as a development tool. Dan Reifsnyder, leading negotiator in the US delegation, jumped on the chance to expand the flexibility available to the USA and its allies in meeting their targets, as well as to involve the South in carbon abatement. It was proposed formally and rapidly became a key part of the Kyoto architecture.

The CDM is thus often described as the 'Kyoto surprise' because it arrived so late in the negotiations that many negotiators did not see it coming.[1] That said, in the Kyoto Protocol agreed in 1997, it existed in name only. The battles over its rules, procedures and the activities it would cover were all still to come. The main operational guidelines of the CDM were only finalised in 2003.

But behind the 'surprise', the CDM responded to many problems left unresolved by restricting JI to projects between Northern countries only. Many in the North, both from governments and business, asked themselves the question: what about the vast untapped potential to invest in countries that don't have obligations under the UNFCCC or Kyoto? It was those areas of the world, where cheap investment opportunities were rife, where 'low-hanging fruit', as it is referred to, was abundant, that attracted the new carbon entrepreneurs. The AIJ pilot phase exposed such entrepreneurs to the potential of such markets, but they came to believe that it was much more viable in a North–South context.

These efforts to enable North–South deals also have to be understood in the context of anxiety on the part of many in the North, but especially the USA, that rapidly industrialising countries in the South were not required to accept legally binding emissions reductions under Kyoto. China, in particular, but also Brazil and India, were fast approaching levels of emissions comparable to those of Northern countries (in absolute terms at least, if not on a per capita basis). So the USA was looking for ways to draw these countries into the regime to ensure US industry was not placed at a competitive disadvantage through controls on its energy use which its economic rivals were not subject to. The Byrd–Hagel resolution, which was passed in the US Senate in 1997, insisted upon Southern reduction commitments as a prerequisite for US support for the Kyoto Protocol. This legislation,

---

[1] J. Werksman, 'The Clean Development Mechanism: Unwrapping the Kyoto surprise' *Review of European Community and International Environmental Law*, **7** (1998), 147–58.

combined with intense levels of industry lobbying, made it impossible for the USA to sign up to an international agreement that did not contain commitments for countries in the South. Though not implying direct commitments on the part of Southern countries themselves, the CDM provided one step towards emissions reductions *actions* from those countries given that they were charged with ensuring that projects delivered the required emissions savings.

FROM FLEXIBILITY MECHANISM TO GLOBAL MARKET

While the CDM started through the search for flexibility and efficiency in meeting commitments, entrepreneurs seized on what they viewed as a market opening. They rapidly started projects, developed methodologies to get projects through, built elaborate market structures to spread investment risk and so on. Indeed, by the time Russia agreed to ratify the Protocol in October 2004, bringing Kyoto into force, more than 120 transactions had already been recorded. Since then, the CDM has exploded to become literally the jewel in the crown of the three mechanisms provided for in the Kyoto Protocol, at least from the point of view of Kyoto's supporters. It is currently anticipated that at least three times as many carbon emissions will be reduced through the CDM than its designers originally thought.[2]

So how does the CDM work? Basically, it creates emissions credits for countries funding projects that reduce GHG emissions overseas. The range of possible projects is diverse – from wind or solar energy, to energy efficiency, to landfill gas capture (of methane, a GHG), to destruction of powerful GHGs like hydrofluorocarbons (HFCs). The projects are also supposed to promote sustainable development, for example through positive social impacts such as on employment, and deliver other environmental benefits such as for biodiversity. So, for example, a country such as Switzerland can invest in a wind energy project in, say, India, and the credits this generates count towards Switzerland meeting its obligations to reduce its own emissions under the Kyoto Protocol.

But if the basic logic is simple enough, the operation of the CDM is highly complex. Mostly this is because its designers wanted to ensure that projects would only be accepted if they could demonstrate 'real' emissions reductions. It works roughly like this (see

[2] Interview with Christine Zumkeller, former senior member of the UNFCCC secretariat, Bonn, 16 October 2007.

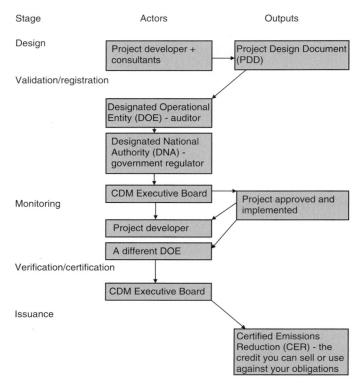

Figure 5.1   The CDM project activity cycle.
Source: adapted from UNFCCC, 'CDM Project activity cycle', available at: http://cdm.unfccc.int/CommonImages/ProjectCycleSlide.

Figure 5.1 for a schematic version). A project sponsor, investor or buyer (PP – project participant) produces a Project Design Document (PDD). Often this is done using a consulting firm. The PDD includes a description of the project, the methodology that will be applied, a discussion of the projected environmental and social benefits of the project and any comments received from stakeholders. A private company, called a Designated Operational Entity (DOE), is then hired to validate the claims made in the PDD. Such companies are usually auditors or certifiers. Once validated, it must be approved by the host country government, through part of that government bureaucracy called a Designated National Authority (DNA) – often a small office in the environment ministry. After this stage, it is passed to the CDM offices in Bonn. If there is a new methodology for measuring the emissions reductions the project developers want to claim for their project, this methodology must first be approved. If not – if the developers are simply using a methodology already approved for use – then it goes to the CDM Executive Board (EB) for registration as a *bona fide* CDM project. The project is then implemented, monitored by the developers themselves as well as by another DOE (auditor). The DOE sends a report to the CDM EB which then, if it accepts the report, issues the credits, which under the CDM are called Certified Emissions Reductions units (CERs). These CERs have become one of the basic currencies in the global carbon market – treated by investors as assets, traded in financial markets and so on.

Central to the CDM (and to JI, which has a similar, but not identical, project cycle) are the methodologies by which projects are judged 'additional'. Projects in the words of the Kyoto Protocol have to be 'additional to any that would occur in the absence of the certified project'. These methodologies are often the source of the criticisms of the CDM which we discuss in Chapter 8. Essentially, project developers have to say what the trajectory of emissions would have been without the project (the 'baseline' emissions), and how much lower the emissions path will be with the project. This part entails all sorts of complexities to do with how the emissions saved should be measured. For example, you (the project developer) have to show that the host government wouldn't simply have required you in any case to do what you are going to do. You also have to show that the project depends on CDM financing to go ahead – without the money created by the credits to be sold to actors in the North, the project would not be financially viable.

All of these are complex hurdles which you have to jump over, but this complexity also raises questions about their efficiency and effectiveness in reducing global emissions. Even those who recognise the value of the projects fear that the high transaction costs exclude many potential participants in the market. When projects can take up to three years from initiation to receiving the CERs, with no guarantees of receiving the latter, the risks and costs are borne up front and can run into the tens of thousands of dollars – a combination of high transaction costs, risk and uncertainty of outcome that serves to deter many potential market entrants.

FROM CDM TO GLOBAL CARBON MARKET

The CDM, along with the European Union Emissions Trading System (EU ETS, see next chapter) has become the central element in what we now call the 'global carbon market'. It is thus a central institution affecting the emergence of what may become climate capitalism. It was thought of originally, however, just as a means of giving rich countries flexibility in meeting their emissions targets, and the South access to new sources of investment. How did this transformation from 'flexibility mechanism' to 'global market' occur?

The essence of the answer is that, while they didn't realise it, those creating the CDM were busy creating what financiers now regard as a set of asset classes. Along with the European Union Allowance (the unit in the European emissions trading system), the CER units have become the central commodity in global carbon markets. Various profit-making strategies have been developed and a series of secondary markets have been created.

These different units have become commodities like any other: traded, hedged, differentially priced according to various conditions and so on. And as the CDM became linked to other emerging carbon markets, especially the EU ETS, this entailed creating ways to make these commodities comparable to each other so the markets could all be linked up. In the language of finance, they have to be made *commensurable* and *fungible*; that is to say, they can be defined according to the same sort of accounting logic (commensurable) in order to become fungible (making different commodities alike so they can be traded).

What has been going on is a sort of reinvention of money. Money enables different things to be compared through their price. Similarly, the construction of units of carbon in different ways enables them to be traded. This unit of account has become the tonne of carbon dioxide equivalent (tCO_2e). All the specific systems for trading carbon have come to adopt this as the unit, measure it in comparable ways, and express it through a simple acronym which traders can then relate to and construct products around. Thus we have the alphabet soup of AAUs (Assigned Amount Units, Kyoto's basic unit), CERs (CDM credits), VERs (Verified Emissions Reductions, voluntary carbon market credits), EUAs (European Union allowances), ERUs (Emission Reduction Units, JI credits), as well as the units being created in the newer markets. All these acronyms express, for traders, different sorts of value, and are the means by which carbon markets link up to each other.

The global carbon market was thus created out of the realisation of the potential of the CDM. This potential – to create markets, commodities and profits – also became part of what has sustained the CDM in the face of many criticisms (on which more in Chapter 8), and has given many a glimpse of how carbon markets may (repeat, *may*) help to decarbonise the global economy.

THE WORLD BANK GETS THE BALL ROLLING

Alongside a few early entrepreneurs, it was the World Bank that stepped in to kick start the process. The Prototype Carbon Fund (PCF) is a fund managed by the World Bank to purchase emission reduction credits under JI and the CDM. It gets over $180 million from six governments and 15 companies. The PCF was the first investor in the CDM. It was established in 1999, became operational in 2000 and signed its first emission reduction purchase agreement for a CDM project in Chile in 2002. It functioned as a learning and implementation network providing participants with an opportunity to learn about JI and the CDM before the Protocol had entered into force and before the guidelines on how to implement such projects had been agreed.[3] It was also intended to have demonstration effects that project-based investments under the Kyoto Protocol could earn revenue for Southern countries and increase the profitability of cleaner energy options. The PCF has shareholders from the public and private sectors, and was set up to create carbon as an asset for trading in the marketplace.

The motivations for actors to get involved in this were mixed. They included:

> learning about this emerging market, gaining competitive and strategic advantage over competitors, influencing ongoing negotiations and acquiring emissions reductions. Although it invested very little of its own resources into the PCF, the World Bank saw carbon finance as an opportunity to channel additional resources, private resources in particular, to developing countries in a period of declining ODA [Overseas Development Assistance].[4]

Though welcoming the effort to enroll the private sector in financing carbon abatement efforts, many in the South and in environmental NGOs were more wary of organisations like the World Bank getting involved. The World Bank still invests heavily in fossil fuel projects, despite the mounting evidence that climate change significantly

[3] C. Streck, 'New partnerships in global environmental policy: The Clean Development Mechanism', *Journal of Environment and Development*, **13**(3) (2004), 295–322.

[4] F. Lecoq and P. Ambrosi, 'The Clean Development Mechanism: History, Status and Prospects' *Review of Environmental Economics and Policy* **1**(1) (2007),134–51.

exacerbates the welfare of its main clients: the poor. For instance in 2008 the World Bank invested in a 4000-megawatt coal-fired power plant in Gujarat, India, which will emit more carbon dioxide annually than the whole of Tunisia.[5] As late as 2007, more than 50 per cent of the World Bank's $1.8 billion energy-sector portfolio did not include climate change considerations at all.[6]

The World Bank's role as a purveyor of neoliberal reform also creates contradictions for its new-found role in enabling a transition to climate capitalism. The bank itself concedes 'unregulated electricity markets are likely to put renewable energy technologies at a disadvantage in the short-run because they favour the cheapest energy as determined purely by price, but do not capture environmental and social externalities'.[7]

Such internal contradictions do not detract from the fact that the World Bank is at the forefront of efforts to finance low-carbon energy transitions. As part of its Strategic Framework on Development and Climate Change, two Climate Investment Funds were approved in July 2008: the Clean Technology Fund and the Strategic Climate Fund. Donors from ten countries have pledged $6.1 billion to the World Bank for these funds, with the largest commitments made by the USA ($2 billion), the UK ($1.5 billion) and Japan (up to $1.2 billion). The Clean Technology Fund's objective is to provide finance for low-carbon energy projects or energy technologies in the South that reduce emissions, while the Strategic Climate fund aims to facilitate demand for a post-2012 market by supporting large-scale programmatic and sectoral investments.[8]

FINANCIERS STEP IN

If the World Bank helped kick-start the CDM, however, private financial actors have since driven its development into a fully fledged

[5] C. Swann, 'Zoellick fossil fuel campaign belied by World Bank's Tata loan' *Bloomberg.com*, 10 August 2008. See http://www.bloomberg.com/apps/news?pid=2 0601080&sid=ap2zaLeAmcdQ.

[6] World Resources Institute, *Correcting the World's greatest market failure: Climate change and multilateral development banks* (Washington, DC: World Resources Institute, 2007). See http://www.wri.org/publication/correcting-the-worlds-greatest-market-failure.

[7] I. Tellam (ed.), *Fuel for Change: World Bank Energy Policy – Rhetoric and Reality* (London: Zed Books, 2000), p. 33.

[8] World Bank, *Climate Investment Funds* (Washington DC: World Bank, 2008). Available at http://www.worldbank.org/cifs; World Bank, *Development And Climate Change: A Strategic Framework For The World Bank Group, Report to the Development*

market. A wide range of buyers have entered the CDM market. Most of these are banks and speculators that do not need CERs to comply with their obligations to regulators, but instead seek to trade them on the secondary market. One estimate is that in at least one-third of all the project-based transactions concluded between January 2005 and April 2006, the buyer had the intention of selling some of the resulting CERs on the secondary market.[9] There was a 5.8-fold increase in one year from 2004 to 2005. The volumes being traded on this carbon market represent about 6 per cent of the total GHG emissions by parties to the Kyoto Protocol, or roughly the annual CO_2 emissions of France and Spain combined. This rapid growth was triggered by the EU ETS described in the next chapter, and the entry into force of the Kyoto Protocol, both of which happened in 2005.

Another indication of the rapid growth of the CDM market is the capitalisation of carbon funds worldwide which surged from $275 million in January 2004 to an estimated $4.6 billion in April 2006 and to an estimated $6.4 billion in September 2006. It is also the case that the market took off more quickly than many had anticipated, and the bodies set up to manage the process struggled to cope. The EB lacked the funding and capacity to process the volume of applications that were received, leading to a backlog of projects and demands for a permanent staff to be able to clear it. It is still struggling to keep up, but DNAs have now been set up in 112 countries, of which 91 are Southern countries, which should make project approval easier.

HOW TO MAKE MONEY IN THE CDM

Businesses have adopted a range of different strategies for making money through CDM activities. Some invest in projects early on, taking on the risk that the project will not be approved by the CDM EB or that it will not secure funding for example. Some gain their profits from having invested early and sold the CERs at their most profitable – that is to say at the end of the process. Others take on less risk, investing later when it is already more expensive, but knowing already that the project is likely to be approved and go ahead. Others wait until the end, just buying up the CERs in the secondary market. This is expensive but very safe – the CERs already exist. Of course many are making

Committee (Washington DC: World Bank, 2008). Available at http://siteresources. worldbank.org/EXTCC/Resources/FullFrameworkDocument1212008Book.pdf.

[9] F. Lecoq and P. Ambrosi, 'The Clean Development Mechanism', pp. 134–51.

their money as intermediaries – consultants on the PDDs, those trad-ing the CERs in the secondary market, lawyers, auditors and so on. A few companies are worth a closer look to see how they make their money.

EcoSecurities operates by providing two sorts of services to pro-ject developers (typically companies in the South). First, it provides technical services – helping with the preparation of a PDD, enabling companies to decide on whether to go for the CDM market or the voluntary market and so on. Second, it signs an 'Emissions Reduction Purchase Agreement' through which it guarantees to purchase the credits from the developer at a fixed price once the credits have been issued. Thus, instead of providing finance upfront, it agrees to reduce the risk to the developer that there will not be a market for the credits. EcoSecurities itself takes on a certain amount of risk in terms of the fluctuation in prices for CERs, while offloading the greater part of the risk that the credits will not be issued onto the project developer.

EcoSecurities has become one of the largest companies work-ing in the market, building on the experience of prototype carbon markets acquired during the 1990s.[10] It has registered more than 110 CDM projects and has more than 400 underway in 34 countries with a portfolio of projects totalling more than 122 million CERs by 2012. With offices in the UK, USA, Indonesia and India, it is one of the key global players. When it was floated on the London Stock Exchange it raised £80 million ($113.9 million), and in 2007 raised a further £100 million ($142.4 million), with Credit Suisse acquiring almost 10 per cent of the shares.[11]

By contrast, companies such as CantorCO2e or IceCap operate simply as brokers. One part of their operations is in what financiers call the 'fully commodified' carbon market. This refers to those parts where you have a range of products (CERs, EUAs, etc – our acronym alphabet soup described above), easily identified by price differences, fully comparable with each other. In this part of the market you buy and sell on behalf of those who need allowances or credits for their obligations (at the moment, this means companies regulated under

[10] H. Lovell, 'Conceptualizing climate governance beyond the international regime: the case of carbon offset organisations', Tyndall Programme One Workshop, Oxford, 19–20 May 2008.

[11] EcoSecurities company history: http://www.ecosecurities.com/Home/EcoSecu rities_the_carbon_market/Company_history/default.aspx. Accessed 16 February 2008.

the EU ETS) and those who have allowances or credits to sell. This sort of operation looks much like any other financial market – a trader sitting with three or four computer screens and a couple of telephones, the screens relaying information about buyers and sellers and what they want and are offering, about average prices of sales and the phone there for negotiation between the two parties.

The principal products in these markets are the EUAs (see the next chapter on emissions trading) and those in what is called the 'secondary CDM market' – that is those credits created by CDM projects that are then sold on to companies that need credits. Most project developers do not themselves need allowances, they just realise there is money to be made and they have an expertise in putting projects together, and then sell on the credits through this secondary market. They also organise these markets through a series of auctions, where buyers present sealed bids and transactions are all decided at a single point in time.

But CantorCO2e is also involved in directly putting together CDM project developers in the South with investors in the North. In this, its principal expertise is its networking skills and experience, its capacity to know who is putting projects together and who might want to finance them. The nature of the projects varies considerably with the range of possible CDM projects.

Energy for Sustainable Development (ESD) is a consultancy. It started in 1989 as a non-profit company working mostly on World Bank small-scale sustainable energy projects. In 1999, it got into the joint implementation business when it realised that its expertise would enable it to develop CDM projects. It has become a project originator, working directly with the project developers in the South to make the projects work. The consultancy works through the project cycle, from initial idea, to the PDD, through to selling the credits. An interesting part of ESD's work is that it makes its money by taking a cut of the CERs from the project developer, instead of directly being paid in hard currency. It then realises that money by selling these credits in the secondary CDM market, through brokers such as CantorCO2e.

CONNECTING TO THE SOUTH

All of this relies on internationally connected carbon entrepreneurs in the global South seeking to position action on climate change as an investment opportunity. Market makers in the South have wasted no time in seeking business opportunities though collaborations and partnerships with their equivalents in the North. Chambers of commerce, sector-based business associations and banks have been leading the charge to connect projects in the South with investors in the North, running seminars and training events and networking at 'Carbon Expo' conferences, persuading investors of the merits of investing in their country.

There has been a proliferation of business organisations, intermediary groups and climate entrepreneurs offering training and services to companies wanting to have their factories upgraded, seeking access to cleaner technologies or just wanting to get money for nothing: compensation for not undertaking actions they claimed they had planned to, and selling this as an emission reduction. In fact, one problem governments in the South have had is dealing with unrealistic expectations about the money to be made from CDM. One member of a DNA told us he had meetings with people claiming to be students interested in the CDM requesting information about how the process worked. They then posted this information, inaccurately, the following day on a company website claiming to offer expert services in project development to the business community! Inflated expectations about the CDM bringing about a gold rush of money from North to South, creating 'Robin Hood' redistribution from rich to poor, proved inflated and premature. Many ill-prepared projects rushed through the process have failed to meet basic criteria of additionality and were thus rejected by the CDM EB, having a negative effect on business confidence in the market. We will return to the question of 'cowboy' climate capitalist, later.

CONCLUSIONS

The Clean Development Mechanism has certainly been tremendously successful in at least three ways. First, it has generated great interest by investors, project developers and traders in the new commodity, the Certified Emissions Reduction or CER, which it has created.

Second, it has also created great enthusiasm amongst the UN climate change secretariat and many national governments because it has expanded much faster than its designers anticipated. This fact is taken as a sign of its value. It has, as people in the policy world say, traction.

Third, and perhaps most important, it has transformed the North–South dynamic in climate negotiations. At the time of the Rio summit in 1992, there was a legitimate fear that money to support action by the South on climate change had to be 'additional' to existing development aid budgets rather than drawn from them. This fear continues in the context of the Copenhagen Accord of 2009. But now, because of the CDM, climate change is seen by some as a welcome opportunity to try to redistribute resources in favour of the global South. So far so good, we might conclude. Why shouldn't people that have contributed very little to global warming make some money from those who don't want to take actions themselves? In a way it could provide a form of *de facto* compensation for tolerating some of the worst effects of climate change.

But, in practice, the CDM has not delivered the benefits that many hoped for and expected. Critics, as we will see in Chapter 8, continue to see it as a fraudulent mechanism that lets rich countries off the hook. Despite its achievements then, the future of this sort of institution is uncertain amid proposals for its reform, overhaul or abandonment. Though economists prefer not to admit it, markets respond to signals from states, the same states that create markets and enforce property rights within them. Unless the climate change negotiations make headway on new targets, the incentives for investors to participate in the buying and selling of carbon credits falls away. Without a clear price signal for credits after Kyoto expires in 2012, buyers are much less likely to invest in CDM projects despite the benefits touted by the carbon entrepreneurs. Indeed, there are already signs of a drop in interest in carbon markets, with some firms taking staff away from carbon projects in the light of the weak outcome to the negotiations in Copenhagen in December 2009. Given that outcome, it is possible even that the CDM will no longer, in practice, be operational from 2013 onwards.

6

Caps, trades and profits

In 1989, sitting newly ensconced in his small ground-floor office at Chatham House, the home of the prestigious think-tank the Royal Institute of International Affairs in London, Michael Grubb had a 'little idea'. This idea was the germ of what would become a vast and continually expanding set of markets which trade, in various ways, the carbon emissions produced by industrial economies and consumer lifestyles. At that point, the Intergovernmental Panel on Climate Change (IPCC) had just started meeting to prepare its first assessment report, and many governments were doing the rounds of international conferences declaring climate change a serious issue that needed a collective response.

Faced with the prospect of long, drawn-out negotiations between countries to work out how to reduce their collective emissions, Grubb, like other commentators at the time who had started to think about future climate negotiations, foresaw many problems. As we now recognise well, climate change is not like many other environmental issues. At the time, ozone depletion provided the most obvious model given that the Montreal Protocol had just successfully agreed to 50 per cent cuts in chlorofluorocarbons (CFCs), with more stringent cuts on the way. It also built on a general agreement (the Vienna Convention) rather like the Framework Convention that governments were trying to negotiate on climate change, so there were parallels. But unlike ozone depletion, climate change touches more or less every aspect of economic life, and goes to the literal engine of the industrial economy – energy use. Grubb looked at other negotiations on simpler issues and concluded that the solutions they proposed would be unlikely to work for climate change.

Could we get all countries to agree the same level of cuts? This was the model of the ozone negotiations, with a simple distinction between countries from North and South being the only differentiation. The issues of fairness were immediately obvious. Why would a country which was already much more energy efficient, like Japan or Italy, accept the same level of cuts as an inefficient country like Canada? Conversely, why would a cold, very sparsely populated country like Canada accept the same level of cuts as a mild, densely packed country like the Netherlands? Most crucially, why would poor countries with low per capita emissions accept the same cuts as rich, heavily emitting countries?

Alternatively, could we get countries to agree on a package of differentiated commitments? For this, Grubb took the model of the Large Combustion Plant Directive in the European Community, designed to deal with emissions causing acid rain. He noted that this took many years of negotiations, with meetings twice a week, among a relatively small group of countries on a simpler issue. How long would it take to get a similar outcome for climate change?

Grubb's answer to this dilemma was to turn to regulation being developed in the United States to deal with acid rain. There, the government was planning to give polluters allowances for their emissions (reducing over time to meet environmental goals), but allow them to trade the allowances amongst themselves. Companies that are able to reduce their emissions would do so in order to be able to sell their extra allowances to those who were finding it more difficult to do so. All companies, however, have an incentive to reduce their emissions beyond the minimum required. The overall costs of reducing emissions would be cut significantly, while the costs for each company would become roughly the same. By dealing with the need to cut emissions efficiently, the scheme does so fairly.

Grubb suggested a similar means of attempting to negotiate climate change multilaterally. Countries would agree to allowances, which they could then buy and sell among themselves in a similar fashion. In the international context, the added bonus was that, with most ways of allocating emissions allowances that could be regarded as fair, countries in the South would have more allowances than they could use, while rich countries would need to buy allowances. The system would thus create significant transfers of resources for clean development in the South.

Grubb's argument, developed by himself and others over the next few years, provides the underlying logic for what we now know as the 'global carbon market'. Alongside their search for flexibility in meeting their commitments, which prompted Hanisch to develop the idea of Joint Implementation (JI), governments have taken the efficiency logic of the market mechanisms, in particular noticing how it might enable them to meet targets cheaply and without having to do it all at home, and applied it in a variety of ways in the Kyoto Protocol and beyond.

The markets have then been developed by traders, investors, project developers, accountants and many others into an elaborate system. At a certain point, the business actors we discussed in the previous two chapters realised that there were many opportunities in these emerging markets, and their enthusiasm for carbon markets helped policy-makers keep them going, even while others were expressing doubts about them as an adequate response to the issue. What then are their main features, and how did they develop?

EMISSIONS TRADING

If JI and Clean Development projects are about sharing costs and spreading benefits, in theory at least, emissions trading (also at times known as 'cap and trade') is about the buying and selling of pollution entitlements. They reflect a more purist sense of the economic logic of pursuing emissions abatement efficiently. Since pollution problems arise because no property rights have been allocated to the problems that pollution causes, the solution is to allocate specific and limited rights to polluters. Though the history of emissions trading on climate change is relatively recent, there is a much longer history of using market-based pollution trading schemes to combat other environmental problems. Tradable quota allocation schemes have been used in fisheries, in wetlands management, in industrial pollution policy and other areas. For climate change, the most obviously relevant model came from the way the USA had managed SO_2 emissions to deal with its acid rain problem.

The US system for managing SO_2 emissions had all the features of an approach to environmental regulation that got neoliberals excited. It seemed to keep the role of big central government to a minimum. It harnessed the power of the market to the goal of environmental protection *and* it was more efficient and less bureaucratic. It even allowed the USA to project itself as an environmental leader and a source of innovation at a time when it was being reviled by activists as an environmental laggard. Placed in the climate context, however, the idea of permit trading is presented with a unique set of challenges. Was it really possible to imagine a global system of permit trading in the absence of stronger international institutions to manage it? Who would prevent countries from buying up and hoarding permits until the price went up? Who could enforce sanctions? What would be the basis for allocating permits in the first place?

This last question was a key one in Grubb's early work on emissions trading. At the international level, it boiled down to two questions.

Should all countries participate in an emissions trading scheme? And how should emissions permits be allocated to countries in the system? For Grubb, some of the original logic favouring emissions trading was precisely that it would facilitate transfers from North to South to help enable clean development in the latter. But, following the similar logic as in the debates about JI, this would imply that Southern emissions should be capped (even at much higher levels than current emissions). There was no way the South would accept this.

At the same time, this suited the rich countries, since they would want a system based on a 'grandfathering' model where permits reflect the current status quo of emissions levels. The targets agreed at Kyoto in effect reflect this; rich countries allocated each other tradable emissions rights in proportion to their 1990 emission levels. While the South was not about to take on emissions obligations themselves, it rightly worried that this rewarded countries that have contributed most to the problem to date. Their preference was for a per capita allocation – so that every individual in the world has the same right to emit carbon within constraints set by how much carbon the world could afford to emit overall. This was the allocation principle Grubb had also originally proposed. This approach has the benefit of being intrinsically fair. To argue against it is to claim some people have more rights to pollute than others, more entitlements to the global commons than others. In practice, this is how the global economy is organised, but to adopt it as a negotiating stance places you on dubious ethical grounds.

One way of allocating emissions could be on the basis of the notion of 'contraction and convergence'. This idea was developed by a little known London outfit called the Global Commons Institute, led by concert violinist and engaging orator Aubrey Meyer. With colourful diagrams and impeccable logic, Meyer's argument moved relatively quickly from the margins of the debate, dismissed as unrealistically radical, to the mainstream. Contraction and convergence meant that while overall global emissions would contract to a level consistent with the overall goal of the UNFCCC – to 'prevent dangerous anthropogenic interference with the climate system' – these emissions would converge at a common per capita level. Emissions in the North would thus decline while those in South grew, albeit at a slowed rate. Figure 6.1 shows this in operation. The top of the curve is global emissions over time, and each different colour is the allocation of emissions for each country or group of countries. By 2030, per capita emissions across the globe converge, while overall global emissions peak about 2020 and then decline.

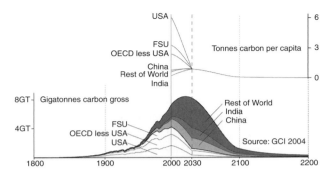

Figure 6.1   Contraction and convergence. This example shows regionally negotiated rates of contraction and convergence for a 450 ppmv contraction budget, converging by 2030.
Source: Global Commons Institute (2004).

The allocations to different countries developed by this method could then be subject to a trading regime. Despite the intrinsic moral and philosophical robustness of a position that holds that in a context where common survival is at stake within limited environmental space, no one has a greater right to pollute than anyone else and everyone, therefore, is entitled to a per capita entitlement to the global commons, the idea met (and continues to meet) with fierce resistance.

The USA, meanwhile, saw emissions trading as another 'flexibility mechanism': a market-based instrument that allowed countries to seek out opportunities to reduce emissions where it was cheapest and most cost-effective to do so – and of course they had their own experience with trading SO_2. In the run-up to Kyoto, they peddled hard the idea that emissions trading was an essential tool in the international community's armoury for tackling climate change. The EU was resistant. Adopting a similar stance to vocal environmental groups, the EU suggested that the emphasis on emissions trading was in practice a way to avoid taking domestic action to reduce greenhouse gas (GHG) emissions. However, resistance was short-lived. Shortly after Kyoto was signed, the EU switched its position on Kyoto flexibility mechanisms like emissions trading and the Clean Development Mechanism (CDM), seeing them as crucial to trying to keep the USA on board, but also increasingly as an opportunity to develop leadership on climate change. After President Bush pulled the USA out of Kyoto in early 2001, the EU took the opportunity to put itself in pole position in climate politics, using emissions trading and the CDM as means to do so.

Compared to the project-based mechanisms such as CDM and JI, the ETS in the Kyoto Protocol is a relatively simple instrument. This is how it works: the Protocol establishes the basic unit of account – the Assigned Amount Unit, or AAU. Each AAU is worth one tonne of carbon dioxide equivalent or tCO_2e. Each country has a certain number of AAUs depending on its target under Kyoto. Each country then aims to keep its average emissions for the 2008–2012 period within that number of AAUs. This can include those credits they have gained through investments in the CDM or in JI. If they can't achieve this, however, they can buy AAUs from other states that have over-complied with their targets, and thus have spare AAUs to sell. The UN climate secretariat maintains a log of transactions which covers all three mechanisms – the emissions trading scheme, the CDM and JI – to prevent double counting. States simply contract with other states to buy or sell AAUs from them and have those trades registered with the secretariat.

THE PROLIFERATION OF EMISSIONS TRADING SCHEMES

Since its initial insertion into the Kyoto Protocol, emissions trading schemes have spread to other sites. They are now in the process of becoming a standard part, even the central element, of states' regulatory tools to deal with climate change.

The first attempt to create such as system was to come from an unlikely source. Shortly after opposing emissions trading throughout most of the Kyoto negotiations, and only accepting it reluctantly, the EU did a complete U-turn in 1998, deciding to create its own internal emissions trading scheme as part of its strategy to meet its Kyoto target.

In fact, European opposition to emissions trading was never as principled or as robust as some of the diplomatic posturing around that time suggested. A consensus about the desirability of a strongly market-based approach to action on climate had been developing for some time. Since the early 1990s there is mention in EU policy documents of the benefits of such schemes, way before the publication in 2000 of the European Commission's Green Paper on GHG Emissions Trading, which launched emissions trading as a key component of EU climate change strategy.

Indeed, a constant source of frustration for advocates of climate action within the EU is that all actions on climate have to be justified in relation to the broader objective of realising full market integration.[1] Proposed measures that impinge upon that goal or which challenge the logic of the market are quickly sidelined. Construction of new carbon markets was always more popular than an EU carbon tax which, as we saw in Chapter 3, produced one of the largest and most ferocious industry lobbying campaigns ever seen in Brussels. While it made sense in political terms to maintain distance from the US stance, the EU's position was never, in truth, so strongly opposed to emissions trading and its neoliberal logic.

On the contrary. Momentum was gathering in Europe for an emissions trading scheme. For a long time the EU had struggled with ways of allocating responsibility for tackling climate change between member states with highly uneven degrees of development. 'Burden-sharing' was the phrase that was used to describe an arrangement whereby wealthier countries with a larger climate footprint such as the UK and Germany would be expected to reduce their emissions by a proportionally greater amount than countries such as Portugal and Spain. But differentiating between collective (EU) and individual country targets caused confusion among negotiating partners such as the USA. How individual member state and collective responsibilities were to be divided and calculated was not always clear, a feature of the division of competence between the EU institutions (the Commission, the Parliament and the Council of Ministers). But the arrangement paved the way for an intra-community emissions trading scheme.

THE EU EMISSIONS TRADING SCHEME

Since New Year's Day 2005, a price has been paid for almost half of the CO_2 emissions generated by the EU, a region that collectively accounts for about 20% of the world's GNP and 17% of the world's energy-related CO_2 emissions.[2] The European Union's Emission Trading Scheme (EU ETS) was, and remains, the world's first large-scale emissions trading programme.

The scheme operates what emissions trading designers call a 'downstream' system. That is to say, anyone who emits a large amount of CO_2 at a point source, such as a large factory, power station or oil refinery, is required to have enough allowances (the acronym in

[1] W. Grant, D. Matthews and P. Newell, *The Effectiveness of EU Environmental Policy* (Basingstoke: MacMillan, 2000).

[2] A. Denny Ellerman and B. K. Buchner, 'The European Union Emissions Trading Scheme: Origins, Allocation and Early Results', *Review of Environmental Economics and Policy*, **1**(1) (2007), 66–87.

the European system is the EUA – European Union Allowance – you guessed, it equals a tonne of CO_2e) to cover their level of emissions. The level of emissions that have to be covered is reasonably small – for example a medium-sized organisation like Edinburgh University with its own power generating system which delivers electricity and heat to its buildings requires allowances to operate.[3] Each permit covers one year only – installations need to make sure they have enough allowances for each year that the scheme operates.

The EU ETS was organised into phases over time. Partly this was to enable the ratcheting up of targets over time, but also to allow for learning about how such a novel scheme might work. Phase I was to last between 2005 and 2007, and was explicitly called a 'learning by doing' phase. Phase II is from 2008–2012, to coincide with the Kyoto commitment period. Phase III was only confirmed later on, and will last from 2013–2020.

In Phase I, there were two key issues that the EU ETS designers had to address. First, the question of allocation. How should those who need allowances to cover their emissions get them? Economists will argue that the pure logic of emissions trading is that allowances should be auctioned – companies should have to pay upfront for allowances, since they are in effect gaining a property right. This then provides them with a clear cost, and thus a strong incentive to reduce their emissions.

But auctioning is politically fraught for at least three reasons. First, when you are implementing a scheme on anything less than a global basis, there are particular industries which are highly exposed to international competition. Imposing the costs of purchasing potentially expensive carbon allowances might simply make them uncompetitive and, worse, encourage them to relocate outside the EU. This would be disastrous economically for the EU, and pointless in climate terms – the 'carbon leakage' effect. Second, even beyond the problem of competitiveness, all industries simply lobby extremely hard against having to pay for their allowances. In the first two phases of the EU ETS, governments and the Commission largely baulked at the issue of auctioning for allowances. Industries lobbied hard for no auctioning, and there was minimal auctioning in each period – slightly increasing in Phase II to a maximum of 8% of all allowances. The third problem with auctioning is that if you are trying to get companies to invest in clean energy, energy efficiency and so on, then slapping them with a

---

[3] D. MacKenzie, 'Finding the ratchet: the political economy of carbon trading', *London Review of Books*, 5 April 2007.

bill for their allowances might seem to reduce the money available for green investments. Those investments will only be profitable over the longer term, while the allowances have to be bought each year.

The second key issue to resolve was about the measurement of emissions at the level of each installation to be covered by the scheme. To give each installation a target, you first needed to know how much they emitted in the baseline period (for the EU ETS this was the average annual emissions over the period 1998–2003). Governments had not needed these detailed data previously, and there was a mad scramble to gather it. In the end, the data that were in place in 2005 as the scheme started were rather imprecise, and more precise data only became available during 2006.

The combination of these two issues meant that, in late 2006, the EU ETS went into crisis. The price of allowances in the market collapsed as it became obvious from the more precise data that too many allowances had been allocated. Companies realised they had enough allowances to cover their emissions, and thus trading in allowances more or less stopped in Phase I. At the same time, given that the vast majority of the allowances had been given out for free, including to electricity companies who could just pass on any costs to consumers without competitiveness worries, it became clear that these companies had just gained considerable windfall profits from their extra free allowances. So the credibility of the system was thrown into question. Commentators inside and outside the EU poured scorn on the ETS.

LEARNING BY DOING

The EU, however, responded clearly by saying that the EU ETS was always supposed to be a phase of 'learning by doing', and that it was better to have had a start-up phase which erred on the side of caution in terms of not imposing too many economic costs while they learnt how to make it operate. In Phase II, it was claimed the data problems would be resolved, and the EU would know how to bargain much harder with governments and industry about the allocations. There would also be more auctioning of allowances. The market players clearly believed this argument – even while the price for Phase I EUAs collapsed in 2006–2007, the future market for Phase II allowances kept trading at a stable price of around €25 (US$35) per tonne.

In Phase II, when it came to bargaining for the allowances, the Commission seemed to have learned to bargain much harder with Member States. Many of the national allocation plans were radically revised downwards. For example, the recently joined states from Eastern Europe are not part of the EU's formal Kyoto target. The Commission nevertheless refused to accept the Kyoto targets of these new Member States as part of the EU ETS, as it would dramatically increase the number of allowances in the system, and thus reduce its effectiveness. They also reduced the allocation of allowances by 30% in some cases compared to the country's own proposals. Some of this is still being disputed in the European courts system, although the Commission is confident of winning.

There is also more auctioning in Phase II, although nothing like what is planned for Phase III. The carbon price has been maintained (at least until the recession started in late 2008), which suggests companies have significant incentives to reduce their emissions where they can. There is regular market exchange and an elaborate derivative market has emerged. The prices for electricity and carbon emissions in the EU track each other, suggesting that the EU ETS is having some impact on the behaviour of companies.

Most importantly, emissions do seem to be going down. Emissions by regulated companies in Phase I were 3% lower than the amount of allowances they had been given. While some of this shows that they were given too many allowances, analysis by researchers at Massachusetts Institute of Technology (MIT) and the International Energy Agency has shown that emissions were in fact reduced by these companies by somewhere between 50 and 100 million tonnes of carbon dioxide.[4] And this was in Phase I. Given that the Commission has been more successful in forcing countries' allocation plans downward in Phase II, and there is more auctioning, we can expect better results in the period through to 2012.

PUSHING FOR DECARBONISATION

It is also clear that the EU plans to continue expanding the scheme as a core part of its GHG reduction strategy. In January 2008 the Commission announced its plans for Phase III. This will involve direct allocation of allowances by the Commission, not member states. This should eliminate governments doing favours to particular industries, as well as enable sector-wide allocations at the EU level. They plan to widen the scope of the scheme to other sectors and gases, notably to

---

[4] A. Denny Ellerman and Barbara K. Buchner, 'Overallocation or abatement? A preliminary analysis of the EU ETS based on the 2005–06 emissions data', *Environmental and Resource Economics*, **41**(2) (2008), 267–87.

include aviation. The latter is highly controversial, prompting challenges at the International Civil Aviation Organization, and perhaps at the World Trade Organization (WTO). Finally, the EU plans to expand considerably the use of auctioning of allowances, with at least two thirds of allowances to be auctioned as of 2013.

From our point of view, the EU ETS has become a success – in political terms at least – because it satisfies one of the key questions raised by the imperative of climate capitalism; it has created a cycle of economic growth which can (in principle) promote decarbonisation, and can generate a whole constituency of interests in maintaining, even ratcheting up the system. This includes the city traders (mostly in London) who do the bulk of the day-to-day trading, the project developers for offset projects, the management consultants helping companies engage in 'carbon asset management', the auditors assessing the emissions of companies and so on. All these now have a vested interest in progressively stronger climate policy, because of the EU ETS.

LINKING EMISSIONS TRADING TO THE CDM

Particular to the success here has been the linkage of EU ETS to the CDM. After the formal declaration of the EU ETS in 2003, which came shortly after the final agreement of the Kyoto institutions in Marrakech in 2001, some actors proposed linking the two. Why should companies regulated under the EU ETS not be able to meet some of their commitment by investing in CDM projects and turning their Certified Emissions Reductions (CERs) into EUAs? This would increase the flexibility for companies in meeting their commitments and should lower their overall costs of meeting reduction targets (since emissions reduction is generally cheaper in poor countries than in rich countries). It would also have the spin-off benefit of making the EU a guarantor of Kyoto, helping it to keep the South on board by generating demand (and thus investment flows) from the EU ETS for CERs generated through the CDM. So in 2004, the EU agreed on a Linking Directive that enabled companies to do this. As shown above, this has made the CDM expand well beyond the expectations of its architects. The EU ETS continues to drive the demand for CERs in the CDM, accounting for about 90% of the overall demand according to the World Bank.[5]

In the discussions about what to do after Kyoto, the EU has come under criticism for its plans for more restrictive limits on how

---

[5] K. Capoor and P. Ambrosi, *State and Trends of the Carbon Market 2008* (Washington DC: World Bank, 2008), p. 23.

companies can use the CDM (or whatever replaces it after 2012) to meet their commitments. This has been proposed to make sure that the EU ETS stimulates a genuine economic-technological transformation within Europe – a shift precisely to climate capitalism. But some sort of linkage will remain, continuing to drive the development of a global carbon market for some years to come.

EMISSIONS TRADING BEYOND THE EU

Whether or not the EU experience makes us optimistic about the usefulness of EU ETS in reducing emissions, many other states and regions are taking up such systems with a vengeance. Since the inception of the EU system, there has been a proliferation of such systems (see Table 6.1). The table shows the expansion of these systems. A number are in the process of coming on stream. The Regional Greenhouse Gas Initiative (RGGI) among the north-eastern US states started in September 2008, while the New Zealand and Australian systems will start probably in 2010. A US system at the federal level now looks highly likely, although it will not be operational until at least 2012, assuming a very optimistic timetable for its adoption in Congress and with the new President Obama pushing it all the way.

These systems (or at least those which have got to the design stage) all deal differently with some of the key issues in designing an emissions trading scheme. Some are 'downstream' like the EU system, imposing obligations on those who actually emit the CO_2; others, such as the New Zealand one, are 'upstream' – producers such as oil companies have to hold enough allowances for the petrol or diesel they sell. This operates rather differently, in that to consumers it simply appears as a tax, although it does enable the application of the scheme to the transport sector. This can only be done in a downstream system with personal carbon allowances, suggested by David Miliband when he was UK environment minister, but unlikely to be implemented anytime in the near future. But all face similar concerns about competitiveness effects or 'carbon leakage', as well as technical questions about the availability of installation-level emissions data.

An interesting trend to watch in the future development of climate capitalism will be how the different emissions trading schemes interact with one another. More players will undoubtedly be drawn into the market if the possibility exists of trading between schemes. We have seen how access to external credits provided by the Linking Directive has had an invigorating effect on the CDM and more generally

Table 6.1 *Emissions trading systems currently operating or being planned*

Names in regular type indicate a venue where an ETS is being planned.
Names in bold type indicate a venue where an ETS is up and running. Shading indicates that the venue on the first line includes the others in the shaded block.

	1998–2001	2002–2004	2005–2008
EUROPE	**British Petroleum (BP)**	**Denmark**	EU
	Shell	**UK**	Denmark, UK, BP,
	Denmark	BP, Shell	Shell, Norway
	United Kingdom (UK)	Norway	**Switzerland**
	Norway	EU	
	European Union (EU)	Switzerland	
	Switzerland		
NORTH	Canada	**CCX**	**CCX**
AMERICA	New Jersey (NJ)	Canada	Canada
	Chicago Climate	MA	NAFTA
	Exchange (CCX)	NH	US Congress
	Massachusetts (MA)	NAFTA	Florida
	New England	US Congress	Ontario-Québec
	Governors – Canadian	Regional	RGGI
	Provinces (NEG-CP)	Greenhouse	NEG-CP, NJ,
	New Hampshire (NH)	Gas Initiative	MA, NH
	North American Free	NEG-CP, NJ	WCI
	Trade Agreement	Western	California,
	(NAFTA)	Climate	New Mexico, OR
		Initiative	MGA
		Oregan (OR)	Illinios
ASIA-PACIFIC	New South Wales (NSW)	**NSW**	**NSW**
		Japan	**Japan**
		Australian	**New Zealand**
		States and	Australian Federal
		Territories	Aus States
		(Aus States)	South Korea

Source: adapted from Michelle Betsill and Matthew Hoffmann, 'The Evolution of Emissions Trading Systems for Greenhouse Gases', paper presented at the International Studies Association Annual Conference, 26–29 March 2008, San Francisco.

on CO_2-reduction projects in the South, creating as it does the possibility of selling credits to the EU ETS. Further efforts to connect different trading schemes so that emissions reductions are tradable among them would provide the basis of a truly global regime and provide incentives for others to join.

CONCLUSIONS

We are a long way from realising Michael Grubb's hopes for combining economic efficiency and global justice, or Ted Hanisch's ambition for the full use of flexibility in meeting commitments. The flourishing of market-based approaches to climate change has in fact been driven less by the neat abstractions of economics, or the pragmatic concerns of negotiators, and more (and increasingly) by the inventiveness and greed of financiers. This inventiveness has been put to use in turning a set of discrete regulatory schemes – the EU ETS, the CDM and so on – into a messy, and highly profitable, global carbon market.

What we have seen in this chapter is that the carbon economy could, in principle, play a key role in the transition to climate capitalism. It has been mediated and created by public institutions, and then taken up with alacrity by private market actors. We have seen a set of institutions and mechanisms created that reflect compromises in the battle to protect the climate. Businesses and governments calculated that if some action is to be taken, it is better that it harnesses the power of business by creating new markets and thus new opportunities to make money. The carbon economy is, nevertheless, driven by states and international institutions who have to demonstrate that market mechanisms can serve social and environmental ends in order to be able to justify why they provide a legitimate response to climate change; this has so far proved difficult to do in practice.

There are key questions still to be answered fully. Can such markets in fact lead to the substantial emissions reductions needed to deal with climate change? Can they stimulate the investment in the 'sunrise' industries essential to the transformation of the global economy? Whether or not they will is a question of politics and governance – how the rules might be made, and how struggles will be fought to shape those rules. Will these political struggles enable the carbon market not just to be an opportunity for money-making, but also one for emissions reductions and industrial transformation? We deal with these questions more fully in Chapters 8 and 9.

In the next chapter we will see how an almost entirely private and financial market has developed, not constrained by such public goals. It provides another insight into the construction and day-to-day operation of the global carbon economy, and the extent to which it might bring about a transition to climate capitalism.

7

Buying our way out of trouble

Most people in wealthier parts of the world have come across invitations to calculate their carbon footprint, offset their carbon emissions or go on a 'low-carbon diet'. Many large firms now do the same in order to market themselves as 'carbon neutral', often as part of broader climate change Corporate Social Responsibility (CSR) strategies as we saw in Chapter 3. Offsets are now routinely sold to firms and individuals, in particular to offset emissions from air travel. Consumers are sold products that both alleviate their sense of guilt and claim to contribute to low-carbon development projects in poor countries. The fact that poorer countries will bear the worst effects of climate change adds to the feeling of culpability. Journalist Mark Honigsbaum writes:

> 'Flying over Kenya's Rift Valley ... it's hard not to feel a pang of guilt ... I feel guilty because as a privileged westerner with an addiction to air travel I am at this very moment spewing carbon dioxide into the atmosphere at the rate of about 1kg a minute, emissions that, according to climate change experts, may be contributing to Kenya's faltering rains.'[1]

Offsets offer the prospect of compensating directly those whose livelihoods are threatened as a result of your actions.

Most European airlines and a growing number of North American ones have direct links to one or other of the firms dealing in carbon offsets, so that when you buy a ticket from their website, at the end of the process the website asks if you would like to offset your carbon emissions. If you tick yes, it takes you to their offset provider to calculate the emissions, and thus the price for offsetting. Swissair and

[1] M. Honigsbaum, 'Is carbon offsetting the solution (or part of the problem)?' *The Observer,* 10 June 2007.

Virgin are linked with myclimate, SAS and others are linked to the CarbonNeutral Company, and so on. On Virgin Atlantic, you can even purchase the offset on the plane with your duty free.

These markets are the result of entrepreneurial activity by environmental NGOs as well as private firms spotting opportunities for new market development. Many of these firms operate also in the carbon markets established by governments or under the Kyoto Protocol. But they have also been instrumental in establishing these private, or 'voluntary' carbon markets. Indeed, the two sorts of market are often connected, as projects that fail to qualify for registration with the Clean Development Mechanism (CDM) may end up on the voluntary market that imposes less stringent criteria. What happens in the broader climate regime in terms of targets, approved methodologies and the like, sends strong market signals to actors involved in voluntary markets. For those involved in voluntary and compliance markets such as offset organisations like EcoSecurities, a workable national and international framework of regulation is hugely important.[2]

What started as a small sector led by a few entrepreneurs has attracted the interest and capital of some of the largest players in the global financial community, such as J. P. Morgan who acquired the offset firm Climate Care. This chapter charts the story of how these markets came about and what issues they raise, as well as asking what might be their contribution to climate capitalism.

THE BIRTH OF OFFSETS

Promoters of the voluntary offset markets never tire of pointing out they precede the regulatory markets. The first such transaction was in 1989 when AES, a US electricity company, invested in a forestry plantation (of pine and eucalyptus) in Guatemala to offset the emissions from its new coal-fired power plant in Connecticut. But most of these markets emerged during the 1990s.

According to the mythology, sitting in a field at Glastonbury Festival in 1996, Clash singer Joe Strummer and Dan Morell came

---

[2] According to Carbon Finance, in 2007 EcoSecurities revised its expected number of carbon credits downwards by a quarter because of the slowness of getting the project approval from the Executive Board and its share price subsequently dropped by 50%. Carbon Finance, 'EcoSecurities' woes prompt CER rethink', *Carbon Finance*, 20 November, 2007. See http://www.carbon-financeonline.com/index.c fm?section+lead&action+view&id=10846. Cited in H. Lovell, 'Conceptualizing climate governance beyond the international regime: The case of carbon offset organisations', Tyndall Programme One Workshop, Oxford, 19–20 May 2008.

up with the brainwave which became Future Forests and later the CarbonNeutral Company. They sat discussing problems of deforestation and climate change, with Strummer musing about the impacts music events like Glastonbury, as well as tours by bands, have on these problems. The two came up with the idea of a company which would enable people to fund forestry projects in order to compensate for the emissions that they produced in their daily lives. While large firms like AES could easily enough find a way to invest in projects to offset its emissions, individuals and smaller firms need well-organised intermediaries to work between them and the projects they might want to finance to offset their emissions.

It is Richard Sandor, nevertheless, who is referred to by many as the 'father of carbon markets'. Along with a few others, at the beginning of concern about climate change at the end of the 1980s, he started to think about the possibility of using financial markets to mitigate climate change. Sandor decided to create a market outside governmental regulatory frameworks. This became the Chicago Climate Exchange (CCX). As the historical home of some of the world's most important commodity markets, Chicago was an appropriate birthplace for this initiative.

Work on this started in 2000 and the Exchange was launched in 2003. It is a member organisation, where large corporations who join agree to reduce their greenhouse gas (GHG) emissions as a condition of membership. All members who have joined to date have agreed to reduce their emissions by 6% by 2010 (roughly tracking the Kyoto target, although the baseline year is not 1990, using instead the average of emissions between 1998 and 2001). The CCX describes their commitments as 'voluntary legally binding commitments'. Member firms can then meet their target by internal reductions or purchasing credits from other members or through offset projects organised through the exchange. It mirrors, therefore, the structure of the EU Emissions Trading Scheme (EU ETS), but at the same time operates as the infrastructure of the market – the site where all its participants meet. The CCX started with just US and Canadian firms (like Ford, DuPont and Motorola), but now has firms participating from other countries, notably Australia, China and India. It has also established the European Climate Exchange, which operates as a registry and exchange in the EU ETS. More recently, in June 2008, the Montreal Climate Exchange started futures trading on the GHG emissions credits due to be given out in the Canadian government's emissions trading system. Some firms have done very well out of these systems. Climate Exchange, which describes itself as the world's leading specialist exchange for trading emissions, has seen its share price soar from $5.50 to $21.50 within a year, bringing a market value in excess of $828 million.[3]

Other entrepreneurs embraced the idea of offsets as a win–win opportunity to promote conservation and make money at the same time. The climate dimension was secondary. Their natural allies were groups working on forestry issues, such as Global Canopy, that were seeking new revenue streams for their work on forest conservation. Individual entrepreneurs also saw an opening. Dorjee Sun, for example, founder and head of Carbon Conservation spent many years trailing around Indonesia trying to persuade governors to guarantee forest protection in exchange for investments from carbon buyers.[4] Despite meeting scepticism from the likes of Starbucks and failed attempts to persuade E-bay to set up virtual trading places, he eventually succeeded in forming a carbon-credits-for-forests partnership with Merrill Lynch.[5] The calculation was that credits bought now will be more valuable in the future, especially if UN negotiators could be persuaded to include Reducing Emissions from Deforestation and Forest Degradation in Developing Countries (REDD) in the CDM. The Bali roadmap, agreed at the climate summit in Bali in 2007, opens up that clear possibility, and if the number of side events on the issue of REDD organised at the Copenhagen negotiations in December 2009 is anything to go by, the momentum behind this issue is irreversible, even if it is still unclear whether it will be linked to the CDM or just introduced as a separate measure.

The voluntary markets have grown spectacularly since 2001 when they started to emerge. They have gone from 3–5 megatonnes of carbon in 2004 to 65 megatonnes of carbon in 2007,[6] tripling in one year in 2006–2007. They are currently worth $331 million including the CCX – without it, $258 million. By 2012 some estimate the voluntary

[3] M. Milner, 'Cornering carbon: the broker that takes a cut when polluters pay', *The Guardian*, 28 April 2008.
[4] BBC4 'The burning season', Documentary, 6 August 2008.
[5] Mongabay.com 'Merill Lynch announces carbon credits-for-forest conservation partnership', *Mongabay.com*, 6 December 2007. See http://news.mongabay.com/2007/1206-ml_carbon.html, accessed 3 January 2010.
[6] R. Bayon, A. Hawn and K. Hamilton, *Voluntary Carbon Markets* (London: Earthscan, 2007), p. 14; K. Capoor and P. Ambrosi, *State and Trends of the Carbon Market 2008* (Washington DC: World Bank, 2008), p. 41.

offset market will be worth $4 billion[7] and by 2020 project-based carbon offsets could rise to $286 billion in value. In the UK alone, in 2007 there were more than 61 different organisations and companies working in this sector.[8] Twenty-five per cent of the total traded volume is used directly to offset emissions, while 75 per cent changed hands and could be resold in the future. This is, nevertheless, a fraction of the size of regulated markets which dominate global carbon markets: trades in the voluntary markets in 2007 were worth $331 million, as opposed to around $62 billion in the EU ETS and CDM combined.

Nevertheless, voluntary markets are an interesting aspect of carbon markets for a number of reasons. The demand in the market comes predominantly from the 'wholesale' part of the trade rather than the 'retail' end – that is to say from companies (often large ones – such as HSBC which has made a big play of its involvement) rather than individuals. According to figures from the UK-based Tyndall Centre on Climate Change, private businesses currently account for 80% of the credits bought (50% to offset emissions, 29% for investment or resale), while individuals account for just 5% of the market.[9] Despite the prominence in public debate of individuals offsetting their emissions through this market, therefore, they play only a minor role in the actual purchase of credits. Many firms have become big enough that there have been a number of buyouts by large finance houses, most prominently the aforementioned purchase of Climate Care by J. P. Morgan.

HOW THE VOLUNTARY MARKET WORKS

The voluntary market has a structure which is fairly similar to the CDM market. Typically, there is a 'project developer' in a country in

[7] Voluntary Carbon Standard Association, 'Leading market providers back new registry system for the Voluntary Carbon Standard: The Voluntary Carbon Standard (VCS) Association reveals the approval of 4 VCS registries', press release, Voluntary Carbon Standard Association, London, 2 July 2008, available at: http://www.v-c-s.org/020708regi.html, accessed 4 January 2010.
[8] A. Bumpus and D. Liverman, 'Accumulation by decarbonisation and the governance of carbon offsets', *Economic Geography*, **84**(2) (2008),127–55.
[9] L. Whitmarsh and S. O'Neill, 'Carbon off-setting behaviour: catalyst for – or evasion of – low-carbon lifestyles?' Paper presented at the International Conference on Climate change impacts and adaptation: Dangerous rates of change, Exeter, 22–24 September 2009.

the South, and a 'project originator' in the North (like myclimate, CarbonNeutral, Climate Change Capital, CantorCO2e and so on). The latter channels money from companies and individuals in the North wishing to offset their emissions, into the Southern project developer, in return for carbon credits which are then passed on to the Northern investors. Sometimes offset providers put out calls for projects, offering carbon finance as a reward for the best projects in Southern countries. Making this market exchange possible are the verification firms (like SGS, DNV and Tüv Süd) who assess the project in terms of criteria set out by one of the main standards which have emerged (see below on standards). This enables the issuance of credits. For example, SGS-Qualifor inspects the forest and assesses the carbon sequestration levels for organisations such as FACE (a Dutch offset organisation) and Climate Care every five years.

There are also a series of intermediaries who act between the project originators (firms working directly with project developers to get the project going) and those purchasing credits. Though there is not the elaborate secondary market in the sale of VERs (Voluntary Emissions Reductions) that has emerged in the EU ETS or the CDM market, projects that fail to be certified through the CDM can still be approved for purchase in voluntary carbon markets. In the CCX (about a third of voluntary market transactions currently go through that exchange), there is then the layer of market exchange, and some derivatives trading (futures, etc.), which is made possible by the fact that it is an allowance-based system. Through specific emissions reductions projects, offsets are made into saleable units that can be quantified, owned and traded.

Business models in the voluntary markets broadly follow those in the CDM. Some firms operate as wholesalers, such as EcoSecurities, buying and selling on credits to other firms such as Climate Care. Both firms were formed in 1997 but play different roles in the market. Climate Care focuses more on the development and retail of voluntary and compliance carbon offsets. It handles anything from individuals' offset requests, to serving the needs of huge corporate clients like British Airways and Land Rover as well as ethical investors such as The Co-operative Bank that in 2005 paid Climate Care $414,000 to offset one-fifth of UK mortgage customers' homes.

But there are two main differences between the CDM and the voluntary markets in this context. First, in the voluntary markets, there is a much bigger link to the specific project that the money is invested in. Corporate buyers want to use this for good PR, so the nature of the specific project matters to them. In many contexts, the challenge for traders is to separate out the multiple values of a project for different buyers. As an example, the Climate Community and Biodiversity Alliance (CCBA) suggest that simultaneously 'a reforestation project with obvious environmental and social co-benefits may attract private investors for the carbon credits, government money for sustainable development and conservation dollars for biodiversity activities'.[10] Second, both because of this and the fact that there are no regulations driving the market, there is no secondary market for VERs like there is for CERs (Certified Emissions Reductions). No firm will want to buy credits for a project that someone else has already gained the green PR for.

It is worth giving a couple of examples of projects to illustrate how they work. In Western Sumatra, myclimate has financed a project to upgrade and bring back into production a small-scale hydroelectric plant, the Salido Kecil plant.[11] The hydroelectric plant had become unviable due to subsidies given to diesel in the 1990s, but these subsidies were withdrawn after the financial crisis of 1997–1998. The aim of myclimate was to invest in the plant to bring it back into production, and thus reduce emissions from electricity generation, which is currently based largely on diesel in that region. The project involves a partnership between myclimate and PT Anggrek Mekar Sari (PT AMS), who own the plant. The former calculated the emissions reductions from the proposed project, based on the baseline assessment of what emissions would be without the project. They used energy consultants Ecofys to develop the Project Design Document (PDD – the same title is used in the voluntary market as in the CDM), which details the project and the emissions reductions in the form required by the Gold Standard. The PDD is then validated by a verification and certification company, in this case Tüv Nord, who assess it against Gold Standard rules about calculating baselines, additionality and so on. After it has been validated, the work will be done on the hydroplant, the implementation is monitored and then the emissions reductions verified (by a different verification company than that which did the validation). The Gold Standard will then issue VER certificates for the project

[10] CCBA. Climate, Community and Biodiversity Project Design Standards,first edition (March 2005). See http://www.climate-standards.org.
[11] myclimate, Salido Kecil Power plant Project Design Document. See http://www.myclimate.org/download/Salido_Kecil_070911_PDD.pdf, accessed 6 November 2007.

which myclimate will pass on to its customers who have financed it through their purchase of offsets.

In a case like a small-scale hydroelectric plant, demonstrating the carbon abatement is relatively straightforward. The project itself emits no carbon, and can be expected to displace emissions from other sources of electricity based on fossil fuels. There are complexities of course. For example, how do we know it will reduce diesel consumption in electricity generation rather than simply add to the total amount of electricity consumed? How do we know that now that the diesel subsidies no longer exist, PT AMS would not be able to raise the finance to bring the plant back into production from general financial markets? The PDD attempts to deal with these sorts of issues.

But demonstrating additionality is much more difficult in many other cases. For example, Climate Care developed a project in the Guguletu township near Cape Town in South Africa. They distributed 10,000 compact fluorescent lightbulbs (CFL) in order to increase the energy efficiency of consumption in the township. But it turned out that Eskom, the electricity company, was itself distributing CFL bulbs free in the township.[12] The methodology required for the offset markets is in principle similar to that of the CDM. You calculate a baseline of what emissions would be without the project, you calculate what emissions will be with the project, and credits are issued based on the difference. In the end it relies on a judgement call about the plausibility of the claims made by the project developer, supported by the verifiers.

In the voluntary market, of course, much is made of the individual projects. Many offsetters like to know something about the project in which they are investing. So many voluntary market firms thus make the projects a very visible and clear part of their marketing. Most of the companies have parts of their website devoted to the projects they are working on, with the documentation, photographs, videos, testimonies by participants and so on, making clear the motivations of the buyers of credits.

CARBON NEUTRALITY

The HSBC bank provides a good example of these motivations in the voluntary market. Its account of the high-profile decision to 'go carbon

---

[12] K. Smith, *The Carbon Neutral Myth: Offset Indulgences for your Climate Sins* (Amsterdam: Carbon Trade Watch, 2007), p. 40.

neutral' reveals an interesting mix of philanthropic and marketing motives. On the one hand, the decision arose from pressure from a variety of sources, though notably not from regulators: 'the pressure to reduce our emissions wasn't overt but it did exist, from peers, from shareholders, from the NGOs we work with and from our own staff'.[13] This aspect is made more obvious with the bank's financing of a variety of partnerships, working with the Climate Group, WWF, the Earthwatch Institute, among others, principally to develop its own employees into a 'green taskforce'. On the other hand, HSBC has sought to gain a first-mover advantage in the carbon market where they hope to 'gain a deeper insight into the emerging low-carbon economy and be exceptionally well placed to understand the needs of and opportunities for their clients'.[14] The bank decided to build its own capacity in-house rather than rely on external brokers, in order to position themselves to profit from the carbon market, principally through providing consultancy services for its existing clients.

Carbon neutrality is a powerful claim to make. In 2006 the Oxford American Dictionary declared it 'word of the year' for the widespread use the concept was attracting.[15] HSBC was one of the first major players to declare itself 'carbon neutral' in 2004 following in the path of Swiss Re (2003). Francis Sullivan at HSBC was the key figure behind this but is in fact rather cautious about the role that voluntary offsets can play in the pursuit of carbon neutrality. He has said 'I'm sure there are people buying offsets in this unregulated market that are not credible. I am sure there are people buying nothing more than hot air'.[16] Amid scepticism about firms using offsets to buy their way out of trouble, as Nick Robins of the bank makes clear, offsets are a last resort to mop up those emissions that can't be reduced by other means.[17] Indeed many people refer to a 'hierarchy' of actions whereby the priority should be to avoid and reduce emissions, then to replace

[13] L. Slade, 'A bank's perspective on the voluntary carbon market: from risk to opportunity – the HSBC carbon neutral experience', in R. Bayon, A. Hawn and K. Hamilton. (eds.) *Voluntary Carbon Markets*, (London: Earthscan, 2007), p. 96.

[14] L. Slade, 'A bank's perspective on the voluntary carbon market…,' p. 95.

[15] Clean Air–Cool Planet and Forum for the Future, 'Getting to zero: defining corporate carbon neutrality', 2008, available at: www.cleanair-coolplanet.org/documents/zero.pdf, accessed 3 January 2010.

[16] As quoted in D. Adam, 'You feel better, but is your carbon offset just hot air?', *The Guardian*, 7 October 2006. See http://www.guardian.co.uk/environment/2006/oct/07/frontpagenews.climatechange, accessed 30 September 2009.

[17] Interview with Nick Robins, HSBC, 19 June 2008.

processes and technologies generating high levels of GHGs, and only then to use offsets.[18]

Given the difficulty of tracking and quantifying all aspects of a business' operations, many firms have been wary of making claims of carbon neutrality and advertising standards authorities have criticised firms making claims that are impossible to prove. The UK's Advertising Standards Authority, for example, ruled against a claim by British Gas that one of its fuel packages was 'zero carbon'.

The big issue for firms attempting to calculate their footprint is where to establish the boundaries. Do you take into account your suppliers' emissions, the travel of your employees, emissions associated with packaging, transportation and end use? Firms' responses have varied considerably.[19] While Ben and Jerry's ice-cream franchise claim to be carbon neutral 'from cow to cone', Manchester airport's claim excludes emissions from flights into and out of the airport! Some have made it sound suspiciously easy: 'you can neutralise the greenhouse gas emissions from your home, office, car and air travel in 5 minutes and for the cost of a cappuccino a week'.[20] As with the offsets market in general, as we will see below, the Climate Neutral Network tries to bring together businesses and NGOs to create guidelines for climate neutral products and enterprises.

For large corporate clients, interest in projects is driven by the nature of their sector and the regions where they are looking to invest. They want projects where they have a client base or projects with a strong element of PR potential attached to them. Priorities will not necessarily include those projects that make most difference socially and environmentally. Inevitably when other actors enter the market with different priorities such as traders, lawyers and financial services providers, things change. A Climate Care employee reflected on his frustration at attending a voluntary carbon markets conference; 'this is not about climate change ... It's about trading these instruments. It's not about how we can do the most good, it's not

---

[18] Clean Air–Cool Planet and Forum for the Future, 'Getting to zero...'.

[19] Clean Air–Cool Planet and Forum for the Future, 'Getting to zero...'; See also Carbonfund.org, 'CArbonFreeTM Product Certification: Carbon Footprint Protocol,' version 1.0, 6 July 2007, available at: http://www.carbonfund.org/site/uploads/Product_Certification_Protocol_-_2007-07.pdf, accessed 3 January 2010.

[20] Carbon Clear website, cited in K. Smith, *The Carbon Neutral Myth: Offset Indulgences for your Climate Sins* (Amsterdam: Carbon Trade Watch, 2007), p.10.

about how we tackle climate change, and that's the absolute danger here'.[21]

In response to that danger, the groups New Economics Foundation and the International Institute for Environment and Development have set up what they call an 'AdMit' scheme, which seeks to fund adaptation to climate change impacts in countries in the South through the purchase of credits. Seen as an alternative to offsetting, 'The AdMit initiative provides a mechanism for emitters of greenhouse gases in developed countries to take care of the impacts of their emissions by investing in projects that enable poor people in developing countries to adapt to the impacts of climate change'.[22] It is a new product (rather than a new standard) running on a pilot basis until the end of 2009, and has been supported by a broad range of development NGOs such as CARE and Action Aid, UN agencies such as UNICEF as well as environmental groups such as Greenpeace.

STANDARDS IN THE VOLUNTARY CARBON MARKET

In the CDM, a central aspect of the creation of the market is the process by which a project is declared to have reduced overall emissions, and credits are issued. A key difference in the voluntary market is that no such centralised means of issuing credits exists. Indeed, firms can (although the number doing so is declining) simply issue credits themselves without any third party verifying their claims. While the CDM market 'product' is the CER, the equivalent in the voluntary market is the VER. Both are equal to one tonne of CO_2 equivalent. But how is it established that a project produces a particular amount of VERs? In the place of a central regulator, a number of different standards have been elaborated by various organisations to provide a sense of governance of these projects. The large buyers of credits, as we have seen, are motivated in part by the PR benefits of claiming carbon neutrality, or some other way of presenting their commitment to dealing with climate change. And when PR is at stake, those companies have an interest in preventing that turning into bad PR. This is why the demand for certification schemes has developed. It may also produce a race to

---

[21] H. Lovell, 'Conceptualizing climate governance...'. beyond the international regime.

[22] See http://www.iied.org/climate-change/key-issues/economics-and-equity-adaptation/admit, accessed 21 July 2009.

the top in standards: the World Bank claims that there is a 'flight to quality' in these standards, both with more ambitious standards being elaborated, and more and more projects being subjected to the most stringent tests.[23] Certainly, from 2006–2007, the proportion of projects which had no standard declined, and the proportion of standards with no third-party verification or with proprietary (and therefore not verifiable by outsiders) standards, like the CCX or other standards which are owned by the offset provider, declined. Meanwhile the number using standards widely regarded as more reliable, like the Voluntary Carbon Standard (VCS), VER+ or Gold Standards, increased significantly.[24] As much as 50% of the transactions conducted in 2007 involved credits verified to a specific third-party standard. Reflecting on this trend, the *State of the Voluntary Carbon Markets* report for 2008 notes:

> Over the past 2 years numerous writers and analysts have likened the voluntary carbon markets to the 'wild west'. In 2007 market trends highlight that this frontier has become a settlement zone. Customers are increasingly savvy about the opportunities and pitfalls in the carbon offset domain and stakeholders are aggressively working to forge the rule of the game and structures to enable smooth transactions.[25]

Table 7.1 illustrates a number of these standards. Most claim to have at least as stringent criteria for measuring additionality – the emissions the project will save as compared to the situation if it did not go ahead – as the CDM. The Gold Standard, developed by WWF, essentially applies an extra set of screens to CDM or voluntary projects, and gives credits only to projects in the areas of renewable and energy efficiency and the conversion of methane to energy. It thus avoids the various problems associated in particular with forestry as well as many biomass projects, which are usually the focus of the critics of offsetting projects. A number of offset organisations, such as myclimate (itself an NGO rather than a for-profit company), based

---

[23] K. Capoor and P. Ambrosi, *State and Trends of the Carbon Market* (Washington DC: World Bank, 2006), p. 41.

[24] See K. Hamilton, M. Sjardin, T. Marcello and G. Xu, *Forging a Frontier: State of the Voluntary Carbon Markets 2008* (Washington DC: Ecosystem Marketplace and New Carbon Finance, 2008), p. 53. In this period, the VCS (the most popular standard) went from 21% to 29% of the share of those projects using standards, the VER+ went from a standing start to 9%, and the Gold Standard went from 4% to 9%. By contrast, the CCX halved its share from 14% to 7%, while those using the retailer's own standard crashed from 23% in 2006 to 2% in 2007.

[25] K. Hamilton *et al.*, *Forging a Frontier: State of the Voluntary Carbon Markets....*

Table 7.1. *Standards in the voluntary carbon market*

Standard	Description	Environmental and social benefits	Includes Land Use, Land Use Change and Forestry
Gold Standard	Certification for offset projects and carbon credits	Yes	Renewable energy and energy efficiency only
The Voluntary Carbon Standard (VCS)	Certification for offset projects and carbon credits	No	Yes, but methodologies to be confirmed
Green-e Climate	Certification for offset projects and carbon credits	No	Accepts other standards with LULUCF
Climate, Community and Biodiversity (CCB) standards	Certification for offset projects and carbon credits	Yes	Only for LULUCF
Chicago Climate Exchange (CCX)	Internal system for CCX offset projects & CCX carbon credits	No	Yes
Plan Vivo	Guidelines for offset projects	Yes	Community based agro-forestry only
Greenhouse Friendly	Certification program for for offset sellers and carbon neutral products	No	Yes
California Climate Action Registry (CCAR)	A registry protocol	No	Yes
VER+	Certification for offset projects, carbon neutral products	No	If CDM/JI approved

Table 7.1. (*cont.*)

Standard	Description	Environmental and social benefits	Includes Land Use, Land Use Change and Forestry
ISO14064	Certification for emissions reporting, offset projects, carbon neutral products	No	Yes
Voluntary Offset Standard (VOS)	Certification for offset projects and carbon credits	No	If CDM/JI approved
Social Carbon	Certification for offset projects and carbon credits	Yes	Focus on reforestation and avoided deforestation
Department of Environment, Food and Rural Affairs (UK)	Proposed consumer code for offsetting and accounting	No	If CDM/JI approved

Source: Adapted from K. Hamilton, M. Sjardin, T. Marcello and G. Xu, *Forging a Frontier: State of the Voluntary Carbon Markets 2008* (Washington DC: Ecosystem Marketplace and New Carbon Finance, 2008), p. 57.

in Zürich, only develop projects which meet Gold Standard criteria. This enables myclimate to situate itself as a provider of 'high quality' carbon offsets, distinguishing itself from other less reliable providers, and thus permitting the company buying the credits to use the Gold Standard label for marketing purposes. That this is effective is shown by the price differential between Gold Standard VERs and others – a project approved under Gold Standard rules attracts around double the price in the market for VERs than the average.[26] Likewise, the VCS, developed by the Climate Group, the International

[26] New Carbon Finance, Voluntary Carbon Index, first edition (September 2008), p. 2. See http://www.newcarbonfinance.com/?p=about&i=freereports, accessed 13 November 2008.

Emissions Trading Association and the World Business Council for Sustainable Development in 2006 as a pilot standard for use in the market, seeks to provide a 'robust global standard, program framework and institutional structure for validation and verification of voluntary GHG emission reductions'.[27]

Besides issues of environmental integrity, some standards address the social dimensions of voluntary projects. For example, The Climate, Community and Biodiversity (CCB) standards,[28] released in 2005, aim to 'identify land-based carbon projects that deliver robust GHG reductions while also delivering net positive benefits to local communities and biodiversity'. These provide gold, silver and standard certification for projects depending on how many of their criteria are satisfied. These range from required criteria which include additionality, baseline issues and leakage assessment through to extras such as employing stakeholders in project management, worker safety and adaptive management. Given the fatigue and confusion generated by the proliferation in voluntary standards, and to build on existing capacity, one thing CCB does is build on the use of existing certifiers authorised under Kyoto or by the Forestry Stewardship Council (a private forestry products certification scheme), for example, as third party evaluators of whether a project deserves to be certified.

As well as standards governing voluntary carbon market projects, there are also standards which govern the voluntary reporting of emissions. These include the WBCSD–WRI Greenhouse Gas Protocol for corporate GHG reporting, the Carbon Trust's Carbon Footprint Measurement Methodology or Le Bilan Carbone in France. There is an interesting dynamic between formal and informal regulation here. The Greenhouse Gas Protocol (GHG Protocol) was designed by the World Resources Institute (WRI) and the World Business Council for Sustainable Development (WBCSD). In 2006, the International Organization for Standardization (ISO), a global industry standards body, adopted the Corporate Standard as the basis for its *ISO 14064-I: Specification with Guidance at the Organization Level for Quantification*

---

[27] VCS, Voluntary Carbon Standard Program Guidelines (18 November 2008). See http://www.v-c-s.org/docs/Voluntary%20Carbon%20Standard%20Program%20 Guidelines%202007_1.pdf.

[28] CCBA, *Climate, Community and Biodiversity Project Design Standards*, second edition. (Arlington, VA: Climate, Community and Biodiversity Alliance, 2008), available at http://www.climate-standards.org/standards/pdf/ccb_standards_second_ Edition_december_2008.pdf.

and Reporting of Greenhouse Gas Emissions and Removals. On December 3rd
2007 ISO, WBCSD and WRI signed a Memorandum of Understanding to
jointly promote both global standards.[29] As well as improving corporate climate governance, organisations such as the Carbon Fund, which
works with over 700 companies, set their goals higher: 'increasing
awareness of products and companies that are compensating for their
carbon footprint while helping to hasten a market transformation'.[30]
Indeed, tools such as the Carbon Fund's 'Carbon Footprint Protocol'
associated with its Carbon*Free*™ product certification programme, as
well as the CCB standards, draw on guidelines and standards that govern the compliance market such as rules for the CDM, since essentially
they are wrestling with the same issues of proving additionality and
using valid baselines.[31]

These private standards always bring with them issues of effect-
iveness and sanctions, accountability and legitimacy. Managing
some of these legitimacy issues may be a role for the International
Emissions Trading Association. There is also, however, the Offset
Quality Initiative, a coalition of six leading non-profit organisations –
the Climate Trust, Pew Center on Global Climate Change, California
Climate Action Registry, Environmental Resources Trust, Greenhouse
Gas Management Institute and the Climate Group founded in
November 2007 to provide leadership on GHG offset policy and best
practices.

Investors moving into this sector such as Merrill Lynch, Credit
Suisse and J. P. Morgan want to see not just a healthy return on their
investments, but evidence that offset products are seen as market
leaders, credible in the eyes of those that buy them. On launching
its own carbon offset service, Merrill Lynch's managing director and
global head of carbon emissions Abyd Karmail said: 'The market must
continue to grow on a foundation of environmental integrity. Demand
in the rapidly growing voluntary carbon offsets market is shifting
towards emission reductions that provide stakeholders with an independent guarantee of environmental sustainability and credibility.'[32]

[29] World Resources Institute (2007). See http://www.wri.org/press/2007/12/iso-wri-
and-wbcsd-announce-cooperation-greenhouse-gas-accounting-and-verification.
[30] Carbonfund.org, 'CArbonFreeTM Product Certification...' p. 3.
[31] Carbonfund.org, 'CArbonFreeTM Product Certification...'.
[32] 'Merrill Lynch enters the Carbon Offset business' *ClimateBiz*, 23 April 2008. See
http://www.climatebiz.com/news/2008/04/23/merrill-lynch-enters-carbon-offset-
business, accessed 8 July 2008.

In some cases leading financial institutions even run VCS registries which are meant to issue, hold, trade and retire VCUs (Voluntary Carbon Units). Players such as the Bank of New York Mellon (USA) and Caisse des Dépôts (France) provide the offset market with what they describe as 'a clean chain of custody and custodial services'. The VCS registries need high levels of financial standing to provide long-term certainty in the market. For Mark Kenber of the Climate Group, the benefits of the registry are obvious: 'a cast iron environmental and financial guarantee for all VCS buyers from the investment banker in Manhattan to the occasional flyer in London'. [33] For Serge Bernou, head of carbon finance at Caisse des Dépôts, the move 'puts carbon markets on a level footing with other financial services'.[34] Without doubt, then, carbon has been incorporated into the world of financial products and services. It has become a currency that people want to buy.

Buyers of credits also interpret interest by major financial players as an endorsement of their status as companies. The press release announcing J. P. Morgan's acquisition of Climate Care suggests the goal is to 'join forces in an acquisition to invest in quality, large-scale carbon emission reduction projects and to advance the development of a liquid financial market that trades in carbon reduction credits'.[35] Tellingly, from J. P. Morgan's side the acquisition 'represents a new milestone in J. P. Morgan's ongoing investment in its commodities business'. Carbon offsets are a commodity much like any other it seems. What Climate Care will get in return from working with a leading global financial services firm with assets of $1.6 trillion and operations in more than 50 countries is access to truly global markets through J. P. Morgan, and the prospect of working 'with hundreds of major partners around the world to facilitate the roll-out of low-carbon technologies at the scale and pace required to make a genuine difference to our environment ... originating projects that will materially increase Climate Care's capacity to reduce carbon emissions'.[36]

But rapid market expansion in the future may also be dependent on addressing a broader range of issues discussed in the next chapter. If

---

[33] Voluntary Carbon Standard, 'The Voluntary Carbon Standard association today reveals the approval of four VCS registries', press release, 2 July 2008. See http://www.v-c-s.org/docs/pr/020708%20VCS%20Approves%20Registries.pdf.

[34] Voluntary Carbon Standard, 'New VCS Registry System to boost carbon market integrity and growth', press release, 17 March 2009. See http://www.v-c-s.org/170309newreg.html.

[35] 'JPMorgan to acquire ClimateCare', joint press release, 26 March 2008.

[36] 'JPMorgan to acquire ClimateCare', joint press release, 26 March 2008.

not, governments may get involved in regulating markets which companies continually claim they do not understand.[37] For companies, the drivers are both voluntarism and regulation, or as Blythe Masters, head of Commodities at J. P. Morgan puts it: 'Clients … seeking to reduce their emissions both due to regulations and out of social responsibility.' There is a lack of transparency and access to information about project methodologies, designs and carbon accounting procedures, however. Taken together with worries about baselines, additionality and third-party verification, this may fuel demands for minimal standards of reporting that allow for comparison across projects and sectors. If not provided by participants in the market, therefore, these standards may be required by government. Some in the offset industry suggest, nevertheless, that while there is no one registry and no standard definition of credits, the markets are more regulated than the allegations of 'cowboy capitalism' we will discuss in Chapter 8 allow for.

CONCLUSION: WHAT ROLE FOR THE VOLUNTARY
CARBON MARKETS?

The two types of carbon economy, voluntary and compliance, will continue to co-exist and shape one another. The voluntary market lives in the shadow of the compliance market, while at the same time playing off its limitations. The initiative by the UK government for a code of conduct emerged because of worries about the voluntary sector's ability to self-regulate. The government's decision also reflected their concern that the voluntary market was a distraction from the existing CDM system whose creation and maintenance required enormous political efforts as part of the Kyoto negotiations. Actors in the voluntary market, therefore, have to show they are adding value in some way. For the President of EcoSecurities, the slow pace and excessive bureaucracy of the compliance market means valuable time is lost in the battle to tackle climate change. This is where the voluntary market comes in: meeting the demand for immediate action, filling a gap in the market, doing the things that Kyoto can't do.[38] Which areas voluntary markets cover will be directly affected by negotiations about what is in and what is out of the CDM. The new battlegrounds

[37] H. Lovell, 'Conceptualizing climate governance beyond the international regime…'.
[38] H. Lovell, 'Conceptualizing climate governance beyond the international regime…'.

include avoided deforestation (REDD) and carbon capture and storage. If the former is to be included in the CDM in the successor to the Kyoto Protocol, this could have an enormous impact on offset markets, which have traditionally served that niche.

The director of Climate Care Mike Mason talks about voluntary markets 'topping up' the compliance markets. Perhaps this is a useful way to understand their role: complementary to compliance markets rather than competing with them or acting as a substitute.[39] At the end of the day, in terms of facilitating the transition to a system of climate capitalism, voluntary markets inevitably only have a small role to play. They serve as a stop-gap, plugging holes and maybe engaging and enrolling actors that would otherwise not be interested. Interestingly, though, this might include bringing on board governments that chose to stay out of Kyoto. Firms that see the potential in carbon markets in countries that until recently were outside the Kyoto regime, such as the USA and Australia, have provided a big market for offsets. Offset firms speak confidently of the ability to 'engineer a shift in political stance' of some key players that had been opposed to action, once they see the money to be made.[40]

Mike Mason is almost evangelical about the value of offsets. His claim, one he made forcefully at a conference at Oxford University in a debate with one of us, to an audience that included many climate activists, was a strong one: only offsets can deliver the scale of emissions reductions required in a short-term time-frame. In other words we cannot afford to do without them. Brushing aside concerns about the integrity of offset projects or the way in which their wholesale purchase by firms like British Airways allow them to increase flights and still claim to be carbon neutral, he can play hard ball with his critics, challenging them to find a solution that can achieve similar cuts in emissions as rapidly as the projects he funds. Perhaps the reasons people are interested in offsets are unimportant given the urgency of taking action. As Climate Care's annual report for 2004 states: 'the climate crisis is so urgent that we should not worry about the motivation of our clients'.[41]

---

[39] H. Lovell, 'Conceptualizing climate governance beyond the international regime...'.

[40] Conversation with Johannes Ehberling, EcoSecurities, Oxford, 28 February 2008.

[41] Quoted in K. Smith, *The Carbon Neutral Myth: Offset Indulgences for your Climate Sins* (Amsterdam: Carbon Trade Watch, 2007), p. 40.

But as well as generating short-term action and creating ways to involve otherwise recalcitrant actors, voluntary markets might be an important testing ground for experiments in carbon projects. They have the flexibility to invent and test out new sorts of projects which may then become suitable for inclusion in regulated markets like the CDM. The freedom which comes from being outside direct government scrutiny can lead to problems in claims about the environmental integrity of the projects (as we discuss in the next chapter), but it can also mean freedom to try out new things which may end up working well.

A simpler justification for their existence is that they are merely meeting a huge demand that exists for emissions reductions projects and carbon credits outside of the Kyoto regime. As the World Bank puts it: 'brokers, consultants, carbon procurement funds, hedge fund managers and other buyers scoured the globe for opportunities to buy credits associated with projects that reduce emissions in developing countries'.[42] In narrow financial terms, the interest they have solicited from some of the world's largest financial services companies suggest they have brought carbon trading to the city.

More broadly, however, we can see in the flourishing of the voluntary carbon markets the fundamental forces of neoliberalism at work that we suggested in Chapter 2 are driving the development of climate capitalism. These markets embody the sorts of entrepreneurial flair and bottom-up innovation that will survive and flourish if they meet a need and will wither away and disappear if not. They clearly reflect the assumption that markets can work wonders in moving capitalism in innovative directions. They reveal again the dominance of finance in responses to climate change – they come about very much through the entrepreneurialism of companies like Climate Care or Cantor CO2e and the big financial players (J. P. Morgan and Cantor Fitzgerald) that back them. They have an interesting relationship with global inequalities. On the one hand offset projects are often marketed in terms of investing in (clean) development in the South, spreading wealth benefits while reducing emissions. But they also only make sense as projects because it is much cheaper to reduce emissions in the South than the North, precisely because income differences are so sharp. Perhaps more than any other aspect of the emergent climate capitalism, they are organised through highly fluid networks. They are

---

[42] K. Capoor and P. Ambrosi, *State and Trends of the Carbon Market 2006* (Washington DC: World Bank, 2006), p. i.

heavily reliant on the networking skills of key firms and intermediaries to bring together the disparate actors (project developers, investors, verifiers, etc.) to make the market 'work'. Finally, they are also, as we will see in detail in the next chapter, heavily contested. There are many who think that voluntary markets can play no role in a serious response to climate change – and the criticisms of these markets are precisely about their neoliberal character.

8

The limits of climate capitalism

One of the questions we raised in the introduction to this book is whether the carbon economy is, frankly, a bit of a scam. That essentially it is more about making money than tackling climate change. If that remains your suspicion having read this far, rest assured you are in good company. Many critics will tell you the whole gamut of carbon trading, offsets and projects under the Clean Development Mechanism (CDM) is based on dodgy accounting, unverifiable assumptions and merely provides new and elaborate ways of escaping obligations to act at home, making money all the while. Let's look at these concerns in a little more detail.

THE LIMITS OF CLEAN DEVELOPMENT

So if clean development is making money, is it delivering benefits for the climate (is it clean?) and is it contributing to development? To be registered under the UN's CDM, projects have to show that they achieve both these things.

The problem is that investors have been attracted to those areas where 'low-hanging fruit' (the easiest and cheapest options) are plentiful, where they have other reasons to invest and where institutions are much stronger. They have not been attracted to weaker states where poverty levels are higher and there are fewer opportunities for high returns over short time-frames. Because of this, flows of carbon finance tend to mirror flows of finance in general in the developing world. Brazil, China and India are the leading hosts of CDM projects, between them accounting for nearly 60% of total registered projects and over 70% of all Certified Emissions Reductions (CERs) issued.[1]

---

[1] See http://cdm.unfccc.int/Statistics/. Accessed 21 July 2009.

The poorest areas of sub-Saharan Africa, meanwhile, have largely not featured in the CDM deal-brokering – the entire continent of Africa is host to just 1.86% of registered CDM projects.[2] Registered projects exist only in South Africa and the Maghreb countries. With a limited supply of large-scale projects, energy or landfill gas (LFG) capture and no hydrofluorocarbon (such as HFC-23) or N_2O destruction opportunities, the lucrative and convenient options that have allowed players like China to reap significant rewards are simply not there for many poorer nations. This accounts for the geographically uneven spread of the benefits of clean development projects across the developing world. It is an issue the World Bank is seeking to address through its Climate Investment Funds and the UNDP through its MDG (Millennium Development Goal) Carbon Facility, as a complement to the CDM; but they face a huge challenge.

Early on the market was also distorted by mega-projects which target greenhouse gases (GHGs) with a high level of what's called Global Warming Potential (GWP). Gases with a higher GWP act as more powerful drivers of the greenhouse effect. Hydrofluorocarbons form one such family of gases where one tonne of HFC-23 is equivalent to 11,700 tonnes of CO_2. The distortion comes from the fact that the credits countries receive for projects are related to this GWP. So a project to phase out HFC-23 for example produces a significantly larger financial return than a CO_2 reduction project for example – in fact it can earn 11,700 times as many CERs as a CO_2 reduction project! Consequently 70% of CERs in the first one and half years of the CDM were issued for abating gases other than CO_2. But many of the opportunities for HFC-23 destruction worldwide appear to have already been exhausted, and the latest figures suggest projects in the chemical industries sector currently account for just over 3% of projects, while projects in the energy industries sector account for 60% of projects.[3]

Questions have also been asked about the sustainable development benefits of projects like the large HFC projects. By contrast, the long-term positive effects for local communities are much clearer with renewable energy and energy efficiency projects. In some cases, CDM finance has provided a new lifeline for waste dumps which become profitable as places to burn methane, to the dismay of communities pushing for their closure – such as the Ensenada landfill site in

[2] UNFCCC (2009) 'Registered projects by region'. See http://cdm.unfccc.int/Statistics/Registration/RegisteredProjByRegionPieChart.html.
[3] See http://cdm.unfccc.int, accessed 29 September 2009.

Argentina, or the 'toxic' dumps in Durban, South Africa.[4] Claims that project promoters make about the positive development benefits they bring are often taken by government authorities and certification companies at face value. Some Designated National Authorities (DNAs), the government bodies set up to approve and register CDM projects in their countries, concede they do not have the capacity to assess them for themselves. Similarly, claims of increased employment, sourcing of local materials or health benefits from host communities are often exaggerated or difficult to verify. The fact that the sustainable development benefits of projects do not have a monetary value, in the way 'additional' savings in GHG emissions do, means they are not a priority in most cases.

Rather than investing equity, as was imagined, investors have shown a clear preference for a 'commodity model'. Buyers are preferring to buy emissions reductions produced by a project without providing equity. Most investors do not have the skills to invest in projects, and those companies that do invest in projects in developing countries do not necessarily need credits. The company Trading Emissions Plc,[5] for example, is looking to invest $300 million in CERs by concluding emission reduction purchase agreements with project developers. Trading Emissions do not need the CERs, they just want to make a profit – buy early and take risks on a project: invest in a project's potential – and sell on the CERs at a higher price. They also lend money to projects and get paid back in CERs. For example, a $5 million loan can generate 200,000 CERs per year.

Nevertheless, in many countries in the South, the CDM is often regarded as a great opportunity to use climate related funds to invest in projects and technologies that they could not otherwise afford, and that may benefit poorer groups in particular.

Though views are now more sanguine and realistic, early on, many companies and project developers were persuaded by the idea that the CDM would bring about a 'gold rush' of easily accessible funds that would deliver a 'Robin Hood effect': a redistribution of resources from the rich to the poor. As we saw in Chapter 5, these expectations were talked up by consultants and brokers who stood

[4] L. Lohmann, *Carbon Trading: A Critical Conversation on Climate Change, Privatisation and Power,* Development Dialogue No. 48 (Uppsala: Dag Hammarsköld & Corner House, 2006).
[5] R. Weiss, Trading Emissions Plc, EEA Fund Management, UK embassy, 'Carbon market business opportunities: creating successful UK–Argentine partnerships', Presentation at Bolsa de Comercio de Buenos Aires event, 29 April 2009.

to gain from overseeing projects and selling CERs. In reality, the time lag between setting up a project and receiving the CERs can be several years. The uncertainty about the outcome, the changing nature of rules about approved methodologies and baselines and the fact that money has to be invested up front (and therefore the risks are on the investor and project developer), is enough to deter many potential actors from getting involved in CDM projects in the first place. The transaction costs in getting a project through all stages of the project cycle mean that it is often only larger players in the market – such as PriceWaterhouseCoopers and EcoSecurities – that can flourish, as they are able to absorb these costs up front.

Besides issues of who is in a position to participate in the CDM market and benefit from CDM projects, other more wide-ranging criticisms focus on the issue of the global South being seen as a sink for Northern emissions, most critically referred to as 'carbon colonialism'.[6] Even senior government officials within the climate change negotiations, such as the 'father of Kyoto', Ambassador Raúl Estrada-Oyuela, noted at the time of the Kyoto agreement:

> My reservation was that the CDM is considered a form of joint implementation but I don't understand how a commitment can be jointly implemented if only one of the parties involved is committed to limit emissions and the other party is free from a qualitative point of view. Such disparity has been at the root of every colonisation since the time of the Greeks.[7]

In an interview with one of the authors, he made clear his view that in his home country of Argentina, not one CDM project is genuinely additional or contributes to development.[8] Others argue, not just that such offsetting mechanisms do no good, but that in fact they can do a great deal of harm. There have been cases of negative impacts on the poor when land is given up for carbon sink purposes, for example. In one such instance, a Norwegian company operating in Uganda, that leased its lands for a sequestration project, allegedly resulted in 8,000 people in thirteen villages being evicted.[9] The project in Bukaleba Forestry Reserve was meant to offset GHG emissions of a coal-fired power plant

---

[6] H. Bachram, 'Climate fraud and carbon colonialism: the new trade in greenhouse gases' *Capitalism, Nature, Socialism*, **15**(4) (2004), 10–12.

[7] R. Estrada-Oyuela, 'First approaches and unanswered questions', in J. Goldemberg (ed.), *Issues and Options: The Clean Development Mechanism* (UNDP, 1998), pp. 23–9.

[8] Interview with Raúl Estrada-Oyuela, 30 April 2009, Buenos Aires.

[9] H. Bachram, 'Climate fraud and carbon colonialism', 10–12.

to be built in Norway. International criticism at the time prevented the project from claiming carbon credits to 'offset' the power plant emissions, but the project continued and the trees were planted. After lengthy negotiations, the Norwegian owners agreed to allocate less than 5% of the land they received from the government at a 'bargain price' to the local people who had previously been evicted. According to one NGO, 'The eucalyptus trees chosen for the project appear to have been a poor choice for the local site. Local people state that they are paid very low wages and that most of their labour is not sourced locally.'[10] The danger then is that carbon finance performs poorly as a means of getting resources to poor people, reinforcing rather than reversing inequalities.

CAN THE CDM DELIVER?

The CDM has certainly been tremendously successful in two ways. It has generated great interest by investors, project developers and traders in the new commodity which it has created, the CER. It has also created great enthusiasm amongst the UNFCCC Secretariat and many national governments because it expanded way faster than its designers anticipated, which is taken as a sign of its value. Proposals in the run-up to the Copenhagen summit in 2009 were about expanding the CDM further to include more sectors (forests, agriculture and land use) and the possibility of moving towards a sectoral approach which reduces transaction costs by funding large-scale shifts in countries' transport or energy bases. The idea of the CDM has, as people in the policy world say, traction.

But does it do the job it was supposed to – reduce emissions by lowering the cost of doing so? And even if it does so, does it do so in a way which doesn't create other major problems? Many identify a series of flaws and problems with the CDM, which raise the basic question we want to ask – what type of climate capitalism do we want to emerge?

At the heart of these problems is the question of methodology. The CDM (and other similar 'project-based mechanisms') is fundamentally different from an allowance-based system like emissions trading (see below). Rather than say to participants, 'you each have this much carbon you can emit, and you can trade these allowances amongst

[10] J. Kill, 'Land grab in Uganda in preparation for CDM sinks project'. *World Rainforest Movement Bulletin*, No. 74, September 2003.

yourselves', in the CDM, one participant has such a limit on its emissions while another doesn't. There is no real way of saying, therefore, that overall, carbon emissions have gone down. Rather, the claim is that in the country in the South where CDM projects have been developed, the CDM has helped slow the rate of emissions growth in that country. But while of course this may not be particularly useful from a strict climate point of view (which needs overall global emissions to decline), it raises the more immediate question, 'how do we know?'

Many criticisms thus focus on the problems raised by the need in CDM projects to develop a counter-factual – what would have happened to emissions if the project had not gone ahead? These counterfactuals (baseline emissions), which underpin CDM methodologies, have given rise to a whole series of problems as they provide incentives for both buyer and seller to exaggerate the scale of emissions saved by not undertaking a particular activity. Many projects were started before the CDM existed, yet have subsequently tried to claim credits for being 'additional',[11] while the availability of CERs provides perverse incentives for HFC producers in China to project expanded HFC production, just so they can be paid not to. The other fear is that the availability of funds through the CDM creates a disincentive for governments to regulate emissions reductions when they can get money for maintaining higher emissions reductions potential.

A related problem is that many of the agencies involved have at least mixed motives in relation to CDM projects. For some Southern countries these projects have become a useful source of foreign investment, and thus the governments have an interest in seeing the projects go through. Designated National Authorities are supposed to play a role in 'quality assurance'– approving projects that look set to reduce emissions and promote sustainable development and requesting more information where they have doubts. However, most DNAs have to trust project developers' accounts of whether local communities object to projects and what measures have been taken to address those concerns, as they don't have the resources or capacity to follow up on applications.

Most companies merely complete that part of the form relating to consultations by suggesting that no feedback was received. This is not so surprising when consultations are often brief, undertaken in

---

[11] Hydro accounted for the majority of projects that failed, with 82 projects failing to progress past the initial validation stage. See http://internationalrivers.org/en/blog/katy-yan/cdm-verifiers-flunking-additionality-school, accessed 21 July 2009.

capital cities far away from where a project will be based and conducted on an invitation-only basis. Unless the company identifies you as a legitimate stakeholder, you often don't get a say. One Project Design Document (PDD) for a project in Argentina even acknowledges that when asked about the environmental benefits of the proposed landfill gas recovery project most participants felt they did not have enough information to answer the question adequately. This is also not so surprising when it is recalled that those presenting at the meeting are from the government and business seeking to sell credits for the projects. Some governments are more stringent than others in the thoroughness of the screening they undertake and the amount of time it takes to get a project approved, with India, for example, having the highest rate of rejections by the CDM Executive Board.

The methodological problems are particularly acute with certain types of projects. One area with currently low levels of investment is forestry. This partly reflects the controversy around LULUCF (Land Use, Land-Use Change and Forestry) projects. Critics feared that forestry projects would flood the market with unsound credits (given the difficultly of quantifying CO_2 saved by absorption), creating incentives for countries to cultivate fast-growing trees on large-scale industrial plantations instead of focusing on sustainable and community-based forestry. Economic rewards handed out by a handful of people on the CDM Executive Board could fundamentally transform the livelihoods of millions of the world's forest dwellers and not necessarily in positive ways.[12] For this reason restrictions were imposed on the way credits achieved through forestry projects could be used, though this may be set to change given proposals for projects which reduce emissions from deforestation and forest degradation (REDD).[13]

LIMITS OF EMISSIONS TRADING

Emissions trading also of course has to overcome a number of technical and political barriers in order to operate effectively. As we saw in

[12] F. Seymour, 'Forests, climate change and human rights'. Note prepared for the meeting of the International Council on Human Rights Policy, Geneva, 12–13 October 2007.

[13] The Marrakesh accords restrict LULUCF projects to afforestation and reforestation projects and the total amount of LULUCF CERs that can be obtained is capped. Climate NGOs also succeeded in insisting that credits from LULUCF CDM projects could not be imported into the EU ETS.

Chapter 6, there are now a wide range of emissions trading schemes in operation around the world, which allocate permits on a different basis and establish a variety of rules to ensure their smooth running. Despite avoiding difficult counter-factual judgments about additionality and without the pressure to demonstrate sustainable development benefits, there are nevertheless problems with the emissions trading scheme in the Kyoto Protocol.

One is the problem of 'hot air': the surplus emissions entitlements available to countries that underwent large-scale de-industrialisation after the baseline year for their agreed targets. The allocations countries agreed to were in relation to 1990 emissions. Since emissions in the former Soviet bloc countries plummeted precisely after 1990 along with those countries' economic collapse, it was obvious that there would be a lot of spare Assigned Amount Units (AAUs) in the system. The emissions of almost all of those countries remain well below 1990 levels despite an economic recovery since the late 1990s. So it would be easy for countries such as Canada and Japan, who will not meet their Kyoto targets, to buy spare AAUs from Russia or the Ukraine fairly cheaply. Overall emissions will not have gone down, but Kyoto will have been complied with. Of course the hot-air problem does not mean an emissions trading system is inevitably flawed, just that the bargain struck at Kyoto over allocation of emissions rights was tainted by *realpolitik*, as all such bargains are.

The second problem may be more fundamental, especially from the point of view of an emergent climate capitalism. A market needs actors who behave in market-like ways – seeking profitable opportunities, comparing prices over time, choosing between a range of alternatives, and so on. In the Kyoto emissions trading scheme (Kyoto ETS), it is governments who do the trading. By and large, governments do not act as profit maximisers. So, for example, many states have said that they would not buy hot air, even though that would almost certainly be the cheapest option for complying with Kyoto. There are also arguably not enough buyers and sellers in the system to make a 'real' market. The number of sellers are few – Russia, Ukraine, perhaps the UK (although most of its over-compliance will simply compensate for the under-achievement of other EU states, given the special 'burden-sharing' arrangements for the EU in the Kyoto Protocol) and a few smaller East European states. The buyers are also few – Canada will be the biggest, but probably also Japan, perhaps Norway or New Zealand. Hardly the basis for a vibrant market. Even then, they can wait until near the end of the commitment period before deciding whether to trade or not, so no active market in AAUs is likely to develop. There have only been a tiny number to date since the transaction log went live in late 2007. The Kyoto ETS is not really the basis for a global carbon market (certainly compared to the CDM). In effect, it will be something like an end-of-tax-year reckoning, where your accountant works out that despite the various allowances and tax credits, you still owe the government a few dollars.

LIMITS OF VOLUNTARY CARBON MARKETS

Voluntary carbon markets present a different set of challenges again. Far less regulated through institutional oversight than compliance markets, the quality of carbon credits traded, and the projects from which they derive, have come under sustained attack. Critics focus on the way they let Northern businesses and consumers off the hook in terms of reducing their own emissions, as well as the social consequences of ill-conceived projects.

In relation to the first criticism, Carbon Trade Watch coined the neat term 'the new indulgences' to encapsulate what they see as their main flaw.[14] In the Middle Ages, the Catholic church introduced a market for indulgences to enable the sinful to get to heaven. The logic was a market one – given monks had a surplus of virtue, the church could sell this surplus virtue to sinners who needed to repent to get to heaven. Similarly, the over-consumer in the rich world is enabled by the offset markets to salve their climate conscience while changing little in their everyday life. They refer to this as 'purchasable legitimacy'. For critics, then, offsets amount to greenwash where, for example, 'British Airways, which opposes aviation taxes and would never advocate that people simply chose not to fly unnecessarily can, through Climate Care, present its climate-conscious passengers with the option of flying free from concern over the impact of its emissions'.[15] Indeed, ludicrous claims such as that the expansion of Heathrow airport will not increase emissions of CO_2 can be sustained by this means, because the purchase of offsets means that emissions growth can be compensated by savings elsewhere in the world. Contrary to the claims of advocates of offsets, therefore, critics argue it does matter *where* the emissions occur because savings made in countries outside of the

[14] K. Smith, *The Carbon Neutral Myth: Offset Indulgences for your Climate Sins* (Amsterdam: Carbon Trade Watch, 2007).

[15] K. Smith, *The Carbon Neutral Myth...*, p. 10.

climate regime, where most offset projects are hosted, do not count towards meeting Kyoto targets.

In relation to the second criticism about the negative social impacts of offset markets, a few examples feature heavily in the debate. An often cited one is the reforestation project on Mount Elgon in Uganda financed by the Forests-Absorbing Carbon Emissions (FACE) Foundation based in the Netherlands, effectively operating as a carbon offset investment fund for Dutch power companies. It started as a reforestation project in 1994. It gained accreditation from the Forestry Stewardship Council (FSC) for its operations. Later on, another Dutch company, GreenSeat, started selling carbon credits from the project. The project has been plagued with accusations of human rights abuses – using the Ugandan Wildlife Authority to evict families, often violently, who had been farming the land for decades.[16] A number of other projects show similar problems, with severe difficulties demonstrating the additionality of the project, its permanence (particularly difficult with forestry projects) or having negative social impacts upon local populations that project developers do not take into account. The voluntary carbon markets thus depend on a motivation by Northern corporations and consumers to salve their consciences for their carbon emissions. It doesn't cost them much to do this. In September 2007, a flight from London to Copenhagen with SAS could be offset through the CarbonNeutral Company for £1.34 ($1.90), representing a value of £10.60 ($15) per tonne of carbon. Credits have been reported as available considerably cheaper than this. In contrast, carbon was selling at that point under the EU Emissions Trading Scheme (ETS) for around £20 ($28.50) per tonne. Remember, in strict emissions trading systems, this price is determined by the overall number of emissions permits in the system and the relative costs of reducing your own emissions versus those of buying emissions credits. In the offset market no such trade-off exists.

This under-valuing of carbon in the offset markets is often regarded as reflecting one of two basic problems (or perhaps both of them). It may simply be 'climate fraud': it may reflect the fact that for a variety of reasons the things which that £1.34 is spent on do not in fact reduce emissions (or increase sinks) equivalent to the emissions produced by the flight. It may alternatively be 'carbon colonialism' – displacing the costs of the flight's emissions onto people in the South

---

[16] K. Smith, *The Carbon Neutral Myth…*, p. 32.

by fixing them in a position as tree planters, or simply by underpaying them for the benefits they provide to the European consumer. Or again, it could be both climate fraud and carbon colonialism at the same time.

What emerges is what critics call 'Enron environmentalism': creative accounting where either what appears on the books bears no relation to activities undertaken, or carbon savings expected to be made in the future are counted as savings made in the present. To be credible, voluntary markets need to address technical issues such as the ability of tree-planting schemes to absorb carbon in the atmosphere to the degree claimed by the advocates of offsets. This is of concern because of inadequate data about rates of carbon absorption and the lack of reliability of forestry projects in terms of their potential to release emissions as they decay over time, which undermine the claim of the equivalence of tree planting to emissions reductions. There are questions over the time-frame of offsets, with emissions (say from a flight) occurring immediately, while the offset may occur over a period of up to a century. This raises issues about guaranteeing that a forest will still be standing and set aside for carbon absorption, especially in areas where land rights are contested and conflict frequently occurs. As Jutta Kill of FERN puts it: 'Who can guarantee a tree planted in Uganda or Kenya will still be standing in 100 years? How many of the countries that host these projects have even existed for 100 years?'[17]

There are questions over the calculation of baselines for projects – of calculating what emissions from a particular project would have been without the project. For critics, a technical solution to this calculation is impossible, and project proponents have inevitable interests in inflating baselines to maximise revenue. Closely related is the calculation of 'additionality' – of proving that the project would not have gone ahead without the finance from carbon markets and thus that the project leads to 'real' reductions in emissions. Without resolving these questions, the ability of the offset markets to contribute to the emergence of a genuine climate capitalism is unclear. In fact offset markets could easily undermine the legitimacy of other elements which have more credibility, derailing the whole process. The story does not stop there though. Advocates of carbon markets have sought to respond to many of these issues – to reassure

---

[17] Quoted in M. Honigsbaum, 'Is carbon offsetting the solution (or part of the problem)?' *The Observer*, 10 June 2007.

sceptical publics and investors, to guarantee government support and to carve a future role for themselves in responses to climate change. To do this, they have had to address governance issues: managing carbon markets to ensure they deliver. It is to this issue that we turn in the next chapter.

9

Governing the carbon economy

The criticisms of carbon markets discussed in the last chapter – whether focused on the effectiveness or inequities of such markets – raise the issue of governance. By what rules should carbon markets be governed? Who should make these rules? To whom should they be accountable?

Many economists, and those pushing for the free-market policies of the last 25 years (who we called neoliberals in Chapter 2) would respond to the question of governing markets with a quizzical look, because for them markets regulate themselves, hence the question of governance is not relevant. That's what markets do. Set up the minimal rules of play, allocate property rights and let the market do the rest. Or, in the case of climate change, hand out the emissions permits (or, better still, auction them) and sit back and let the trading begin. According to this logic, investors will seek out the best opportunities to profit from clean technology and projects that reduce overall emissions of greenhouse gases (GHGs) without the need for government steering. The rhetoric behind the trading schemes we discussed in Chapters 5 and 6, whether it is the EU's Emissions Trading Scheme (EU ETS) or the private-sector Chicago Climate Exchange, embody this logic. Many market actors like Point Carbon or the International Emissions Trading Association are currently pushing for the Clean Development Mechanism (CDM) rules to be relaxed to make it easier to get projects approved, using similar rhetoric.

However, while it may be true, as free-marketeers suggest, that markets to some extent govern themselves (hence the popular phrase 'market discipline'), to construct a market nevertheless entails a considerable amount of governance from 'outside' the market. When you actually try to create a market, it turns out you can't just do the minimum of creating property rights and enforcing contracts. You also need to define rules by which trading can occur, set up elaborate accounting systems to measure emissions and make companies report on them and create complex methodologies by which a project may be deemed to have reduced emissions. Seen in this light, the claim that the market regulates itself is naïve to say the least. Adam Smith's famous invisible hand (by which left to their own devices markets will deliver the most efficient outcomes) in practice needs, if not direct guidance, then a lot of regulatory infrastructure behind it, in order to work.

But if they are naïve, then free-market neoliberals are equally irresponsible. As highlighted in the previous chapter, the critics of carbon markets ably point out the various problems involved in these markets where ideology favours the minimum regulation possible, and weak institutions result. As Larry Lohmann suggests, '... trading is often a singularly *inefficient* way of attaining goals ... when the necessary conditions for trading – measurement instruments, legal institutions and so forth – are inadequate'.[1] We don't have to look too far in other directions (think Enron, Long Term Capital Management, the sub-prime-cum-'credit crunch' crisis) to see how, if financiers are left to their own devices, making money as quickly as they can with minimal supervision, all sorts of scams, injustices and crises inevitably result. Carbon markets risk being no different – the problem of 'subprime carbon' has already been identified.[2]

Beyond the problem of scams and exploitation, carbon markets are rather different to other markets. They do not exist for the sake of it. They are not *ends* in themselves, but exist as a *means* to achieve a specific social purpose – to enable societies to reduce GHG emissions. Free-marketeers struggle to understand this aspect of carbon markets, seeing them as neutral and natural social institutions that have no goal other than enabling market participants to maximise profit, and thus ought not to be interfered with since they know best how to do this.

The danger that cowboy operations pose to the credibility of carbon markets as a whole may, however, persuade some market believers that a measure of regulation may be necessary to secure the collective good of a market-based response to climate change. The parallel with

---

[1] L. Lohmann (ed.), *Carbon Trading: A Critical Conversation on Climate Change, Privatisation and Power.* Development Dialogue No. 48, September (Uppsala: Dag Hammarsköld & Corner House, 2006).

[2] Friends of the Earth US, 'Subprime carbon? Re-thinking the world's largest new derivatives market.' See http://www.foe.org/pdf/SubprimeCarbonReport.pdf.

the current financial crisis is again striking, with neoliberal econo-mists having to concede that there may be a case for greater regula-tion of the banking and financial services sector, that greed doesn't always mean good.

The critics are in effect right that an under-regulated carbon economy will produce enormous problems. But they are often mis-taken on two things. One is a similar mistake to the one neoliberals make: to assume that carbon markets exist largely without inter-vention and oversight, when in fact the carbon economy is already highly governed. Once we accept this, the question rather becomes what sorts of governance, for whose benefit and towards what ends? The second mistake is to see themselves – the critics – as existing out-side the dynamics of carbon markets, looking on, protesting about carbon markets, but not having any impact on them. However, as we saw in the previous chapter in relation to how standards have devel-oped in the voluntary carbon markets, protest and criticism in fact stimulates efforts to govern these markets more carefully. It creates legitimacy crises that affect levels of confidence and interest in carbon markets and so ultimately their value. Other examples of this dynamic would include efforts to create a CDM Gold Standard that privileges projects that meet tougher sustainable development criteria, or the shift towards auctioning in the EU ETS. The former was a response to concerns about the CDM not bringing sustainable development ben-efits to host communities and being overly focused on projects which eliminate industrial gases with few positive spin-offs. The latter can be seen in the light of protests about the windfall profits earned by some companies in the first phase of the EU ETS because of the over-allocation of permits. Governance often develops, then, in response to NGO campaigns and criticisms.

The question, then, is not to assume (for good or ill) that there is no carbon market governance, but to understand how those mar-kets are governed, in order to identify what the principal weaknesses and strengths of that governance are, how different bits of governance interact with each other and then to think about how to improve the system of governance. So how then is the carbon market governed and what is its purpose?

ACTUALLY EXISTING CARBON ECONOMY GOVERNANCE

First, a word about governance. At least two things are entailed in this bit of academic and policy jargon. One is that governance is not confined to those ways that rules are developed and enforced through some central power that can impose its will by force. Governance implies that many rules may be followed not because of the threat posed by state power, but rather because of a range of more subtle pressures – to conform to collectively agreed norms, because your actions are highly visible and you value your reputation; or because you understand that your interests are served by the general observance of the rule, and that requires you to do what you expect of others.

The second point of the term governance is that it is no longer only governments who get to make the rules. As we have seen, many of the rules in the carbon markets are being made by private-sector actors and occasionally by NGOs.[3] Some people are, of course, nostalgic for the good old days when states exercised greater sovereignty. But the sorts of changes in the powers of actors like large corporations or transnational NGOs associated with that other over-used buzzword 'globalisation', are both probably irreversible, and in fact also might be put to good use in responding to climate change.

Table 9.1 shows the different types of governance operating in the carbon economy we have discussed in earlier chapters. It illustrates well the point made above that the carbon economy is fundamentally already governed – it entails a complex set of rules which aim to shape the behaviour of governments, companies and individuals. The question is whether it works well and whether it is enough.

Three basic sorts of governance can be identified. Some parts of the carbon economy are governed by quantity; that is to say, rules are set which establish overall limits for carbon emissions, allocate them among different players and attempt to enforce those limits. Governments do this when they set a national target, or specific targets, for economic sectors. Governments also do this collectively when they negotiate among themselves individual national targets, as in the Kyoto Protocol or the EU agreement for sharing the burden of the EU's overall target among its member states. But private actors can also do this, as in the Chicago Climate Exchange, where member companies have agreed to an overall cut of 6% in their emissions by 2010. Individual companies of course also set themselves targets for emissions reductions – most radically in those that attempt to become 'carbon neutral', like HSBC, as we saw in Chapter 3. Governing by quantity involves a series of secondary rules – to measure emissions, report on them and to allocate targets among actors.

---

[3] H. Bulkeley, and P. Newell, *Governing Climate Change* (London: Routledge, 2010).

Table 9.1. *Types of governance*

Primary mode of governance	Goal	Agents of governance	Examples	Secondary forms of governance
Governance by quantity	Direct control of emissions levels	National governments, international agreements, Chicago Climate Exchange	Emissions trading systems, emissions targets	Allocation rules, data reporting rules
Governance by price	Structuring incentives of consumers and investors	National governments (including EU institutions), CDM institutions, VCM certification systems, the market itself as institution	[Carbon taxes], emissions trading systems, CDM, VCM	Methodologies – for baselines, additionality, verification (for project-based mechanisms); methodologies for producing commensurability of instruments, fungibility of products (including linkage between systems such as between CDM and EU ETS); trading rules – transaction logs, exchange systems; certification systems – CDM Executive Board, Methodology Panel, VCM certification schemes
Governance by information disclosure	Shifting investor behaviour	Private investors, self-regulation of companies	Carbon Disclosure Project, Global Reporting Initiative, [Securities and Exchanges Commission disclosure rules]	Accounting rules for reporting, investor behaviour

Note: measures in square brackets indicate governance measures not currently widely adopted.

Governance by price is, in emissions trading systems, a logical extension of governing by quantity. Allocating emissions targets, as long as it produces scarcity, creates demand for trading, which will create a price for carbon emissions permits. As in other markets, this price then exerts a governing effect on behaviour, creating an incentive to reduce emissions so as not to have to buy so many permits. Other carbon markets, especially when they are linked to an emissions trading scheme (as in the CDM–EU ETS link) function similarly – through the creation of monetary incentives to reduce emissions. But price can also be affected directly, through carbon taxes. Some governments have instituted such taxes (despite their unpopularity) and they remain a possibility for transforming the incentives individuals and companies face.

Governing by price, especially through carbon markets (carbon taxes are rather simpler) entails the development of considerably more complex rules than just governing by quantity. Not only do you have to measure and report on emissions, but you have to decide how and when they can be traded and by whom. You have to work out accounting rules which prevent double-counting, and how to enable trading across different systems, assuming that linking different markets makes them more efficient. For project-based mechanisms like the CDM, you then also need rules to deal with all the counterfactuals involved in such a project – how to measure the emissions foregone because of the project (its 'additionality'), how to verify that the emissions reductions have occurred, and how to award credits for the projects. Figure 9.1 illustrates just how many actors are involved in the CDM to make this market work. There are roles for national government agencies (Designated National Authorities), for international institutions (CDM Executive Board), as well as a range of private actors that help investors develop project proposals and then the Designated Operating Entities that audit and verify whether claimed emissions reductions have taken place. There is a highly elaborate web of governance actors that oversee the creation of Certified Emissions Reductions (CERs).

Governing by disclosure is perhaps more simple. Businesses and other actors are required to report on their emissions profiles. Still, to enable investors to make decisions based on a company's carbon intensity or its policies to reduce its emissions, good quality data reporting and consistent reporting across companies to make them comparable is necessary; this entails elaborate rules about how to measure and calculate emissions. If it is to achieve its goal, it also then entails a more

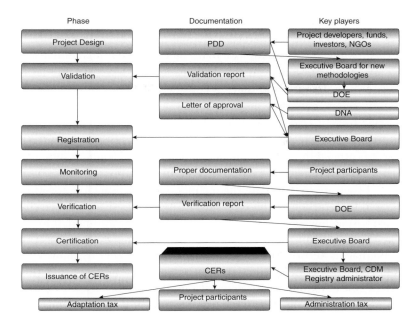

Figure 9.1   The CDM project cycle.
Source: E. Boyd, N. E. Hultman, T. Roberts *et al.*, 'The Clean Development Mechanism: an assessment of current practice and future approaches for policy,' *Tyndall Centre Working Paper*, no. 114, October (2007).

crude form of governance – as investors either disinvest from carbon-intensive companies or (more plausibly) become active in managing companies to reduce their emissions.

HOW GOOD IS ALL THIS GOVERNANCE?

In the last chapter we reviewed many of the limitations of the carbon economy. At the heart of these problems are weak governance rules, and, as a consequence, reductions in carbon emissions do not go far enough. What then are the main weaknesses in the way this governance works?

First, where there are targets, they are too weak, and governments find ways of weakening them further. The Kyoto target, of a 5.2% reduction in the emissions of industrialised countries by 2008–2012, is woefully inadequate to address climate change. Governments have more recently started to acknowledge the need for much deeper cuts, with the G8 meeting in July 2009 for example proclaiming a goal to limit temperature change to 2°C over pre-industrial levels, reducing G8 emissions by 80% by 2050 and global emissions by 50% by 2050.[4] But even this is considerably less than the IPCC regards as necessary, and there is considerable doubt as to whether the emissions cuts they propose would actually limit temperature change to 2°C. This much is well known and accepted (apart from by the vocal but relatively small in number climate change deniers), but it is crucial in terms of the effectiveness of carbon markets. The latter depend fundamentally on scarcity in the supply of carbon permits if they are to stimulate the technological and social innovation needed to decarbonise the economy. If there is no scarcity, then the price will be low and changes in behaviour will be minimal. It looks like the targets for the post-Kyoto era will be stronger, but gives the Copenhagen Accord it is unlikely that collective cuts by industrialised countries will be more than 20% (and may be less), and this leaves out emissions reductions in rapidly growing countries like China, for whom no legally binding limits will be in place (even if they accept some voluntary reductions commitments).

The targets that governments have imposed on companies have also often been weak. The allocation problems in the EU ETS are a perfect example here. Behind the weaknesses of the EU ETS is a failure of governance by EU institutions and national governments. Because national governments over-allocated permits in the first round of the emissions trading scheme there was no scarcity in emissions permits, and companies were thus able to reap windfall profits without doing anything to reduce their emissions. As Larry Lohmann puts it: 'In April 2006 it became clear that corporate participants in the EU ETS had been granted around 10% more allowances than they had needed to cover their 2005 emissions. That translated to between 44 and 150 million tonnes of surplus carbon permits or, at €13 [US$18.60] per tonne, up to €1.8bn [US$2.57bn] of free money.'[5] As a consequence of this over-allocation, not only were windfall profits realised, but the price collapsed – so that mode of governance also didn't work. Even the major consulting firm, Ernst and Young, who have vested interests in carbon trading, conceded: 'The EU ETS has not encouraged

[4] ENDS Europe, 'G8 leaders agree two degrees climate goal', *ENDS Europe DAILY*, 8 July 2009.

[5] L. Lohmann, 'A Critical Conversation on Climate Change, Privatisation and Power...,' p. 87.

meaningful investment in carbon-reducing technologies.'[6] While this is perhaps an exaggeration – the World Bank, for example, claims that the EU ETS has helped reduce emissions from regulated companies – it is a systemic problem. Ultimately this is because of the dilemmas faced by governments – while committed to regulating companies to limit emissions, they also want to make sure their own companies are not disadvantaged in European and international markets, and may even offer generous allocations to help particular sectors develop, or exempt them from the scheme altogether.

The second weakness is that flexibility in meeting commitments enables governments and companies to undermine the targets that have been set. Particularly important here is the problem in defining 'additionality' in the carbon offset markets. The Kyoto offset market in the CDM is where these problems are most obvious. The rules fail to prevent various weaknesses – as in the example of large hydrofluoro-carbon (HFC) or hydro projects that would probably have gone ahead in any case. Governance systems are also weak in terms of addressing the maldistribution of projects and investments between and within countries. They currently fall short in their capacity to steer invest-ments to where they are most needed and where they can make a difference. The large, rapidly industrialising countries of China, India and Brazil capture the lion's share of CDM projects, while sub-Saharan Africa hardly gets a look in, as we saw in Chapter 7. The CDM is densely regulated with a complex set of methodological rules. Many individ-ual states have their own rules on top of those. The CDM projects are meant to deliver sustainable development, something that individual countries can define for themselves. But only governments that are highly attractive to investors are able to lay down conditions such as this. China remains the leading player in the CDM, despite rules that require 51% ownership of CDM projects by the Chinese state, arrange-ments that guarantee the Chinese state a share of the CERs that accrue, as well as revenue from taxes on CDM transactions. Most poorer countries, which are less attractive to investors, have less bargaining leverage to shape carbon finance on their own terms.[7]

[6] T. Ward, energy director Ernst and Young, May 2006. Cited in Open Europe, 'The High Price of Hot Air: why the EU ETS is an environmental and economic failure'. See http://www.openeurope.org.uk/research/ets.pdf, accessed 1 October 2009.

[7] P. Newell, L. Jenner and L. Baker, 'Governing Clean Development: A Framework for Analysis', *The Governance of Clean Development Working Paper Series*, no. 1, Univer-sity of East Anglia (2009). See www.clean-development.com.

Third, the voluntary market is even more prone to such problems. Offsets are far less regulated, with offset markets often being equated with the 'wild west' when compared with the CDM.[8] Because it is largely uncoordinated and has little institutional oversight in terms of the monitoring of claimed reductions, multiple investors can claim emission reductions from the same project. This has raised a series of problems about quality and credibility, which new standards in the voluntary sector, discussed below, have sought to address. Private and self-regulation, where companies set their own targets, as we saw in Chapter 3, face similar issues of lack of sanctions and comparability across initiatives. This is not to say that voluntary commitments do not make an important contribution, but we simply don't know how much of a contribution they make. Recent attempts to calculate the net effect of carbon saved by the range of existing voluntary initiatives on climate change have concluded that it is simply impossible to say.[9] The benchmarks used are different, the range of gases covered varies and the time-frames employed are highly variable.

Given the uncertainties involved and the discretion powerful actors have to set their own targets and establish their own preferred systems of governance, it is easy to see why climate activists cry foul and level the charge of 'climate fraud' at the money-makers, brokers and intermediaries that manage the carbon economy. Some might argue that letting all flowers bloom in a carbon-constrained world might not be a bad thing, especially in a context of diplomatic stalemate over a future climate regime. Harnessing the energy and dynamism of private actors to the goal of climate change may well be a good thing. But someone has to do the sums. What is the net effect of all these private, dispersed and only loosely regulated actions? Only by knowing this can we know what progress we are making.

Part of this governance gap results from the legacy that neoliberalism has bequeathed climate politics. While it has created the possibility of carbon markets as a 'solution' to climate change, it also instinctively favours very light-touch regulation that can leave space for climate fraud. Its presumption is that voluntarism and

[8] M. Estrada, E. Corbera and K. Brown, 'How do regulated and voluntary carbon offset schemes compare?' *Tyndall Centre Working Paper*, no. 116, May (2008). See http://www.tyndall.ac.uk/content/how-do-regulated-and-voluntary-carbon-offset-schemes-compare.

[9] P. Mann, and D. Liverman, 'An empirical study of climate mitigation commitments and achievements by non-state actors', presented at the Amsterdam Human Dimensions of Global Environmental Change conference, 24 May 2007.

self-regulation are more efficient and effective than state-led, legally binding approaches. But it is also true that experiments in de-regulation and non-regulation in carbon markets have often led to regulation and re-regulation. When EU car-makers argued in 1998 that regulation from the European Commission was not needed and provided too clumsy an instrument to improve the fuel efficiency of cars being produced, they suggested a voluntary approach, which was indeed developed. Following ongoing talks between the European Commission and the car industry, the two parties concluded a voluntary agreement, setting a mid-term target of 25% reduction on CO_2 emissions from motor-cars by 2008. However, by February 2007, the European Commission had to insist on mandatory targets for CO_2 emissions from cars after it had become clear that the car industry was failing to meet targets agreed under the 10-year voluntary agreement on CO_2 emissions.[10] Even industry lobbyists from Business Europe, that had trumpeted the scheme, admitted that the car-makers' failure to make good on their promises was 'highly embarrassing', undermining the general credibility of voluntary approaches.[11]

For market-based solutions to climate change to help address climate change, they thus need to be governed by strong rules. The Stern Review, commissioned by the British government, which made a strong economic case for early action on climate change, argues that global warming is the biggest example of market failure ever. It argues that the state has to play a significant part in redressing the balance, even if it is an 'ensuring state' as suggested by Anthony Giddens.[12] Some of the world's leading carbon entrepreneurs would welcome more direction through regulation. Many business leaders are hesitant to go further with action on climate change because of uncertainty regarding the overall policy framework and, related, the price of carbon. In a recent open letter to President Obama and Congress a group of leading firms, including household names such as Starbucks, Hewlett Packard, Levis and E-bay, leant their weight to calls for climate legislation. The letter stated: 'We support this legislation because certainty and rules of the road enable us to plan, build, innovate and expand our businesses. Putting a price on carbon will drive investment

[10] Corporate Europe, 'Car industry flexes its muscles, Commission bows down', Briefing paper, Observatory (CEO), 16 March 2007. See http://www.corporateeurope.org/carlobby.html.

[11] Meeting with representative from Business Europe, European Parliament, Brussels, April 2008,

[12] A. Giddens, *The Politics of Climate Change* (Cambridge: Polity, 2009).

into cost-saving, energy-saving technologies, and will create the next wave of jobs in the new energy economy.'[13] The same is true for traders of offsets in the carbon economy. If there is no value for CERs in a regime to replace the Kyoto Protocol in 2012, the bottom may fall out of the market.

LEARNING: IS IT GETTING BETTER?

So the actual governance of carbon markets has a number of major inadequacies. But it is also fair to say that there is a certain amount of learning already going on in governance, precisely in response to weaknesses in the way they are currently governed. The model of 'learning by doing', which underpins many of these systems of governance, notably the CDM and the EU ETS, should perhaps be taken seriously. With such innovative forms of policy design, and the range of actors and networks that have to be brought on board, it is unlikely that any institutions could get it right first time.

The EU, for example, has responded to the problems experienced in the first phase – especially the allocation and data problems. The data collection was tightened up in the first round itself. In fact it was the release of better data that prompted the price collapse – since the new data demonstrated that states had over-allocated permits. The Commission bargained much more strongly in the second phase, for 2008–2012, rejecting many countries' submissions, radically reducing the overall allocations of a number of them.[14] There are still some problems of over-allocation to specific industries,[15] and thus windfalls for them, but much less so at the level of the overall allocation. For the third phase for after 2012, which is currently being developed, the Commission is proposing both an expansion of the sectors to be covered, but, more importantly, a great expansion in the use of auctioning, where companies don't get given permits for free, but instead have to bid for them. This is precisely to respond to the problem of windfall profits.

A similar logic can be seen in the voluntary carbon market, as we have already seen in the previous chapter. The danger for companies

---

[13] 'Competing by leading', an open letter to President Obama and Congress. See http://wecanlead.org/ad0623.html, accessed 1 October 2009.

[14] J. Birger Skjaerseth and J. Wettestad, *EU Emissions Trading: Initiation, Decision-Making and Implementation* (London: Ashgate, 2008), pp. 173–4.

[15] O. Tickell, 'A licence to print money', *The Guardian*, 12 September 2008.

in those markets is that the potential for making money is undermined by the loss of faith in the effect of those actions. If all of this rests on guilt – allowing people to buy their way out of trouble while someone else offsets their contributions to global warming – then people parting with their cash want to know they are buying a credible product. Otherwise they will be castigated for paying into a scam – not good for appeasing guilt or generating 'green PR'. For example, a wave of exposés in the mainstream media caused the share value of Climate Care and EcoSecurities to plummet. Carbon brokers are then caught in a bind in the face of companies using offsets to 'greenwash' their activities on the one hand, and the environment lobby on the other waiting to pounce on acts of 'climate fraud'.

This is the driver behind the certification schemes like the Voluntary Carbon Standard (VCS), the Gold Standard and the Offset Quality Initiative. People like the Climate Group together with the IETA (International Emissions Trading Association) have played a key part in coming up with such schemes. As we saw in Chapter 7, some of the standards such as the Climate, Community and Biodiversity standard, or the Social Carbon standard, focus on the social dimensions of offsets, in response to activist critiques of their impacts on host communities. The UK government waded in to provide a code of conduct for offsets, suggesting they had to be accredited by the CDM or bought from left-over allowances not traded under the EU ETS. Its DEFRA (Department for the Environment, Food and Rural Affairs) department announced in February 2008 the framework for the Code of Best Practice for Carbon Offsetting. The Code is voluntary and offset providers can choose whether to seek accreditation for all, or some, of their offsetting products.[16] The Code initially covers only CERs that are compliant with the Kyoto Protocol. The UK Secretary of State for Energy and Climate Change, Ed Miliband, has also challenged industry to develop a standard for Voluntary Emissions Reduction credits (VERs), which could be included in the Code in the future, subject to the verification of their robustness. Companies are rarely happy when the government gets involved in what they consider to be their business, and so it is unsurprising that they have sought to develop their own standards of self-regulation. Indeed, recent evidence suggests that offsetters may even be ignoring this Code.

---

[16] DEFRA, 'Government offsetting code announced'. See http://www.defra.gov.uk/news/latest/2008/climate-0219.htm.

COHERENCE: HOW DOES IT HANG TOGETHER?

Individually, the governance of carbon markets can therefore be improved, and, arguably, is being so. But what about when we put all these governance systems together? Do they all pull in the same direction in driving low-carbon growth? Can we imagine ways that the whole might become larger than the individual parts?

At the moment, there is only patchy coherence between the various governance institutions discussed above and summarised in Table 9.1. There are some direct linkages. All are linked through the basic measurement tools which each have adopted by mimicking the others – the tonne of carbon dioxide equivalent. The EU ETS is closely connected to the CDM through a linking directive and drives demand for CDM projects. Other emissions trading systems are being designed to link not only vertically to the CDM, but also horizontally to the EU system. The CDM and the voluntary carbon market are linked not only through the companies that operate in both, but through the methodologies for assessing projects and the technical infrastructure that supports them. Other parts of these governance institutions are totally separate; the CDP and the other investor-led mechanisms operate in almost total abstraction from the carbon markets. There are some companies operating in both, but without a linkage between them.

It is also not necessarily the case that the links work towards better governance. The EU ETS–CDM link in some ways weakens the effectiveness of the EU ETS, making it possible for the overall system to have greater actual emissions than the number of allowances that have been handed out. Managers of the EU ETS recognise this problem – a tension between wanting to stimulate a transformation in the European economy towards decarbonisation, and wanting to pursue abatement as cost-effectively (read: cheaply) as possible.

But it is possible to think through ways that the systems of governance could link up. One particular way is the relationship between 'governance by price' and 'governance by disclosure'. At present, a key limit to the CDP (see Chapter 4) and other similar systems is that the member companies are motivated principally by the business risk – rather than other sorts of risk, such as reputation or climate change itself. They want to know what the carbon emissions are of a firm they invest in, because that might become a measure of whether the firm concerned will be more or less profitable in the future. But whether or not this is the case depends on the carbon price, a reasonable certainty that carbon prices will apply generally across the global economy, and that they will steadily rise. So the worldwide spread of emissions trading systems, and the (increasing) stringency of targets that create scarcity in those trading systems, are key to the CDP realising its potential. As yet, the CDP does not affect investor behaviour in any quantifiable way (although there are signs of more diffuse effects in investor culture), principally because the CO_2-intensity of a firm is not yet a reliable indicator of the riskiness of the investment. We're back of course here to the problem of the weakness of the targets set by governments. Thinking through this sort of coherence problem is an important element in pursuing more effective climate governance, a point we follow up in the following chapter.

A bigger problem is the coherence between climate governance and the more general governance of the global economy. For example, the World Bank has been a central player in the emergence of carbon markets. But its propensity for large-scale lending for infrastructural projects has meant that ongoing investments in the fossil fuel economy are undermining the Bank's, and everyone else's efforts to bring down global emissions overall. As Ian Tellam puts it; 'While the governments of industrialised countries continue to publicly state their commitment to dealing with the climate issue under the Kyoto Protocol, they continue to work with the World Bank, with multilateral development banks and with export credit agencies to directly or indirectly finance the development of energy systems in low-income countries based on fossil-fuels.'[17] The same might be said for trade agreements which, in their current form, are on a 'collision course' with efforts to act on climate change.[18] We turn to some of these challenges in the final chapter because they are essentially about the overall governance of the economy, which will be critical to whether or not climate capitalism comes about. The very rationale of *for whom* and *for what* trade, finance and production are governed would have to change.

---

[17] I. Tellam, (ed.), *Fuel for Change: World Bank Energy Policy – Rhetoric and Reality* (London: Zed Books, 2000), p. 185.

[18] New Economics Foundation, *Collision Course: Free Trade's Free Ride on the Global Climate* (London: New Economics Foundation, 2003); Peter Newell, 'Fit for

GOVERNANCE FOR WHOM?

So while there are clearly problems in the way that carbon markets are being governed, it is clear that such governance can be improved, and that well-governed carbon markets might be able to deliver emissions reductions. But the governance of those markets can also be evaluated according to criteria other than just the effectiveness in pursuing emissions reductions. Behind the problems in achieving these reductions are weaknesses in terms of basic political principles such as justice and accountability. To make carbon markets more effective will involve dealing with these issues as well. These are essentially questions of the *process* of governance – who gets to make the rules, impose them on others, and who has to live with the consequences. This point is worth elaborating, as it underlies the claims about 'carbon colonialism' we saw in the previous chapter.

The core of the justice question is that decisions by large polluters (countries or companies) about whether or not to act on climate change amount to decisions about whether or not to gamble with the lives of poor people that already do, and will increasingly, live with the consequences of climate change. The injustice flows from the fact that those who have contributed least to the problem of climate change will suffer many of its worst effects. It is this situation that animates what has come to be called the climate justice movement.[19] Groups that are part of that movement are deeply sceptical about the notion that carbon markets can deliver social and ecological justice.[20] A number of these groups met in October 2004 and produced the Durban Declaration on Carbon Trading that stated, 'As representatives of peoples' movements and independent organisations, we reject the claim that carbon trading will halt the climate crisis.'[21] Groups signing up to the declaration claim, 'Through this process of creating a new commodity – carbon – the Earth's ability and capacity to support a climate

purpose: Towards a development architecture that can deliver', in E. Paluso (ed.), *Re-thinking Development in a Carbon-Constrained World: Development Cooperation and Climate Change* (Finland: Ministry of Foreign Affairs, 2009), pp. 184–196.

[19] P. Newell, 'Climate for change: civil society and the politics of global warming', in M. Glasius, M. Kaldor and H. Anheier (eds.), *Global Civil Society Yearbook* (London: SAGE, 2005).

[20] I. Angus, D. Wall and D. Tanuro, *The Global Fight for Climate Justice: Anti-Capitalist Responses to Global Warming and Environmental Destruction* (London: IMG publishers, 2009).

[21] Durban Declaration, 'Climate Justice Now! The Durban Declaration on Carbon Trading', signed 10 October 2004. Glenmore Centre, Durban, South Africa.

conducive to life and human societies is now passing into the same corporate hands that are destroying the climate.'[22]

This is not just a problem of inequities between societies, however; great inequalities also exist within societies. National statistics of climate emissions disguise the vast inequalities within countries along the lines of class, gender and race for example in terms of contribution to the problem on the one hand, and vulnerability to its effects on the other. The Indian and Chinese middle class is rapidly approaching levels of energy consumption that rival those of the middle class in Europe or North America, even while the majority of citizens in those countries do not have any access to commercial energy. This means governments face a huge challenge in designing policies and efforts to allocate burden that recognise these vast differences within their populations.

In terms of climate impacts, studies also often fail to identify exactly who will lose. Often it is difficult to speculate beyond the probability that the elderly and the very young suffer more from heat stress, but recent events give us a taste of what we can expect. Hurricane Katrina brought into sharp relief the horror of how environmental change and social inequalities interact to make each other worse. The toxic waste generated by plants located in poorer neighbourhoods in Louisiana, that had been the target of environmental justice activists for decades,[23] was rapidly dispersed by the flooding that followed the breaching of the city's walls. The infrastructure to cope with this emergency was just not there. In fact, funding for flood defences in these areas had been cut by the Bush administration. It became abundantly clear that the ability to adapt to climate change is a function of wealth, and in many contexts this closely intertwines with the politics of race.[24] Natural disasters become social disasters because poorer people tend to live in flimsier housing, nearer more polluting industry and in neighbourhoods with inadequate infrastructure. Climate change reproduces this tendency for environmental change to magnify existing social inequalities.[25]

---

[22] Durban Declaration, 'Climate Justice Now! The Durban Declaration on Carbon Trading'.

[23] B. Allen, *Citizens and Experts in Louisiana's Chemical Corridor Disputes* (Cambridge, MA: MIT Press, 2003); S. Lerner, *Diamond: A Struggle for Environmental Justice in Louisiana's Chemical Corridor* (Cambridge, MA: MIT Press, 2005).

[24] B. Parks, and J. Timmons Roberts, 'Globalization, vulnerability to climate change and perceived injustice', *Society and Natural Resources*, **19** (2006): pp. 337–355.

[25] B. Parks and J. Timmons Roberts, 'Globalization, vulnerability to climate change and perceived injustice' pp. 337–355.

Adaptation has also received increasing attention in climate policy debates because of this dynamic. Until recently, many environmentalists have resisted talking about adaptation, fearing it would take attention away from the need to mobilise action on mitigation. But it is now clear we are already committing the planet to an unprecedented level of climate change, which is already starting to produce major disruptions in the livelihoods of the world's poorest people. Justice demands, therefore, that we think about adaptation, and one possibility is to govern carbon markets in such a way as to help finance this. One suggestion is that carbon trading should be taxed to meet the enormous need for new funds to pay for adaptation. Hence, all transactions might be subject to a levy. This already exists in the CDM market, where 2% of the value of all transactions goes to the UN Adaptation Fund. This scheme could be made more general. Other proposals have also been made. The French government under Chirac advocated a tax on flying whose revenues would be used to fund adaptation.[26] Such global 'Robin Hood' schemes, taking from the world's airborne elite to pay for impacts on the poor, may provide useful ways of generating funds – despite the irony of tying resourcing for adaptation to an increase in an activity that contributes to climate change in the first place.

So we could imagine governing carbon markets so that they mitigate some of the injustices produced by climate change impacts. It is less clear that this helps decarbonise the economy, however, unless it also leads to the reductions in the amount that wealthy people fly.

And there are distinct limits to how markets can in principle deal with questions of justice. Carbon markets govern, as we showed above, principally through the price of carbon. For their proponents, the logic is that such a carbon price should operate universally, affecting all carbon-emitting activities equally. The mantra of carbon markets is often that the atmosphere doesn't care where the carbon is emitted or which activity it comes from. But from a justice point of view, we absolutely do want to distinguish between different types of emissions. As the late Anil Agarwal of India's Centre for Science and Environment put it: 'Is one tonne of a greenhouse gas produced by a New Yorker or a Londoner equal to a tonne of the same gas produced by a peasant in Guatemala, Chad or Bangladesh? The simple, moral answer is "no". The first tonne is the result of luxury. The second tonne

---

[26] R. Klein and B. Muller, 'Adaptation financing instruments', Policy Brief (2009). See http://www.oxfordclimatepolicy.org/publications/KigaliPolicyBrief3.pdf.

for basic survival. Both of them go into the atmosphere. But one needs to be controlled and the other needs to be supported.'[27] Following this logic, justice requires that we do not attempt to increase the price of carbon for survival activities, only for luxury ones. Governing carbon markets justly, therefore, implies limiting their scope somewhat.

As with the effectiveness question, there is a certain amount of learning involved in governing carbon markets towards more just outcomes. Concerns about the uneven distribution and poor quality of CDM projects have prompted proposals for quota systems to encourage flows to areas currently not receiving them, especially sub-Saharan Africa, or to include sectors such as land-use projects where poorer regions are more likely to be attractive hosts. This is exactly the sort of quality control which is required to manage a global system: making sure that, as far as possible, fair play prevails. Governing investment flows to address this imbalance is unlikely to come through the market alone. One way of trying to stimulate particular forms of climate capitalism has been through the multilateral development banks, particularly the World Bank. Because it is funded with public money and operates according to a public mandate – to alleviate poverty – it is able (in principle) to engineer investment flows that deliver a social rather than purely financial return, and to distribute projects more evenly around the world. The Community Development Carbon Fund (CDCF) launched by the World Bank in 2002, with initial capital of $128.6 million, is intended to encourage CDM-like development-focused project funding. It provides financial support to small-scale emission reduction projects through the CDM in the least developed countries and poorest communities within the developing world. The UN's Development Programme (UNDP) has also set up an MDG (Millennium Development Goal) Carbon Facility that seeks to steer investments towards projects which help achieve broader development objectives. Again, emphasising the potential and the perils of getting private finance on board, the scheme is underwritten by Fortin bank, and now faces an uncertain future because the bank has taken a hit in the financial crisis.

CONCLUSIONS

In order, then, that a response to climate change organised around carbon markets might realise its potential in helping to transform the

---

[27] A. Agarwal, 'Global warming in an unequal world', *Equity Watch*, 15 November. See http://www.cseindia.org/campaign/ew/art20001115_2.htm.

global economy, it needs to be well governed. It is by no means clear that such effective governance will emerge, although we have tried to show here that there are signs that it is improving.

Effective governance of carbon markets needs a number of things. First, and most crudely, it needs governments to set strong targets. These create the scarcity in the markets, increase the carbon price, and create incentives for companies to transform their operations away from fossil fuel dependence. Second, it needs rigorous rules for measuring, reporting, monitoring and verifying emissions. Third, those involved in governing offset markets like the CDM need to hold fast against pressure from some carbon market companies to relax rules about the 'additionality' of projects. Without credible claims about additionality, these markets simply become playthings for investors and traders, and more or less useless in responding to climate change. Fourth, if the whole world is to be transformed towards decarbonisation, global markets need to be structured to create incentives and to spread technologies across the world – not just among the rich countries and a few rapidly growing countries in the South like China and India. Fifth, the markets also need to be directed to help with adaptation to climate change, especially for those in particularly vulnerable situations. Finally, the question of who gets to make the rules needs to be addressed – if carbon markets are to achieve their potential, the rule-making needs to be broadened to include more than the small club of currently dominant countries, the carbon traders and a few well-organised international NGOs.

Can we do this? At present, we would have to say it looks fairly unlikely that all these changes will be made. Certainly Copenhagen Accord provides few signs that a new 'grand bargain' will be struck, although progress on some fronts (notably the re-entry of the USA into the multilateral system, and the tightening of targets) is being made. But we need to think through how a well-governed carbon market might emerge in the next few years. In other words, what sorts of climate capitalism could we imagine coming into being? It is to this that we now turn.

What futures for climate capitalism?

So where might all this be heading? In the introduction, we ended by suggesting that the issue is less whether we have climate capitalism or not, but rather what sort of climate capitalism we end up with. Capitalism of one form or another will provide the context in which near-term solutions to climate change have to be found. The governance questions we have just discussed, as well as the critiques of carbon markets we looked at in Chapter 8, suggest the issues climate capitalism will have to address if it is to be effective. The forces behind the development of carbon markets – those forces dominant under neoliberalism that we discussed in Chapter 2 – also provide clues as to the possible forms that climate capitalism might take as it develops. But how might we imagine the current ways that climate change is being managed developing into a more fully fledged, coherent system that could lead to decarbonisation of the economy? And what then might be done to make one or other scenario more likely? We sketch out here four possible scenarios. We should emphasise, they are scenarios, not predictions. They are, in effect, scenario-building exercises thinking through how the various elements of climate change politics we have explored throughout the book might play out in the coming decades.

SCENARIO 1: CLIMATE CAPITALIST UTOPIA

One possibility is that the various elements of climate capitalism we discuss in the previous chapters develop fully and are able to produce a rapid decarbonisation of the global economy. Through mechanisms such as the Carbon Disclosure Project (CDP) and other reporting standards, institutional investors are able to lead a process of investment in renewable energy, energy efficiency and conservation, carbon capture and storage, advanced public transport and urban infrastructure reform, which collectively produce rapid shifts away from fossil fuels, prevent a switching back to coal as gas runs out and secure the carbon from remaining fossil fuel use in underground, geologically viable storage sites.

They are aided by regulators of financial markets such as the Securities and Exchange Commission (SEC) who force companies to disclose their CO_2-intensity, by governments who give indications of the rising price of fossil energy through taxation reforms and who send appropriate signals through the carbon allowances allocated and auctioned in the various markets in Kyoto (and its successor regime) as well as through national and regional policy. These decisions by governments create scarcity in carbon allowances and thus produce reliably high carbon prices, give a clear steer to business about future opportunities and create big incentives to find alternatives to fossil fuels. These price signals from public and private agencies give investors the appropriate signals and the necessary support (in the form of feed-in laws etc) to go full steam ahead in investing in renewable energy, investment which then produces a virtuous cycle as prices for renewable electricity, hydrogen for fuel cells and so on, drop, thus making such investment even more attractive on a purely economic basis. The logic of carbon markets is expanded with the creation of Personal Carbon Allowances, thus creating similar incentives to change behaviour amongst individual consumers and driving demand for low-carbon products and services.

At the same time, the emissions trading begins to work as their designers hoped, reducing substantially the costs of meeting emissions targets, thus enabling both the pursuit of more aggressive targets and the buy-in by a progressively wider range of actors. In the multilateral context, they help enable developing countries to take on targets to limit (the growth of) their emissions, as they see the benefits of being inside an emissions trading system because of the money to be made by selling their excess allowances. They also realise that levels of demand are high for exported renewable energy and other clean energy technologies and construct an industrial base to meet the growing demand for low-carbon technologies. An energy round of trade negotiations might facilitate this. According to the World Bank, the removal of tariffs for four basic clean energy technologies (solar, wind, clean coal and efficient lighting) in 18 developing countries with high levels of greenhouse gas (GHG) emissions would result in trade gains of up to 7%. The removal of both tariffs and non-tariff barriers could boost trade by as much as 13%.[1] Creative issue-linkages to development issues of more immediate concern to developing countries such as trade, debt and aid and enlightened self-interest on the part of leading developed countries in making key concessions, succeed in enrolling them in efforts to decarbonise the global economy.

Those with a vested interest in such markets become successful at pressuring governments to set progressively more aggressive targets. Michael Grubb's original rationale for emissions trading as a mechanism for redistributing resources from larger to smaller polluters and from rich to poor, is realised. A switch in the approach of developing countries is also facilitated by their increasingly positive experience with the Clean Development Mechanism (CDM). This becomes an effective way to channel investment by Northern governments and institutional investors into emerging markets. These investments are increasingly focused on 'win–win' projects in renewable energy and energy efficiency, and less and less in forestry projects, thus overcoming worries about 'carbon colonialism' and pacifying internal critics that long-lasting social benefits are not accruing to host countries. The CDM is reformed to expand the range of possible investments from individual projects towards sectoral reform and even whole policy reform programmes. Sectoral approaches dramatically reduce transaction costs and enable more actors to participate in these markets, thus enabling key transitions in energy production, transport and agriculture.

The World Bank likewise 'decarbonises' its lending programme, realising the need to shift completely away from lending for fossil fuel projects in order to be a credible leader on climate change. This is driven both by the returns to be gained from rapidly developing renewables markets, the cue it takes from its main funders that are also investing heavily in these areas, the demand for sustainable energy options in developing countries and NGOs pressuring the World Bank. Northern tax payers are no longer willing to allow their money to be used to underwrite financial backing for fossil fuel projects when they are trying hard to reduce their own emissions through domestic measures. This enables Northern investment to contribute to wholesale structural reform in the South away from reliance on coal and oil, and thus enables developing countries to 'tunnel through' to a low-carbon economy. This means that the emergence of the low-carbon economy

---

[1] World Bank, *International Trade and Climate Change: Economic, Legal and Institutional Perspectives* (Washington, DC: World Bank, 2007).

also contributes significantly to poverty reduction in the South, opening up an array of new employment and training opportunities, new sources of revenue and ultimately contributes to the reduction of global inequalities.

Early on, some countries clearly benefit more from the emerging carbon economy than others. The UK is perhaps one of the biggest early winners, gaining competitive advantage in the emissions trading markets (around 70% of all carbon trades are currently brokered through London) and seeking to further consolidate its position as the nerve centre of the global carbon economy. In addition, it seeks to make up ground on previous leaders in renewable energy (Denmark for example) through policy support for wind and solar energy. China is also an early winner as it takes a huge share of the investment through the rapidly expanding CDM, given the size of its market and the scale of opportunities it presents. It uses its attractiveness as a market for foreign investors to set terms which make it a leader among the BRICS (Brazil, Russia, India, China and South Africa) in developing its own self-reliant model of renewable energy production. This allows it to protect itself from dependence on unstable or hostile suppliers and to guarantee secure supplies of energy to underwrite its continuing pace of economic growth.

But rather than causing other countries to resent the gains made by these countries, this competitive advantage works to stimulate other countries to compete in the new carbon economy, seeking to emulate China's success. Other developing countries realise the need to create an effective infrastructure to attract CDM investment in order to compete with China, thus enhancing investment in their countries and adopting a suite of policy measures to attract and keep investors in low-carbon sectors of the economy. The pressure in the USA, from the Climate Action Partnership, the Pew Center on Climate Change, and others, forces the US federal government, as well as many state-level governments, to regulate CO_2 and impose reductions targets across the US economy. This helps to further develop existing policies such as Renewable Energy Certificates as support for the rapid expansion of wind and solar energy to compete with European companies. Canada realises it still has a slim competitive advantage in fuel-cell technology and aggressively expands policy support to maintain that advantage. This contributes both to the development of fuel cells and thus the rapid phase-out of internal combustion engines, thereby undermining opposition to climate action, in particular from oil-rich Alberta. Overall, then, competitiveness pressures lead to a race to the top, where countries build policy support for the new carbon economy to maintain their competitive edge in that economy.

The overall effect of these dynamics is to produce a rapid shift from a fossil fuel based economy to one based on renewable energy. Perhaps over a 20–30-year time period, global demand for energy stabilises because of the rapid uptake of efficiency technologies, switching away from car dependence, changes in building codes and practice towards 'zero emissions' buildings. At the same time, the fuel mix in the global economy moves from 90% based on coal, oil and gas, to being 70% based on renewable forms of energy. The vast majority of emissions from remaining fossil energy sources are removed from the atmosphere through various types of carbon capture and storage or atmospheric sequestration projects. The costs of these latter projects reduce to such an extent that the setting of carbon prices is sufficient to make them financially viable (which is not currently the case) and the technical barriers to their diffusion are overcome.

The plausibility of this scenario rests on the assumption, common to many advocates of the neoliberal approach to climate change, that the key to decarbonisation is to set appropriate carbon prices. This would create such a powerful incentive across the globe that financial markets will do the rest, directing investment towards ever greater energy efficiency and towards non-carbon energy sources. We would add that it depends on transparent information, and thus that the CDP, and consistent and comparable reporting mechanisms, are also crucial. In this scenario it is the interaction of carbon prices and information about the CO_2-intensity of companies which is crucial. There is a very strong faith in the powers of markets underpinning this scenario. Yet there are many reasons to be sceptical that the simple effect of a high carbon price would be able to affect all aspects of the global economy without other efforts by governments and others.

The plausibility of the scenario also depends politically on an awkward alliance of technocratic civil servants,[2] opportunistic environmental NGOs and profit-seeking financiers. To support any particular sort of capitalism, political coalitions are necessary. Climate capitalism is no different. All such coalitions entail compromises, especially from the coalition's junior partner. In this case, many environmentalists

---

[2] See J. B. Skjaerseth and J. Wettestad, *EU Emissions Trading: Initiation, Decision-making and Implementation* (Ashgate Publishing, 2008). While discussing the EU ETS, the authors nicely call the civil servants in the EU who pioneered the ETS the 'Bureaucrats for Emissions Trading' group.

have to live with aspects of the management of the economy that they may be distinctly uneasy with. But the coalition more or less holds together, seeing off opposition both from more radical environmentalists who oppose the commodification of the atmosphere, as well as those with strong interests in the carboniferous form that capitalism currently takes – the coal manufacturers and some trade unions and the oil companies, in particular.

SCENARIO 2: STAGNATION

This rosy image can be contrasted with a rather darker one. In this, the various aspects of the carbon economy we have discussed fail to achieve their potential, and governments fail to take the decisions necessary for them to do so.

Carbon markets come to be widely seen as simply another scam by an already tainted financial sector. Climate fraud becomes the next Enron and the next sub-prime crisis rolled into one, with both its dodgy accounting and its bubble economy easily exposed. Many have already made connections between the financial crisis that began in 2008 and 'sub-prime carbon' to challenge our reliance on financial actors to take the right sort of action on climate change. Speculators start to gamble on the carbon price, precisely at a time where general trust in financiers is very low. Carbon markets thus lose legitimacy. The effect of an economic downturn and recurrent financial crises is to force companies and financial investors into even shorter time-frames for securing returns on their investments rather than taking a risk on buying into longer-term decarbonised scenarios. Focus then returns to more cautious and predictable sources of funding and corporate strategy oriented towards keeping the fossil fuel economy buoyant for as long as possible. Recent moves by Shell and BP to reduce their investments in renewable technologies might be indicative of how these trends could play out.

Governments cease to invest much effort in carbon markets and the aggressive targets that might sustain interest in them do not materialise. Pressures to prioritise support to 'old manufacturing' – such as car companies – or to resist 'new deal' demands for a windfall tax on oil and gas companies, especially in a time of financial crisis, are heeded and pressure on these sectors to reform dissipates. In debates about emissions trading systems, the regulated companies – the steel and electricity companies – gain (or keep) the upper hand over financiers, keeping such targets weak, limiting the use of auctioning and thus the scandals of windfall profits continue. Carbon markets remain and the voluntary offset market in particular continues to serve a niche market, but they remain small and do not produce any transformational effects on carbon emissions. Most actors engaged in voluntary markets are widely seen as cowboys, but they are sustained by those companies driven mainly by the desire to present a positive image as a responsible corporation rather than shift their corporate strategies towards low-carbon investments.

In the international negotiations, positive outcomes remain plagued by geopolitical wrangling. In the debates about what to replace Kyoto with, the USA gets fixated with making sure that whatever regime exists, it looks like an American-led one, as opposed to the 'Euro-centric' regime which Kyoto had come to be seen in the USA (despite its US origins). So the results become an incoherent mess rather than an expanded, coherent architecture. Similarly, the North–South struggles that have characterised climate negotiations from the beginning continue in stalemate. Developing countries, even rapidly developing ones like China, continue to refuse any sort of limitation on their expansion of fossil energy use, and the USA correspondingly refuses to set any ambitious targets for itself. No one finds creative ways round this impasse. Ideas such as an expanded CDM or 'no-lose' targets for developing countries (where they get benefits from exceeding a target in terms of carbon credits they can sell, but have no penalties for not meeting them) fall by the wayside. Those developing countries that have gained very little from the CDM to date, most notably sub-Saharan African countries, resist moves towards its expansion unless efforts are made to address its uneven nature, which play-safe investors are reluctant to endorse and governments are wary of imposing in a more cautious economic climate.

As the carbon markets falter, so do projects like the CDP. Investors lose interest in knowing the CO_2 emissions of companies they invest in when it becomes clear that the governments and markets between them cannot be relied on to give a consistent and credible signal that would turn CO_2-intensive companies into a business risk. Shareholder activists and NGOs fail to persuade investors that they should be more proactive or companies to see climate change as a central aspect of Corporate Social Responsibility (CSR), since fossil fuels remain too cheap and ubiquitous for investors and businesses to ignore. The business case becomes business as usual.

In fact, the rising tide of legal activism and liability claims has a perverse effect, inhibiting bolder and more adventurous moves by companies, who retreat into modes of crisis management rather than proactive prevention. As has been the approach of some oil companies to climate change, they act on the maxim that 'the spouting whale gets harpooned', as one Exxon official put it.[3] As companies that make strong claims for CSR or for carbon neutrality get more easily attacked for failing to live up to that claim, companies learn to simply keep their mouths shut.

Efforts by environmental NGOs to forge coalitions with different parts of business as a consequence largely fail. They increasingly have doors shut in their face, as companies prefer to keep their heads down on climate change. Environmental groups return to confrontational tactics, helpful in keeping the issue in the public eye, but making it difficult to build a political coalition that could sustain projects towards decarbonisation against those who would lose from such a transformation.

As climate change itself progresses, periodic crises from hurricanes, sea-level rise, droughts and the large-scale movement of climate refugees serve to keep climate change on the agenda. The response of the insurance industry is to withdraw coverage from ever more areas of the world, rather than use its power to invest in renewables. Some efforts are made to mitigate carbon emissions, and countries do manage to depart from the 'business-as-usual' emissions path. But there is nothing like the coherence in the way these efforts combine, necessary to turn them into something which could create the transformational effect to decarbonise the global economy.

Cynicism and fatalism starts to set in about the possibility of doing anything except adapt to whatever climate change has to offer. The fact that most of those hardest hit are in already marginal situations contributes to this cynicism. The affluent see those displaced by sea-level rise or flooded out of their homes and shrug their shoulders. They feel they have seen it all before and don't feel guilty about turning away climate refugees at their borders. This happens even within rich countries, as in reactions to Katrina in the USA in 2004, where climate change exposes, but does little to heal, deep social rifts and economic inequalities. In the absence of definitive lines of responsibility, and the failure of human-rights-based approaches to advance further,

---

[3] D. Levy, 'Business and the evolution of the climate regime: the dynamics of corporate strategies,' in D. Levy and P. Newell (eds.), *The Business of Global Environmental Governance*, (Cambridge MA: MIT Press, 2005), pp. 73–105.

climate change remains everyone's and no one's responsibility as the world drifts towards a world of 5°C warming.

This scenario is highly plausible, especially in the light of the weak Copenhagen Accord of 2009. One could say it is currently the most likely outcome, depressing as that might be. But there are two other broad possibilities which lie somewhere between climate capitalist utopia and this scenario of stagnation.

SCENARIO 3: DECARBONISED DYSTOPIA

Believers in carbon markets suggest that they can both help us decarbonise and do so equitably. Their critics suggest that such markets are plagued by 'climate fraud' and 'carbon colonialism'. What if the critics are right about the latter, but wrong about the former? That is, we end up with a form of climate capitalism which does create a low-carbon global economy, but which does so in a highly inegalitarian manner?

As carbon prices start to have an effect on behaviour, investment is drawn more to a series of quick-fixes, techno-fixes and drastic solutions that reduce transaction costs and produce economies of scale for their sponsors, but which lead to a range of negative social consequences.

First, the recurrent climate impacts of ever greater magnitude start to provoke panic measures. Urgency is invoked to legitimise the implementation of the fantasies of a number of scientists – to install large mirrors in the sky which reflect back incoming radiation from the Sun, to spread iron filings in the ocean to accelerate the rate at which the sea absorbs CO_2, to artificially create cloud cover or to install large-scale atmospheric CO_2 absorption devices. Indeed, many governments are already exploring seriously the potential of large-scale geo-engineering solutions.[4] The rising price of carbon helps to make these measures seem reasonable, while the military supports such measures, having interpreted climate change as a security threat needing such a response and fears about climate-induced immigration fuel populist measures by governments.

In terms of investments which produce decarbonisation, money pours into biofuels both in the North and South, producing large mono-crop plantations with appalling working conditions, the

---

[4] D. G. Victor, M. Granger Morgan, J. Apt, J. Steinbruner and K. Ricke, 'The geoengineering option: a last resort against global warming?' *Foreign Affairs*, March/April; POST (Parliamentary Office of Science and Technology, 2009), 'Geo-engineering research', *POSTnote*, March, no. 327.

destruction of biodiversity, and price rises of key food crops which place them beyond the reach of the poor. The panic about food price rises during 2007–2008, created in part by the push for biofuels, starts to become the norm, but the rich are able to insulate themselves from criticism. Biotech companies realise that carbon markets are a means to sell the genetically modified (GM) trees that they have already cultivated, which grow much faster than conventional trees and are able to absorb considerably more CO_2 and over longer periods of time, while drought-resistant GM crops are held out as a solution for farmers seeking to adapt to the consequences of climate change. The nightmares of GM activists are thus realised as rapid climate change provides a window to roll out biotech on an unprecedented scale.

And not just the nightmares of GM activists. High carbon prices, rather than creating a wave of investment in renewable energy, help to boost the renaissance of nuclear energy as the solution to climate change in a carbon-constrained world. As in the past, new plants are sited predominantly in remote and poorer areas where the opposition can be more easily overcome. In the USA, many nuclear sites are hosted on Native American lands, while in many other countries poorer communities become the hosts of rapidly assembled nuclear reactors. The injustices produced by the social side effects of technologies, exposed over the years by the environmental justice movement, continue, legitimised this time by the threat of climate change, while terrorists seek to access nuclear materials produced by these plants.

Alongside nuclear, most investment goes into carbon capture and storage. The lack of investment in renewables means the benefits of decarbonisation in developing countries are not realised. The spread of small-scale, decentralised technologies, not requiring an elaborate electricity grid, which could radically increase access to electricity services among the rural poor, does not occur. Micro-energy projects at the village level to meet local basic needs (rather than fuel a new consumer class in countries like India and China) fall by the wayside. Instead, developing countries get large-scale investments in coal plants with CCS (carbon capture and storage) and in nuclear, benefiting primarily urban elites and large transnational business.

The development of the CDM, and the changing investment practices produced by the CDP, end up locking most developing countries precisely into a dynamic of carbon colonialism. The large powerful ones – China, India and Brazil in particular – are able to insulate themselves from this dynamic, or rather their elites are able not only to insulate themselves, but rather to profit from it, increasing both their wealth and power relative to the rest of their societies. Investment through the CDM still predominantly goes to a handful of countries, and more low-hanging fruit such as hydrofluorocarbon (HFC) or methane capture projects are found. Reforms of the CDM open up much greater possibilities for forestry projects, which lock large areas of the developing world into the status of being a heritage park for carbon sequestration or host to large-scale forest plantations. Those inhabiting forest areas that attract money from carbon finance are driven off the land their ancestors have occupied for centuries in the rush to cut emissions and make money whatever the social cost. The voluntary offset market similarly increases its focus on forestry projects, as businesses and individuals wanting to be 'carbon neutral' lose interest in treating such projects as investments in the South, preferring to concentrate on just offsetting their emissions. The World Bank continues its role as major financer of CDM projects, and continues also its tradition of funding large projects with only very concentrated benefits amongst Southern elites and largely based on support to fossil fuels as demanded by the largest recipients of its loans. Large populations in the South become increasingly consigned to the role of guarding forests, while people in the North continue to enjoy high-consumption lives.

The institutional investors behind the CDP contribute to this tendency. The project entails an attempt to enhance investor power over other businesses. In the North–South context, this serves to deny access to capital markets for many Southern businesses, unable to guarantee their products or processes are 'carbon neutral', and without access to the technology which would make them so. Instead of mobilising investment to spread access to those technologies, investor-led governance creates new barriers to entry for Southern companies into world markets.

Similarly, governments shift the burden of implementing carbon cuts squarely onto individuals. Personal Carbon Allowance schemes proliferate, but end up operating more as surveillance schemes, enabling the state to monitor personal behaviour ever more intensively, rather than produce egalitarian outcomes. The rich manage to buy up extra credits easily, following the well-known maxim that 'the poor sell cheap'. The poor get locked ever further into fuel poverty, decarbonising through not consuming, selling surplus allowances for a pittance while experiencing lives that are more and more intrusively monitored.

In this scenario, environmental NGOs are largely co-opted into a world ruled by global finance. Enough of them either don't see the importance of the injustices being caused in the name of climate change, or choose to look away while they support, implicitly or otherwise, the development of carbon colonialism as a less bad choice than stagnation and climate chaos. Elites in the South are also co-opted into this ruling coalition, bought off by creaming off the benefits of large-scale projects and the political pay-off of the power that these bring.

This form of climate capitalism is thus the extension of neoliberalism as it has operated for the most part to date – highly inegalitarian, creating great vulnerabilities for those on the economic margins and concentrating wealth and power in the hands of a few. Carbon markets do, however, deliver real reductions in overall GHG emissions, but in ways which do not spread benefits beyond the core of the carbon economy. While climate capitalism flourishes in Chicago and one or two other places, and the city of London maintains its dominance, the carbon economy does not redistribute the wealth it accumulates, but rather extends its control across the planet from a well-protected centre. This is a world in which the insurance industry responds to rises in climate-related damage by withdrawing cover from people living in vulnerable and fragile environments, in which inequalities associated with fuel poverty are exacerbated as prices rise, but no redistribution is forthcoming. Climate refugees are correspondingly treated with contempt, either refused access at all or held in camps for years as 'illegal aliens'.

SCENARIO 4: CLIMATE KEYNESIANISM

The problems of legitimising carbon markets could go in one of four directions. They could turn out to be unfounded, in which case the climate capitalist utopia could come about. They could become insurmountable, bringing about the collapse of carbon markets, and lead to stagnation. They could be well founded but the critics could be easily ignored, leading to the previous scenario. But they could turn into a dynamic which leads to much stronger governance of the carbon markets that enables those markets to do their job in producing climate capitalism.

In this scenario, the critics of the carbon economy who argue that its neoliberal, laissez-faire character is the source of its ineffectiveness, turn out to be spot on. As they start to win political arguments, and as the inability of carbon markets to exercise an invisible hand that drives down carbon emissions becomes increasingly obvious, more and more political forces come together to strengthen their governance. Markets are not abandoned, merely better governed to direct them more closely towards the goal of decarbonisation and to ensure the 'environmental integrity' of offsets both in the CDM and the voluntary markets.

But at the same time, the market actors themselves realise the limits of what they can achieve autonomously. To work well, carbon markets need to be well integrated across the world. They need to be based on consistent units so that trading can occur easily and their value can be recognised by traders in a range of regulatory environments. They need reliable reporting regimes so that the emissions of companies can be readily checked against their permit allowances. All of this requires sound intervention by governments and coordination amongst them internationally. Through lobby groups like the International Emissions Trading Association (IETA) and the Carbon Markets and Investors Association, financiers start to play a more active role not only in pushing for stronger targets, which benefit them as they stimulate trading activity, but also for better coordinated rules among the different countries in the world, and predictability and transparency in the rules being developed.

As a consequence, governments use their power to shape how carbon markets operate. They set stringent targets, set about closing loopholes and addressing weaknesses (such as the windfall profits problem in the EU ETS) and set stringent rules for offset projects in the CDM. They act to limit speculation in emissions trading markets to ensure that prices reflect the scarcity in the allocation of permits rather than the short-term strategies of finance houses. Collectively, they act on institutions like the World Bank to get it to abandon finance for fossil fuels and greatly expand investment in renewables and energy efficiency in developing countries, and not only in its CDM or other 'carbon finance' investments, but across its development lending portfolio.

Governments also start to realise, as carbon prices go up, that additional policies are necessary to reach those parts of society that carbon markets can't reach. They realise that no level of carbon price will be high enough to stimulate the retrofitting of large amounts of housing stock to realise the potential for savings in households, and develop aggressive 'command-and-control' policies to roll out such a programme. They realise that without infrastructure investment in urban areas, high carbon prices will not be sufficient to get enough people out of their cars and onto bikes or into trains and buses. They, therefore, reorganise urban planning processes to systematically favour such sustainable transport modes. Such policies, far from damaging the economy, however, stabilise the construction industry at a time when the housing market is in recurrent crisis. They create jobs, increase skill levels, as well as address other problems like fuel poverty and urban congestion.

In the voluntary carbon markets, the continuous pressure caused by the problem of 'climate fraud' means that the certification systems like the Gold Standard become essential for project operators. There are repeated scandals about the worth and effectiveness of offsets that do not meet increasingly stringent criteria (including and beyond the Voluntary Carbon Standard (VCS), Offset Quality Initiative, Gold Standard and the Climate Community and Biodiversity (CCB) standards. This means that the space in the market for fly-by-night offset providers, less concerned about tangible environmental gains or social side effects, closes down. If there is less easy and quick money to be made, over time interest declines and actors move out of these markets. This leaves behind a small regulated market and most cowboys move on as transaction costs for them increase and demand declines as poorly perceived carbon credits are self-defeating for companies looking to generate good publicity. It becomes impossible to have offset projects without certification – no one would buy the product – and there is pressure to adopt ever more stringent standards in the projects. Offset projects thus become progressively more useful in pursuing both decarbonisation – eschewing large-scale 'low-hanging fruit' projects in favour of ones which are transformational – and serve broader sustainable development goals. Forestry projects, for example, become restricted to small-scale community forestry projects; large-scale plantations are avoided.

At the same time, the current signs of movement in North–South diplomacy develop further. In negotiations about the international regime beyond 2012, there are increasing discussions about some developing countries taking on some commitments, such as 'no-lose' targets, where they gain financial benefits if they meet or exceed their targets, but are not penalised if they don't. This is combined with a greatly expanded CDM organised to generate investment in broad programmes across whole economic sectors rather than just individual projects. This, in effect, becomes a 'grand bargain' between North and South, facilitating a great expansion in investment to the South, more evenly distributed among Southern countries. This is facilitated by a quota system in the case of the CDM, which ensures a fairer share of carbon finance for sub-Saharan Africa and agreement on new and increased levels of additional aid for mitigation – a fixed per cent (up to 1 per cent) of Northern countries' GNP as currently proposed by China and the G77. Some see this as a new 'Marshall Plan' for the climate, ironically noting that the UN climate change secretariat is housed in the building in Bonn, the Haus Carstanjen, where the original Marshall Plan was signed in 1947.

This form of climate capitalism, therefore, regulates those areas of the carbon economy that are currently under-regulated. It deepens and strengthens regulation of those areas that are already subject to regulation and tries to steer a nascent carbon economy towards a fully fledged form of climate capitalism that delivers growth (as any form of capitalism must) but in so doing achieves a significant degree of de-carbonisation. Importantly, however, it does this in a way that seeks to address inequalities in the carbon economy.

We call it climate Keynesianism after John Maynard Keynes, the British economist. His ideas about the importance of planned economies with strong mechanisms of redistribution had an important influence over post-war economic policy in the West; the last time a similar transformation of capitalism occurred by bringing it under more collectivised control. Rather like with the development of capitalism after the Second World War, this sort of climate capitalism is also based on a broad social compromise. In 1945, that was based on an accommodation between capital and labour, combined with a multilateral bargain between countries. With climate Keynesianism, it is based on a compromise between environmentalist critics and city financiers, combined with new sorts of global governance designed to address unequal contributions to climate change and unequal exposure to its effects.

As governments negotiate turning the CDM into a climate Marshall Plan, they also realise the need to embed this in broader shifts in the ways they manage the global economy multilaterally. The World Bank, as it decarbonises its own projects, at the same time starts to play the coordinating role conceived for it by Keynes and Dexter White in managing a global economy along more sustainable and predictable lines. This time, their focus would be ensuring that its future course is compatible with the goal of preventing dangerous climate change. Similarly, increasing demands to make sure carbon markets do not create 'carbon leakage' turn into demands for tougher minimal standards that apply to companies across the world. In the meantime, countries with commitments to reduce emissions implement border-tax adjustments to tax carbon and energy-intensive products from countries not subject to those commitments (as the USA and the EU have both already suggested they could do) so as not to suffer a comparative disadvantage.[5] In order to do this, reforms in the World Trade Organization's rules are developed so that this does not become simply an excuse for protectionism; rather, it enables such adjustments as long as they are well designed, and thus helps to create pressure for action on climate change in rapidly industrialising countries.

As China and other 'rising powers' play a leading role in the global economy, countries seek to address issues of carbon leakage and capital mobility through international law, as well as the forms of national regulation outlined above. To be effective this would not just occur through the climate regime, but be a component of trade and investment regimes that impact flows of trade and finance more profoundly. This might take the form of calls to set common basic commitments – written into multilateral and bilateral trade agreements such that investor rights are contingent on investor responsibilities to use best available technologies and to screen and conduct impact assessments on the climate footprint of their investments. Over time then, climate change objectives are mainstreamed into other areas of public international law and multilateralism in a way which addresses some of the policy incoherence that current exists.[6]

But the 're-embedding' of the global economy within a framework of strong rules is not only achieved through states. In 1945, states were the only agents capable of making and implementing such rules. Now they have been joined by a whole host of governance actors and processes which exceed their control. But these new governance arrangements start to complement the work of governments.

These include the sorts of voluntary and CSR-led initiatives that we described in Chapter 3, which would send strong signals down

[5] For example in the Waxman-Markey Bill which passed the House of Representatives in the USA in June 2009, and, initially by the EC-mandated High Level Group on Competitiveness, Energy and Environmental Policies, though in its second report the Border Carbon Adjustment proposal was dropped. Some proposals would require importers to purchase offsets in a domestic cap and trade scheme at the point of import.

[6] P. Newell, 'Fit for purpose: towards a development architecture that can deliver', in Paluso, E. (ed.), Re-thinking Development in a Carbon-Constrained World: Development Cooperation and Climate Change (Finland: Ministry of Foreign Affairs, 2009), pp. 184–96.

supply chains from buyers to suppliers that lower carbon production is required. Large supermarkets such as Tesco in the UK have said they will label the carbon footprint of all their product ranges (which run into the hundreds of thousands). Many exporters are already feeling the pressure to reduce the fossil fuels associated with the manufacture and transportation of their products amid concerns about 'food miles', for example. Whilst the age of voluntarism would not come to an end, CSR is transformed by constant pressure from NGOs, as well as shifts in government regulation, into a much stronger driver of corporate transformation. As businesses become subject to much greater scrutiny about their emissions profile, the corporate governance scandals which look like 'Enron environmentalism' prompt efforts beyond voluntary codes, making businesses increasingly accountable not only to shareholders but to a much wider range of interests. The entrenchment of shareholder activism has the same effect – shareholders make more demands of companies that go beyond narrow measures of self-regulation. Threats of litigation by indigenous peoples and others affected by the inactions of leading polluters (as has already occurred against the US government)[7] about climate impacts also make investors jumpy, sending ever stronger signals to companies they invest in to avoid complicity in exacerbating climate change. Those companies then turn to states for stronger regulation to create level playing fields and clear signs of what is and isn't acceptable and to avoid future damaging litigation. Disclosure projects like the CDP start to work in clear synergy with government regulation; companies act to make sure there is one single reporting framework (to avoid duplication of effort), enhancing transparency and allowing investors to make informed choices.

So, in part, states develop stronger forms of regulation in reaction to the limits of these sorts of softer, voluntary forms of governance and private regulation. The pressure exerted by climate activists through shareholder activism, company boycotts and engagement in the construction of private standards discussed in Chapter 8 comes over time to be considered inadequate, problematic or both. This scepticism about the excessive engagement of civil society actors with market initiatives comes to be seen as a distraction from the need for regulation and redistribution, which in turn feeds demands for a state-led approach. Questions are also posed, especially by climate

---

[7] P. Newell, 'Civil society, corporate accountability and the politics of climate change', *Global Environmental Politics*, **8**(3) (2008), 124–55.

justice groups, about the legitimacy of civil society actors setting social and environmental benchmarks for assessing performance. Groups engaged in those strategies find themselves questioned about the lack of sanctions that apply to forms of soft and private regulation and the uneven and non-universal nature of voluntary schemes. This prompts calls for leadership on the issue by the UN and governments who are increasingly expected to use public regulation to fill the gap left by market-led initiatives in the carbon economy. These pressures strengthen calls for a 'Green new deal'.

The development of strong rules to guide carbon markets, policies to reach areas that markets cannot affect and a global bargain to create an integrated decarbonisation of the economy across the world become the central elements in creating a genuinely new form of capitalism. By re-regulating the carbon markets and producing redistributive mechanisms both within countries and across the world, governments create stable conditions for investment in carbon markets and in renewable energy, energy efficiency and so on. The potential benefits of such an economy become more evenly spread around the world. But at the heart of this coalition remains global finance – whose coordinating power is mobilised and channelled by governments to achieve decarbonisation.

PURSUING CLIMATE CAPITALISMS

These are of course imaginative exercises, and ideal types, not predictions. All, however, seem to us intrinsically plausible ways that the development of responses to climate change might play out over the next 20–30 years. In all likelihood some messy mix of them will co-exist – some areas of the world stagnating, others going ahead with a pure neoliberal version, while others still regulate the carbon economy more stringently. These differences could even be deliberately chosen as competitive strategies by states in a global economy, just as states regulate their economies differently as competition strategies at the moment. High levels of transnational investment, integrated strategies and the global reach of many key players in the carbon economy may generate pressures for higher levels of uniformity and convergence in the governance of carbon markets, even if these take some time to be realised.

There are also of course a series of contingencies whose impact is difficult to assess. Perhaps top of the list, how will climate change itself play out in the near term, and how will it be interpreted politically?

Will a series of climate-related disasters help to keep pressure up for stronger targets, or will the rich start to pull up the ladder on 'climate refugees'? Or will a few relatively calm years cause people to become blasé?

But beyond the course of climate change itself, plenty of other factors will have an effect on responses to climate change and the development of climate capitalism. How will the financial crisis of 2008 have an impact? It could lead to a broad re-regulation of finance which might favour the 'climate Keynesianism' scenario. But it could equally cause financial companies to withdraw from 'risky business' like carbon trading as well as cause others to mistrust finance even more, leading to stagnation. What about oil prices? If the high oil prices are here to stay, because 'peak oil' has been reached perhaps, they could intensify pressure to wean economies off oil, contributing to either climate capitalists' utopia or climate Keynesianism. But they could also lead simply to more oil exploitation, the further development of disastrous projects like the Alberta oil tar sands, intensive development of biofuels and a focus on carbon capture and storage policies, which produce decarbonised dystopia. How will the continued rise of China affect things? Will it mean China starts to accept the need to accept commitments, or will it increase the difficulty of reaching any diplomatic agreement which markets need to create reasonable certainty about the future of carbon markets? Numerous other contingencies can be imagined – broader legitimacy crises for neoliberalism, shifting population demographics, how widespread protest campaigns become and the longer-term impact of the 2008 US presidential election. All of these, in some sense, will act as drivers of the development of climate capitalism, but in ways that are impossible to predict.

If prediction is impossible, making claims about which of these scenarios is desirable and how it might be pursued is less complex. Our writing of them is of course tendentious, leading to a favoured version at the end. Our assumption is that either climate capitalist utopia or climate Keynesianism is in principle desirable. But given the various drivers just discussed, and how deregulated markets in practice work, pursuing a pure neoliberal version of climate capitalism is likely to lead to either stagnation or to decarbonised dystopia. The question is then for us how best to pursue climate Keynesianism.

By historical analogy, we can infer a good deal. In the aftermath of the crash of 1929, the depression which followed, and the Second World War, the global economy was radically reorganised. Global finance was restricted using capital controls. Economies were managed closely to prevent booms and slumps (using Keynes' ideas) and to pursue full employment. A whole set of novel multilateral institutions were created to stabilise and facilitate the expansion of trade and investment between countries. But at the heart of this was also a dynamic of social unrest and the way that big business responded to it. Unions and political parties that represented them played a key role in forcing business to adapt, to accept a place for labour in economic management and significant limits on businesses' freedom of action. But most businesses also came to realise that such limits could actually be beneficial; that by spreading wealth more evenly, more people would have money to buy the products created in their factories.

Climate Keynesianism will clearly have its own features, but the response of business to protest and contestation will again be crucial. The basis for the political compromise on which climate Keynesianism would need to be based would require that the financiers realise that strong rules facilitate the smooth operation of carbon markets, even while it might eliminate some opportunities, such as the dodgier carbon offset schemes. The activities of critics of carbon markets, as we discussed in Chapter 8, are thus crucial to producing the pressure to regulate those markets, which might make those markets actually achieve their potential. This is of course ironic given that the critics, for the most part, want to abolish carbon markets. But then many of the union activists in the 1930s wanted to abolish capitalism, but in practice contributed to a better-regulated and more successful version of it.

The multilateral dimension is more complex. In 1945, much of the world was still ruled in a directly colonial fashion, and the rules established either didn't apply to colonies or were simply applied to them as an extension of the obligations of colonial powers like Britain and France. Now, the whole world is engaged in negotiating the rules, and the inequalities across the world are much more complex than simply a question of rich and poor countries (despite the rhetoric of developing countries in UN negotiations and the fragile solidarity of the G77 + China grouping). The situation is also more complex in that multilateral governance by states is accompanied by growing numbers of private governance schemes like the CDP. A grand multilateral bargain is thus perhaps harder to produce. But its essence is similar to the compromise made by financiers. Implicitly, a bargain already exists whereby industrialised countries take the lead in emissions reductions, but do so in a way which facilitates investment in developing countries that might (repeat, *might*) help decarbonise the latter. This was the logic which underpinned the CDM. A green Marshall Plan that would be the basis of such a bargain would require a greatly expanded CDM, aided by a reformed and refocused World Bank and other shifts in institutions like the World Trade Organization (WTO), but also by the investment switching activity helped by private governance projects like the CDP.

There are of course no guarantees. There are no guarantees that we will avoid stagnation, with the accelerated climate change and extensive social and political disruption that this is likely to produce. There is no magic lever we can pull to ensure a desirable outcome. It will be, rather, the result of politics – the messy world of struggle and compromise over visions of how the world should be organised. The world has always been thus.

Conclusions

What if these transformations fail? If you have bought this book and are reading this now, chances are you are concerned about climate change. But we have managed to write a book about climate change while hardly mentioning it as a physical phenomenon – of higher temperatures, sea-level rise, changed rainfall and the social disruptions those changes bring. One of the ironies of carbon markets, though, is that you don't really have to care about climate change to contribute towards tackling the issue. The market, in theory at least, allows you do it while making money.

It is worth reminding ourselves, however, that the costs of not decarbonising the global economy are that life for many on the planet will be, in the classic words of seventeenth-century political philosopher Thomas Hobbes, 'solitary, poor, nasty, brutish and short'. As Kevin Watkins, speaking as editor of the 2008 UN *Human Development Report* on climate change and development, reflects: 'It is about social justice and the human rights of the world's poor and marginalised. Failure to act on climate change would be tantamount to a systematic violation of the human rights of the poor.'[1] For this reason, President Museveni of Uganda described climate change as 'an act of aggression by the rich against the poor'. Hundreds of millions are expected to be made homeless by sea-level rise and droughts as rainfall patterns change.

As those people attempt to find new places to live or ways to make a living, the communities they want to host them may not always be welcoming. Many refugees or migrants are already shunned, as with those people leaving Tuvalu whose call to be offered refuge

---

[1] Kevin Watkins, Editor of the UNDP Human Development Report, at its launch in Brazil, 27 November. Quoted in Larry Elliot and Ashley Seager, 'Cut carbon by up to third to save poor, UN tells west' *The Guardian,* 28 November 2007. www.guardian.co.uk/environment/2007/nov/28/climatechange.

in Australia was rejected by (former) Australian Prime Minister John Howard. Diseases that affect humans as well as crops and farm animals migrate faster. Mechanisms which accelerate global warming (ironically called 'positive feedbacks') such as the release of methane gases from permafrost or the deep ocean, reduced albedo in the high arctic and effects of the loss of arctic sea ice and the Greenland ice sheet, will accelerate warming and may take it out of human control altogether. Many scientists expect these feedbacks to kick in at about 2 °C higher than pre-industrial temperatures. In the extreme scenarios – at 4 °C or higher above pre-industrial levels, for example – sea levels inundate the majority of the world's largest cities, and temperature levels exceed those experienced by the planet for many hundreds of thousands, if not millions, of years. The continued existence of large-scale, organised human societies becomes far from secure.

So for those whose interest in climate change is driven not by the potential to make a quick buck, but the gravity the issue poses to life as we know it, we have to understand how capitalism works in order to work out our collective prospects for dealing with climate change. Seemingly abstract exchanges and flows of fictitious commodities have real life consequences. They determine who is exposed to famine and disease, who will be exposed to extreme weather events and who has the means to survive. The circuits of capital are literally aligned with the cycles of life and death.

This poses the question of 'what if we fail?' rather differently. We may manage to decarbonise the economy sufficiently quickly to avoid the extreme scenarios mentioned above. But we may do so in a brutal, unjust manner. Hobbes' alternative to his anarchic 'state of nature' was the 'Leviathan', a despotic sovereign who could dispose of human lives as he saw fit. Hobbes thought the Leviathan preferable to anarchy, as at least it provided order. But a form of climate capitalism that combines decarbonisation with a fair way of managing that transformation globally and a well-governed system of carbon markets seems to us possible to pursue. We do not need to accept the scams, injustices and uncertainties associated with unregulated carbon markets and over-reliance on the market to achieve decarbonisation. The choice between despotism and anarchy is a false one.

But achieving a humane form of climate capitalism will not be easy. Financiers may not always accept the need for more regulation, even in the current climate of rebuke about their conduct, and political conflict will be involved. We see this now even in the face of a financial crisis that has threatened to bring the global economy to its knees. It will entail, therefore, negotiating a complicated and irresolvable dilemma between the promise and pitfalls of carbon markets. And on top of that is the question of urgency. When we accept the need for a serious and radical move towards a decarbonised economy we also need to be clear how this will happen and the time-frame within which it needs to happen. Andrew Simms and his colleagues at the New Economics Foundation put the figure at 100 months (and counting).[2] Whichever way you look at it, the challenge is both enormous and pressing.

HISTORICAL PARALLELS

We drew on historical analogies in constructing our final scenario. It is worth emphasising them again here. If we are to try to shape climate capitalism and produce a big transformation in the global economy, we need to have some sense of how equivalent changes have been effected in the past. Radical transformations of this sort do not come along very often. Two such examples stand out.

The global capitalist economy was dramatically reorganised between the onset of the Depression after the Wall Street crash in 1929 and the period shortly after 1945. Countries started to manage their economies not along laissez-faire lines, but required states to inter-vene in the economy to promote full employment, stabilise patterns of growth, regulate finance and in many countries directly manage industries. Countries cooperated in the management of the economy through a series of multilateral governance arrangements known as the Bretton Woods system. Global empires were shortly afterwards dismantled. Many states treated both business and trade unions as partners in national economic management.

The Bretton Woods system created by the victors of the Second World War sought to create a new global deal that would ensure peace and prosperity. Their challenge was to set rules for the integration of economies without the resort to beggar-thy-neighbour policies and competitive controls on trade and capital. They were able to organise capitalism such that it produced an unprecedented period of smooth, rapid economic growth. They were also, instructively, able to do so in a relatively short period of time – around 15 years.

There is a key difference between the Bretton Woods transform-ation and the one that we want to see to respond to climate change.

---

[2] A. Simms, 'The final countdown', *The Guardian*, 1 August 1 2008. http://www.guardian.co.uk/environment/2008/aug/01/climatechange.carbonemissions.

Instead of being a pact largely involving a few leading states, their business leaders and selected trade unionists, the range of actors that have to be enrolled in a transformation to climate capitalism is vast. Cities, regional decision-making bodies, citizens, bankers, business people, workers and of course states, all have a role to play. Market signals and political priorities have to reach down to all levels of decision-making all over the world. But the governance mechanisms can no longer depend only on states acting together. They entail a rather messy complex of public and private governance, as we have seen. Coordination of such a complex combination of actors is arguably much more difficult than it was in 1945.

But more importantly, with climate change, the character of the change is not only to produce a period of growth, but to do so with radical changes in the technologies underpinning that global economic growth. The better analogy for this dimension of the challenge is the development of the railways. The emergence of the railways in the mid-nineteenth century produced a similarly radical transformation of the economy, not only in narrow terms – expanding trade networks, rapidly increasing the distribution of goods and people and so on – but also with far-reaching impacts on daily life and military affairs, to name just two. The uniqueness amongst environmental problems of the political challenge posed by tackling climate change is precisely that it demands a similar socio-technical transformation. It is implicated in all aspects of our lives and has to be addressed through a broad array of channels that influence how we produce, consume, trade, move and eat. The railways produced wide-ranging effects. But unlike the Bretton Woods system, the development of the railways was a much more messy, unplanned affair. It was brought about by a number of entrepreneurial engineers acting competitively to out-do the other, but often speculatively, putting huge amounts of money into long-term projects where they had no guarantee of realising profits.

Many climate capitalists may in practice be in a similar situation at the moment. Their economy currently subsists on enthusiasm, energy and optimism, and as such may well be susceptible to a financial bubble, just as the railways were in their early days. But the railways took time – more like 50 years before there was an effective network in place in most Northern countries that realised the transformative potential of the technology. It is clear that we do not have 50 years to decarbonise.

Transformations such as these two normally come about during periods of crisis and dramatic upheaval produced by war or economic depression. We are faced with dealing with climate change during a period of relative affluence, in which large-scale wars that envelop the whole world are thankfully a distant prospect, even if oil wars and regional and civil conflicts continue. Indeed, the conflict in the Darfur region of Sudan has been dubbed the first climate war. But even if, as some suggest, 'Climate change is arguably the most persistent threat to global stability in the coming century,'[3] it is unlikely that war itself will be the catalyst for action on climate change. Many have also sought to advance green proposals in the midst of the current financial meltdown, but it is unclear that such a volatile environment provides the right conditions for a transition towards a sustainable economy. Moreover, those that will be expected to take the lead on climate change and play the largest part in restructuring their economies are not those who are suffering its worst effects and thus experiencing it directly as a crisis.

But these transformations are also the product of political struggle. The Bretton Woods era was in part a product of unions struggling for a fairer share of the fruits of their labour, and the reactions of business and governments to this in a time of acute social and political turmoil, the 1930s. The fear of communism taking hold on the part of leading western governments in the absence of decisive action was widespread. Political struggles about the character of climate capitalism can be similarly fruitful in shaping it.

A GREEN NEW DEAL FOR THE CLIMATE

The goal of decarbonisation must be central to the activities of all the world's main institutions of governance that need to be enrolled in this transformation. For a humane version – climate Keynesianism – to succeed, it must be underpinned by a new global bargain. Some have talked about a Green new deal,[4] a Marshall Plan type global scheme or the creation of a World Environment Organisation equivalent in its power to the WTO. There is no question that the WTO, IMF and World Bank can continue to operate as they do today in this new context.

---

[3] N. Adger, S. Huq, K. Brown, D. Conway and M. Hulme, 'Adaptation to climate change: setting the agenda for development policy and research,' *Tyndall Centre Working Paper* no. 16, April (2002), p. 4.

[4] New Economics Foundation, *A Green New Deal: Joined-up policies to solve the triple crunch of the credit crisis, climate change and high oil prices*, Available at: http://www.neweconomics.org/gen/z_sys_publicationdetail.aspx?pid=258, Accessed 10 August 2008.

Their goals and means of operating will have to be aligned with the imperative of bringing about a low-carbon economy.

The World Bank currently still lends huge amounts of money for fossil fuel projects; this would have to stop. To the extent that there are tensions between free trade imperatives and climate change ones, the latter must prevail. The WTO, backed by the World Bank, had been promoting the idea of an environmental services agreement which, for example, could prioritise market access for energy goods, services and materials critical to the CDM market. The crisis in world trade talks in relation to the stalling of the Doha round may provide an opportunity to go for a carbon markets and services agreement aimed at reducing barriers to trade in low-carbon technologies and products that help to reduce greenhouse gases (GHGs), perhaps cast as a broader 'energy round'.[5] This would allow market leaders, such as China, Mexico and India, to export the latest in renewable technologies. These countries are already among the top 10 exporters of environmental goods relevant to climate change mitigation.[6]

Carbon markets need to be designed and expanded to make sure that the wider economy is unable to ignore the limits implied by aiming for a maximum of 2 °C warming, as it currently does. Climate capitalism needs to seep into capitalism-as-usual and transform it, not be subsumed by it or become an irrelevance: an island of carbon finance in a sea of climate-change-accelerating financial flows. As the NGO CDM Watch argues: 'If it operates within the current policy perversity in which the Kyoto Protocol and CDM exist alongside massive North–South financial flows to fossil fuels, then it will fail. A real solution to climate change and sustainable development must divert these flows, not create carbon markets alongside them.'[7]

To be effective, to be coherent, the global system will need to engage, enrol and change the actors that govern the global economy at the moment. It will require an acceptance by many leading market actors that market failures will have to be corrected through collective action, which markets alone cannot coordinate or deliver.

[5] P. Newell, 'Fit for purpose: Towards a development architecture that can deliver' in E. Paluso (ed.) *Re-thinking Development in a Carbon-Constrained World: Development Cooperation and Climate Change* (Finland: Ministry of Foreign Affairs, 2009), pp. 184–196.

[6] World Bank, *International Trade and Climate Change: Economic, Legal and Institutional Perspectives* (Washington D.C: World Bank, 2007).

[7] B. Pearson, 'Market failure: why the Clean Development Mechanism won't promote clean development', *CDM Watch*, November, p. 8.

Strong institutions with broad-based political support will be critical to addressing the social conflicts produced by carbon markets and the challenges we have described here in terms of 'climate fraud' and 'climate colonialism'.

Constructing the political case for a new global bargain and for the degree of change required to shift from capitalism-as-usual to climate capitalism will require novel and imaginative forms of coalition and alliance-building. This is a consequence of the necessity of political struggles to construct new ways of organising capitalism, as in the shift to Keynesian policies in the 1930s. But also, because of the complex, multilevel, public–private character of contemporary global governance, new avenues – and new dilemmas – are opened up.

This is not, then, about persuading states to sign up to a new agreement or charter, or to establish new institutions such as with Bretton Woods. It is about bringing together people who could never have previously imagined working together – environmentalists with venture capitalists, trade unionists and business leaders, local government officials with UN bureaucrats. They will probably work together in different ways; through networks and diverse organisational forms rather than mega-organisations. There are plenty of examples of such novel, and uneasy, alliances, from Greenpeace courting insurance companies, to the way many environmentalists have created groups like the Climate Group or gone directly into the carbon market business themselves.

This process will not, of course, be smooth or consensual. What we have seen throughout this book is how struggles around how markets work and how they should be governed (and for whom) provide the basis to improve upon them or to construct new markets or other forms of policy intervention. There will be a great deal of learning by doing and muddling through as we seek to assemble the necessary winning coalitions to rewrite the rules of the global economy. More surprises can be expected, in the course of climate change itself of course, but also in the ways that the politics of responding to it unfold.

Glossary

adaptation initiatives and measures to reduce the vulnerability of natural and human systems against actual or expected *climate change* effects. Adaptation can be anticipatory, taking place before observed changes, or reactive. It can also be autonomous or spontaneous, being triggered by non-climate-related stimuli. Examples include raising dyke levels or the substitution of more temperature shock resistant plants for sensitive ones.

additionality reduction in *greenhouse gas* emissions or enhancement of *greenhouse gas* removals by sinks that would not occur without a *Joint Implementation (JI)* or a *Clean Development Mechanism (CDM)* project activity as defined in the *Kyoto Protocol*.

AdMit scheme an initiative set up by the International Institute for Environment and Development seen as an alternative to *carbon offsetting*. It provides a mechanism for direct payments from emitters of *greenhouse gases* in developed countries to invest in those communities directly affected by the impacts of *climate change*. A consortium of organisations was set up to run AdMit schemes on a pilot basis for 18 months, ending in January 2010, to establish project standards.

Asia Pacific Partnership on Clean Development and Climate an international initiative, launched in January 2006, between Australia, Canada, India, Japan, the People's Republic of China, South Korea and the United States, who collectively account for more than half the world's economy, population and energy use. It brings together governments and the private sector to meet goals for *energy security*, national air pollution reduction, and *climate change* in ways that promote sustainable economic growth and poverty reduction. The partners have approved eight public–private sector task forces covering issues such as cleaner fossil energy and power generation and transmission. Critics suggest it was an attempt by the Bush administration to undermine the *Kyoto Protocol*.

baseline the state against which a change is measured. For example the *EU ETS* uses average annual emissions for the baseline period of 1998–2003 against which to measure emission reductions.

benchmarking uses a measurable variable such as a *baseline* to evaluate the performance of an organisation over time. Benchmarks may be drawn from internal experience, that of other organisations or from legal requirement. *Carbon dioxide* benchmarking is designed to make the carbon emissions of organisations transparent.

Bretton Woods system the system set up after a conference in Bretton Woods, New Hampshire, in 1944 to stabilise the global economy after the Second World War. It involved Western countries fixing their exchange rates to each other, thus providing stability for exporters and investors. They also agreed to progressively cut trade barriers. The system was managed by new global institutions, the World Bank, the International Monetary Fund and the General Agreement on Tariffs and Trade.

burden sharing a system to fairly *mitigate climate change* across individual countries. The EU commitment to reduce its *greenhouse gas* emissions by 8% under the *Kyoto Protocol* is shared between the Member States under a legally binding 'Burden Sharing Agreement', which sets individual emissions targets for each Member State.

Byrd–Hagel resolution a resolution passed in the US Senate in 1997 insisting upon 'meaningful participation' by *Southern* countries as a prerequisite for US support for the *Kyoto Protocol*.

carbon asset management carbon emissions and associated permits and offsets are marketable assets for companies. Carbon asset management services are provided to advise and assist companies in managing their carbon emissions through a combination of emission reductions and offsets.

carbon capture and storage a process comprising the separation of *Carbon dioxide* from industrial and energy-related sources, transportation to a storage location, and long-term isolation from the atmosphere. Most current approaches seek to store the carbon deep underground. See also *Sequestration*.

carbon colonialism the term used by critics of carbon trading to describe the way in which *carbon offset* projects can be used by rich consumers in the *North* to displace their high-carbon consuming practices by offsetting their emissions cheaply in the *South*. This opens the door to a new form of colonialism, which in the name of action on climate change can lead to the acquisition of poorer peoples' land, their displacement and impoverishment; practices associated with traditional means of colonial domination.

carbon cycle the flow of carbon (in various forms, e.g. *carbon dioxide*) through the atmosphere, ocean, terrestrial biosphere and lithosphere.

carbon dioxide (CO_2) a naturally occurring gas and a by-product of burning *fossil fuels* or biomass, of land-use changes and of industrial processes. It is the principal anthropogenic *greenhouse gas* causing *global warming* due to the volumes occurring in the atmosphere. It is also the reference gas against which other *greenhouse gases* are measured and therefore it has a *Global Warming Potential* of one.

carbon dioxide equivalent (CO_2e) the atmospheric warming effect of a *greenhouse gas* expressed in terms of the warming effect of *carbon dioxide*. This has also become the basic unit of measurement for *carbon permits* in carbon markets.

Carbon Disclosure Project (CDP) a project whereby investors attempt to shape the activities of other companies by getting them to disclose their *carbon intensity* and their strategies to limit emissions.

carbon intensity   the amount of emissions of *carbon dioxide* per unit of Gross Domestic Product.

carbon leakage   refers to carbon emissions in countries without obligations to reduce their emissions, usually in the *South*, which result directly from reductions in a country where emissions are constrained. This can occur, for example, through relocation of energy-intensive production into non-constrained regions, or the knock-on effects of CDM projects set up in the *South*, if they simply displace emissions elsewhere.

carbon neutral   being carbon neutral refers to achieving net zero carbon emissions by balancing a measured amount of carbon released with an equivalent amount *sequestered* or *offset*.

carbon offsets   a financial instrument aimed at reducing *greenhouse gas* emissions. One carbon offset credit represents the reduction of one metric tonne of *carbon dioxide* or its equivalent (tCO_2e) in other *greenhouse gases*. Individuals, companies, or governments can purchase carbon offsets to mitigate their *greenhouse gas* emissions from sources such as transportation or electricity use.

carbon permits (or allowances)   in an *emissions trading* scheme, companies are issued with pieces of paper that grant them permission to emit a certain quantity of CO_2 into the atmosphere in a particular year. Companies that do not have enough permits to cover their actual emissions have to buy them from someone who does. In the *EU ETS*, such allowances are known as EUAs.

carbon sink   a natural or man-made reservoir that accumulates and stores some carbon-containing chemical compound for an indefinite period. Examples of natural sinks are the oceans and biosphere and man-made sinks include *carbon capture and storage* projects. See also *sequestration*.

carbon taxes   a levy on the carbon content of *fossil fuels*. Such taxes are often considered less favourable than *emissions trading* due to their perceived regulatory nature.

catastrophe bonds   risk-linked securities that transfer a specified set of risks from a sponsor to investors who will pay out against losses in the event of a catastrophe such as a hurricane.

Certified Emissions Reductions (CERs)   the credit created by a project developed under the *Clean Development Mechanism*. It is equivalent to one metric tonne of CO_2e emissions reduced or sequestered, calculated using *Global Warming Potentials*.

Chicago Climate Exchange (CCX)   launched in 2003, the CCX is a membership organisation for large corporations who agree to reduce their *greenhouse gas* emissions as a condition of membership. Member firms can meet their target by internal reductions, purchasing credits on the exchange from other members or through offset projects organised through the exchange.

Clean Development Mechanism (CDM)   a *flexibility mechanism* under the *Kyoto Protocol*, allowing industrialised nations and their private corporations to invest in *greenhouse gas* emissions reductions projects in developing countries in order to achieve their own reduction commitments. Under the *Kyoto Protocol*, the other objective of CDM projects is to promote *sustainable development*.

Clean Technology Fund   a fund set up alongside the Strategic Climate Fund by the World Bank in July 2008 to provide finance for low-carbon energy projects or energy technologies in the *South* that reduce *greenhouse gas* emissions.

climate change   refers to any change in climate over an extended period of time, typically decades, whether due to natural variability or as a result of human activity.

climate fraud   the term used by critics of carbon markets to describe a range of strategies for claiming *greenhouse gas* emissions reductions that are either exaggerated or non-existent.

Climate Justice Programme   comprises a collaboration of lawyers and campaigners around the world encouraging, supporting and tracking enforcement of the law to combat *climate change.*

Community Development Carbon Fund (CDCF)   set up by the World Bank, the CDCF provides carbon finance to projects in the poorer areas of the developing world. It supports projects that combine community development attributes with emissions reductions to create 'development plus carbon' credits.

Conference of the Parties (COP)   conference of the supreme body of the *UNFCCC*, comprising countries that have ratified or acceded to the convention. It meets every year to review progress on implementation of the Convention's aims and to negotiate future commitments.

contraction and convergence   a *greenhouse gas* abatement methodology developed by the Global Commons Institute. It requires contraction of *carbon dioxide* by more industrialised countries to an agreed per capita entitlement consistent with avoiding dangerous interference in the climate system and convergence of emissions to this level by poorer countries.

Corporate Social Responsibility (CSR)   describes a suite of voluntary tools and measures which allow businesses to demonstrate their social and environmental commitments to society, going beyond simply complying with legal obligations. Includes reporting, codes of conduct and certification schemes, many of which increasingly address contributions to *climate change.*

cost–benefit analysis   a tool or process to weigh the total expected costs against the total expected benefits of one or more actions in order to choose the best or most profitable option.

Designated National Authority (DNA)   a government office of a host country, authorised to approve a *CDM Project Design Document.*

Designated Operational Entity (DOE)   a private company, usually an auditor or certifier, hired to validate the claims made in a *Project Design Document* produced for a *CDM* project, and the emissions actually reduced once the project is operational.

El Niño   a warm-water current that periodically flows along the coast of Ecuador and Peru. This event also has great impact on the wind, sea surface temperature, and precipitation patterns in the tropical Pacific. It affects the climate throughout the Pacific region and in many other parts of the world.

emissions trading   a market-based approach to achieving environmental objectives. It allows those reducing *greenhouse gas* emissions below their emission cap to use or trade the excess reductions to offset emissions at another source inside or outside the country. Emissions trading systems are already operational in the *Kyoto Protocol*, the *EU ETS* and a number of other jurisdictions.

energy efficiency   the ratio of useful energy output of a system, conversion process or activity to its energy input.

energy intensity   the ratio of energy use to economic output.

energy security   the various security measures that a country, or whole global community, must carry out in order to maintain an adequate energy supply.

environmental integrity   most often refers to the need to safeguard the quality and authenticity of emissions reductions funded and verified through the *Clean Development Mechanism* against practices associated with *climate fraud*.

European Union Emissions Trading Scheme/System (EU ETS)   one of the key policies introduced by the European Union to help meet the EU's *greenhouse gas* emissions reduction target of 8% below 1990 levels under the *Kyoto Protocol*. Plans by Member States set an overall 'cap' on the total amount of emissions allowed from all the heavy industry installations covered by the scheme that are required to monitor and report their emissions. At the end of each year they are required to surrender allowances to account for their installation's actual emissions. They may use all or part of their allocation and have the flexibility to buy additional allowances or to sell any surplus allowances generated from reducing their emissions below their allocation.

flexibility mechanisms   economic mechanisms based on market principles that parties to the *Kyoto Protocol* can use in an attempt to lessen the potential economic impacts of *greenhouse gas* emission-reduction requirements. The three mechanisms are *Joint Implementation*, the *Clean Development Mechanism* and *emissions trading*.

fossil fuels   carbon-based fuels from fossil hydrocarbon deposits, including coal, peat, oil and natural gas.

global commons   aspects of the natural environment that are owned or controlled by no individual state. Examples include forests, oceans, Antarctica or the atmosphere.

Global Reporting Initiative   a network-based organization that developed a widely used sustainability reporting framework for use worldwide.

Global Warming Potential (GWP)   an index, based upon radiative properties of *greenhouse gases*, compared to that of *carbon dioxide*. The GWP represents the combined effect of the differing lengths of time that these gases remain in the atmosphere and their relative effectiveness in absorbing outgoing infrared radiation.

global warming   the increase in global surface temperatures, as a consequence of radiative forcing caused by anthropogenic *greenhouse gas* emissions.

Gold Standard   a certification scheme for carbon credits. Project developers submit their *CDM* or voluntary carbon market projects for approval by the Gold Standard management system.

grandfathering   an allocation of permits which reflect the current status quo of *carbon dioxide* emissions. The targets agreed at Kyoto reflect this allocation principle; rich countries were allocated tradable emissions rights in proportion to their 1990 emission levels.

green taxes   a range of fiscal and economic instruments used to internalise externalities, making the polluter pay for their emissions. Examples include carbon taxes and taxes on aviation.

greenhouse gas (GHG)   a gas within the atmosphere which allows the entry of solar radiation but blocks the infrared radiation from the earth's surface. Greenhouse gases can be both natural and anthropogenic and the primary gases are water vapour, *carbon dioxide*, nitrous oxide, methane and ozone.

Greenhouse Gas Protocol   a widely used international accounting tool for managing *greenhouse gas* emissions by governments and business leaders. Standards and guidance regarding corporate *greenhouse gas* accounting and reporting are provided.

greenwash   a term used to describe the practice of companies disingenuously describing their products and policies as environmentally friendly, such as by presenting cost cuts as reductions in use of resources.

Gulf stream   a powerful, warm, and swift ocean current that originates in the Gulf of Mexico and extends towards Europe as the North Atlantic drift. The climate of Western Europe and Northern Europe is warmer than it would be without this current.

hot air   for countries in the former Soviet Union and Eastern Europe their *baseline* carbon emissions under the *Kyoto Protocol* are higher than their current and projected emissions because of the slump in their economies after 1990. These allowances are sometimes referred to as hot air because, while they can be traded under the *Kyoto Protocol's flexibility mechanisms*, they did not result from *mitigation* activities.

Intergovernmental Panel on Climate Change (IPCC)   a global scientific body for the assessment of climate change, established in 1988 by the United Nations Environment Programme (UNEP) and the World Meteorological Organization (WMO). Its purpose is to report on the current state of scientific knowledge about climate change and its potential environmental and socio-economic consequences. The preparation of the Assessment Reports on Climate Change is a key activity of the IPCC, reviewing and assessing the most recent scientific, technical and socio-economic information produced worldwide relevant to the understanding of climate change. There have been four of these to date, from the first in 1990 to the fourth in 2007.

Joint Implementation (JI)   one of the *flexible mechanisms* of the *Kyoto Protocol*, JI allows industrialised countries or companies to implement projects jointly that limit or reduce emissions or enhance sinks, and to share the Emissions Reduction Units.

Kyoto Protocol   a protocol of the *UNFCCC* containing legally binding commitments for countries of the *North* to reduce their anthropogenic *greenhouse gas* emissions by at least 5% below 1990 levels in the commitment period 2008–2012. The Kyoto Protocol came into force on 16 February 2005.

Large Combustion Plant Directive   a European Union Directive that aims to reduce acidification, ground-level ozone and particulates by controlling the emissions of sulphur dioxide, oxides of nitrogen and dust from large combustion plants.

Linking Directive   A Directive which allows operators in the *EU ETS* to use credits from the *Kyoto Protocol* project mechanisms – *Joint Implementation* and the *Clean Development Mechanism* to meet their targets in the EU.

low-carbon economy   an economy which minimises the output of *greenhouse gas* emissions into the biosphere, but specifically *carbon dioxide* emissions.

Marshall Plan   the United States plan created in 1947 for rebuilding the countries of Western Europe. The Marshall Plan has also long been seen as one of the first elements of European integration, as it erased tariff trade barriers and set up institutions to coordinate the economy on a continental level.

Millennium Development Goal (MDG) Carbon Facility   Launched in June 2007 by UNDP, this facility offers a comprehensive package of project development services to emission reduction projects.

mitigation   mitigation means implementing policies to minimise the effect of climate change. It includes strategies to reduce *greenhouse gas* sources and emissions and enhance *greenhouse gas* sinks.

monetarism   an approach to economic policy focused on the control of the money supply which forms a key part of *neoliberalism*. In a de-regulated system, where banks and other institutions are much freer to lend money, the main, if not the only, way to do that is to use interest rates.

neoliberalism   a label for a form of political-economic management which became dominant in the early 1980s, associated most strongly with the governments of Margaret Thatcher in the UK and Ronald Reagan in the USA. It aimed to minimise government intervention in the economy and create 'free' markets.

Green new deal   a report released on 21 July 2008 published by the New Economics Foundation and inspired by Franklin D. Roosevelt's New Deal programme launched in the wake of the Great Crash of 1929. It outlines a series of joined-up policies to tackle the triple crisis of *climate change*, depleting energy supplies and the financial crisis.

new indulgences   interpretation of *carbon offsets* as analogous to the indulgences granted by the Catholic Church in the Middle Ages. It refers to the ability of the rich consumer to continue to indulge in a carbon-intensive lifestyle whilst salving their climate conscience through the purchase of *carbon offsets*.

North   a term used in this book to represent developed, industrialised countries with high carbon emissions per capita. They are responsible for most of the activities that have caused existing anthropogenic *climate change*.

Official Development Assistance (ODA)   flows of official finance and technical assistance, from governments to developing countries, administered with the objective of promoting the economic development and welfare of the country.

oil sands   see *tar sands*

personal carbon allowances   allocation of carbon emission credits to adult individuals to surrender when buying fuel or electricity. Such a scheme would allow for the trading of allowances between individuals in ways similar to companies within an *emissions trading* scheme.

Project Design Document (PDD)   required for all *CDM* projects. It presents information on the essential technical and organisational aspects of the project activity and is a key input into the validation, registration and verification of the project as required under the *Kyoto Protocol*.

Prototype Carbon Fund (PCF)   set up by the World Bank in 1999, this is a fund to purchase emission reduction credits under *Joint Implementation* and the *Clean Development Mechanism* With the operational objective of mitigating *climate change*, it aspires to promote sustainable development, to demonstrate the possibilities of public–private partnerships, and to offer a 'learning-by-doing' opportunity to its stakeholders.

Reducing Emissions from Deforestation and Degradation (REDD)   set up by the UNDP, REDD is a multi-donor trust fund, pooling resources in an effort to create a financial value for the carbon stored in forests, offering incentives for developing countries to reduce emissions from deforestation and degradation of their lands. Advocates claim such a *North–South* flow of funds will support new, pro-poor development, help conserve biodiversity and ecosystem services, and contribute to increased resilience to *climate change*.

renewable energy   power generated from resources such as sunlight, wind, tides and geothermal heat which are naturally replenished.

Renewable Energy Certificate (REC)   a tradable environmental commodity in the USA which represents proof that one megawatt-hour of electricity was generated from an eligible *renewable energy* resource. Certificates can be traded and the owner of REC can claim to have purchased renewable energy.

Rio Summit   the United Nations Conference on Environment and Development, held in June 1992 was also known as the Rio Summit. The most important achievement of the conference was the agreement of the United Nations Framework Convention on Climate Change, which in turn led to the *Kyoto Protocol*.

sequestration   refers to the removal of carbon from the atmosphere and storage in terrestrial or marine reservoirs. This can take place biologically through afforestation, reforestation and practices that enhance soil carbon in agriculture. Large-scale, permanent artificial capture and sequestration of industrially-produced *carbon dioxide* using subsurface saline aquifers, reservoirs, ocean water, aging oil fields, for example, are also under investigation and represent the storage element of *carbon capture and storage*.

Socially Responsible Investment (SRI)   an investment strategy which aims to maximise both financial return and social good.

South / Southern countries   a term used in this book to represent developing countries with comparatively low levels of industrialisation and consequently low-carbon emissions per capita. In many cases they are also considered to be more vulnerable to the effects of *climate change* than those countries in the *North*.

Stern Review   shorthand for **The Stern Review on the Economics of Climate Change** published by the UK Treasury in 2007. The principal author was the economist and banker Sir Nicholas Stern. Its main messages were that there is still time to avoid the worst impacts of climate change, if we take strong action now, and that the costs of stabilising the climate are significant but manageable.

Strategic Climate Fund   a fund set up by the World Bank in July 2008, together with the *Clean Technology Fund* to provide financing to pilot new development approaches or to scale-up activities aimed at specific *climate change* challenges through targeted programs.

tar sands   unconsolidated porous sands, sandstone rock and shales containing bituminous material that can be mined and converted to a liquid fuel occurring in particularly large quantities in Canada and Venezuela. Higher oil prices and new technology enable them to be profitably extracted and upgraded to usable products. However, they involve significantly more *greenhouse gas* emissions in their production than conventional fuel oil sources.

United Nations Framework Convention on Climate Change (UNFCCC)   signed at the *Rio Summit* in 1992 by over 150 countries, sets an overall framework for intergovernmental efforts to tackle the challenge posed by *climate change*. Its ultimate objective is the 'stabilisation of *greenhouse gas* concentrations in the atmosphere at a level that would prevent dangerous anthropogenic interference with the climate system'. The Convention now enjoys near universal membership, with 192 countries having ratified it.

Voluntary Carbon Standard (VCS)   like the *Gold Standard*, this programme provides a global standard for approving credits from carbon offset projects in the voluntary carbon market. Initiated by The Climate Group, the International Emissions Trading Association and the World Economic Forum in late 2005, a 19-member Steering Committee provides advice on VCS governance, additionality, validation and verification, registries, land-use change and forestry, general policy issues and performance standards. VCS 2007 was released on 19 November 2007.

Voluntary Carbon Units (VCUs)   a tradable voluntary offset credit created by the *Voluntary Carbon Standard*.

Voluntary Emissions Reductions (VERs)   carbon credits developed by *carbon offset* providers. Through these schemes, industries and individuals voluntarily compensate their emissions or provide an additional contribution to mitigating *climate change*.

weather derivatives   financial instruments that can be used by organisations or individuals as part of a risk management strategy to reduce risk associated with adverse or unexpected weather conditions. Increasing volatility in the weather is helping to fuel such trading which allows investors to bet on or hedge against fluctuations in the weather.

Index